VOCABULARY
BLASTER

VOCABULARY BLASTER

WORD BY ASSOCIATION

DR. ROBERT MCCLERREN

Haystack Creatives
8270 Woodland Center Blvd
Tampa, Florida 33614
www.haystackcreatives.com

ISBN: 978-1-953115-23-2 (sc)
ISBN: 978-1-953115-22-5 (e)

BIOGRAPHY

Through the past 43 years, Dr. McClerren has worked in education in various capacities.

Dr. McClerren's developed his academic expertise through undergraduate work in Elementary Education, graduate studies in Adult Education, and a Doctorate in Religious Studies.

Dr. McClerren is a committed life long learner: a 21st century Renaissance man. Among his accomplishments are those of, USN veteran, private pilot and Licensed Local Pastor in the United Methodist Church.

Dr. McClerren's tenure in education includes:

- USN Advanced Electronics Tech Core Instructor
- San Diego City College Technical Instructor
- ITT Technical Institute General Education Instructor
- University of Oklahoma Continuing Education Instructor
- Nation Center for Training and Development (USPS) Technical Instructor
- Navy College Program Education Advisor

Dr. McClerren is married; and lives with his wife in Lake County Illinois.

aback	adv	suddenly	surprised	unawares	unexpectedly
abaft	adv	aft	astern	behind	rearward
abandon	v	desert	forsake	leave	strand
abase	v	degrade	demean	humble	humiliate
abash	v	confound	embarrass	humiliate	mortify
abate	v	decrease	lapse	lesson	subside
abatement	n	alleviation	decrease	reduction	remission
abattoir	n	bloodbath	butchery	shambles	slaughter-house
abbey	n	cloister	convent	monastery	nunnery
abbreviate	v	abridge	condense	curtail	shorten
abdicate	v	abandon	quit	relinquish	yield
abdication	n	renunciation	resignation	abandonment	relinquish-ment
abdomen	n	belly	middle	stomach	tummy
abduct	v	kidnap	Shanghai	grab	seize
abecedarian	n	amateur	beginner	learner	novice
aberrant	n	abnormal	anomalous	atypical	deviating
aberration	n	abnormality	deviation	distortion	irregularity
abet	v	assist	encourage	support	promote
abeyance	n	dormancy	inaction	pause	suspension
abhor	v	detest	disgust	hate	loath
abhorrence	n	aversion	hatred	horror	loathing
abhorrent	adj	abominable	loathsome	repulsive	repugnant
abide	v	endure	remain	reside	stay
ability	n	aptitude	capacity	skill	talent
abiosis	n	harmony	mutualism	synergy	teamwork
abject	adj	contemptible	debased	degraded	wretched
abjure	v	deny	recant	renounce	withdraw
ablate	v	consume	corrode	erase	erode
ablation	n	abstraction	cutting out	excision	removal
ablution	n	bath	cleaning	cleansing	wash
abnegate	v	abstain	deny	reject	renounce
abnegation	n	abstinence	denial	refusal	temperance
abode	n	dwelling	habitation	home	residence
abolishment	n	annulment	abolition	cancellation	invalidation
abominable	adj	detestable	horrible	repulsive	vile

abominate	v	abhor	detest	hate	loathe
aboriginal	adj	indigenous	native	original	primitive
aborigine	n	bushman	inhabitant	native	primitive
abort	v	cancel	end	stop	terminate
abortifacient	n	aborticide	causative	causing abortion	feticide
abortive	adj	futile	unsuccessful	useless	vain
abound	v	flourish	prevail	swarm	teem
abrade	v	file	chafe	rub	scrape
abreast	adv	acquainted	informed	familiar	versed
abridge	v	compress	condense	reduce	shorten
abroad	adj	away	distant	elsewhere	overseas
abrogate	v	abolish	annul	cancel	revoke
abrupt	adj	brusque	hasty	short	sudden
abscess	n	boil	pustule	sore	ulcer
abscond	v	decamp	flee	hide	skip
absence	n	deficiency	emptiness	lack	scarcity
absolute	adj	complete	definite	positive	unconditional
absolutism	n	authoritarianism	autocracy	dictatorship	tyranny
absolutize	v	complete	perfect	philosophize	theologize
absolve	v	acquit	clear	exonerate	vindicate
absquatulate	v	abscond	bolt	flee	run away
abstain	v	avoid	desist	forbear	refrain
abstemious	adj	abstinent	moderate	sparing	temperate
abstinence	n	asceticism	sobriety	teetotalism	temperance
abstinent	adj	abstemious	ascetic	sober	temperate
abstract	v	detach	extract	isolate	remove
abstract	n	digest	outline	summary	synopsis
abstract	adj	conceptual	intangible	philosophical	theoretical
abstraction	n	concept	generalization	musing	reverie
abstruse	adj	abstract	mysterious	obscure	scholarly
absurd	adj	ludicrous	preposterous	ridiculous	unreasonable
abundance	n	bounty	plenty	prosperity	wealth
abundant	adj	ample	bountiful	copious	extravagant
abuse	n	disservice	harm	interference	maltreatment
abuse	v	assault	attack	exploit	mistreat

abut	v	adjoin	border	meet	touch
abutment	n	buttress	connection	joint	junction
abysm	n	chasm	deep	depth	gulf
abysmal	adj	appalling	awful	bottomless	deep
abyss	n	chasm	crevasse	gulf	pit
academic	adj	learned	pedantic	scholarly	theoretical
academy	n	college	institute	school	seminary
accede	v	comply	concur	submit	yield
accelerability	n	acceptable-ness	admissibility	eligibility	plausibility
accelerate	v	expedite	hasten	hurry	quicken
accentuate	v	accent	emphasize	stress	underline
accept	v	admit	allow	receive	take
access	n	approach	capability	entrance	entry
accession	n	assent	acquiescence	increase	addition
accessory	n	accomplice	associate	confederate	helper
accident	n	casualty	chance	fluke	mishap
acclaim	n	admiration	fame	recognition	tribute
acclaim	v	approve	commend	declare	welcome
acclimate	v	adapt	adjust	acclimatize	accustom
acclivity	n	ascent	incline	grade	slope
accolade	n	applause	award	praise	respect
accommodate	v	acclimate	adapt	adjust	familiarize
accompanies	v	attends	escorts	joins	succeeds
accompaniment	n	addition	accessory	companion	supplement
accompaniment	n	backup	instrumental	soundtrack	support
accomplice	n	ally	associate	assistant	partner
accomplish	v	achieve	complete	execute	perform
accomplishment	n	achievement	attainment	completion	fulfillment
accord	n	agreement	harmony	pact	understanding
accordance	n	agreement	conformity	correspondence	harmony
accost	v	address	greet	hail	salute
accountant	n	auditor	bookkeeper	clerk	comptroller

5

accounting	v	counting	inventorying	reckoning	tallying
accouter	v	equip	fit	outfit	rig
accouterment	n	apparatus	equipment	paraphernalia	stuff
accredit	v	assign	attribute	authorize	approve
accrete	v	accumulate	amass	collect	concentrate
accretion	n	accumulation	buildup	formation	growth
accrue	v	accumulate	collect	grow	increase
acculturate	v	assimilate	civilize	educate	socialize
accumbent	adj	horizontal	prone	prostrate	reclining
accumulate	v	amass	assemble	collect	gather
accurate	adj	correct	exact	precise	true
accuse	v	blame	charge	denounce	indict
accustom	v	acclimate	adapt	familiarize	train
acerbic	adj	bitter	harsh	sour	tart
acerbity	n	acidity	bitterness	harshness	sharpness
acerose	adj	acicular	needlelike	nee-dle-shaped	pointed
acetic	adj	biting	bitter	sharp	sour
Achates	n	companion	comrade	confidant	friend
Acheron	n	abyss	Gehenna	Hades	Sheol
achieve	v	accomplish	complete	attain	gain
acidulous	adj	acid	biting	sour	tart
acknowledge	v	accept	admit	concede	confess
acme	n	crest	peak	summit	top
acolyte	n	aide	assistant	attendant	helper
acoustic	adj	audio	hearing	phonic	sound
acquaint	v	familiarize	inform	notify	present
acquiesce	v	agree	comply	consent	submit
acquiescence	n	agreement	compliance	consent	submission
acquiescing	v	acceding	allowing	granting	permitting
acquire	v	attain	gain	obtain	procure
acquisition	n	acquirement	attainment	gain	purchase
acquisitive	adj	covetous	desirous	greedy	selfish
acquit	v	absolve	discharge	exonerate	liberate
acquittal	n	absolution	clearing	discharge	exoneration
acrid	adj	bitter	caustic	pungent	sharp

acrimonious	adj	angry	bitter	caustic	harsh
acrimony	n	animosity	bitterness	hatred	malice
actuary	n	accountant	auditor	bookkeeper	comptroller
actuate	v	activate	impel	move	motivate
acuity	n	aptitude	keenness	perception	sharpness
acumen	n	insight	keenness	sharpness	shrewdness
acute	adj	intense	perceptive	sharp	shrewd
adage	n	motto	proverb	truism	saying
adamant	adj	immovable	insistent	unshakable	unyielding
adamantine	adj	inflexible	tough	unrelenting	unyielding
adapt	v	adjust	altar	change	modify
adaptable	adj	adjustable	compliant	flexible	pliable
adaption	n	acclimation	compliance	conformation	modification
addendum	n	addition	appendix	extension	supplement
addict	n	devotee	enthusiast	fanatic	junkie
addle	v	befuddle	bewilder	confuse	confound
addled	adj	confused	dazed	disoriented	muddled
adduce	v	allege	cite	evidence	reason
adducing	v	attesting	carrying	declaring	fetching
adept	adj	able	clever	handy	skillful
adequate	adj	acceptable	enough	satisfactory	sufficient
adequately	adv	amply	satisfactorily	sufficiently	tolerably
adhere	v	attach	bond	cleave	cling
adherent	n	devotee	disciple	follower	supporter
adhesion	n	adherence	bonding	allegiance	devotion
adieu	n	cheerio	farewell	goodbye	so long
adipose	adj	fatty	greasy	oily	sebaceous
adjacent	adj	abutting	adjoining	bordering	proximate
adjourn	v	discontinue	defer	delay	postpone
adjudicate	v	arbitrate	decide	judge	settle
adjudication	n	arbitration	decision	determination	verdict
adjunct	n	accessory	addition	appendage	auxiliary
adjure	v	appeal	beseech	implore	plead
adjustment	n	adaptation	accommodation	modification	refinement
administer	v	control	direct	govern	manage

admirable	adj	applaudable	commendable	creditable	praiseworthy
admire	v	adore	esteem	respect	revere
admissible	adj	acceptable	allowable	permissible	tolerable
admission	n	acceptance	acknowledg-ment	affirmation	declaration
admit	v	accept	allow	acknowledge	confess
admittance	n	access	entrance	entry	ingress
admonish	v	advise	counsel	criticize	warn
admonition	n	advice	caution	counsel	warning
admonitory	adj	advisory	cautionary	reproving	warning
ado	n	bustle	commotion	fuss	stir
adolescence	n	teenage	juvenility	puberty	youth
adolescent	adj	immature	juvenile	pubescent	teenage
adopt	v	appropriate	choose	embrace	espouse
adoptive	adj	choosing	discriminating	constituent	elective
adoration	n	admiration	devotion	respect	worship
adorn	v	beautify	decorate	embellish	garnish
adornment	n	decoration	embellish-ment	garnish	ornament
adroit	adj	adept	clever	ingenious	skillful
adscititious	adj	additional	extra	incidental	secondary
adulate	v	adore	love	flatter	glorify
adulation	n	admiration	adoration	idolization	veneration
adulator	n	apple-polisher	bootlicker	flatterer	flunkey
adulterate	v	contaminate	corrupt	spoil	taint
adulteration	n	contamination	corruption	defilement	pollution
adumbrate	v	forecast	foretell	foreshadow	predict
adumbration	n	allusion	foreshadow-ing	obscureness	shroud
advance	n	improvement	refinement	furtherance	headway
advantage	n	benefit	gain	good	profit
advantageous	adj	beneficial	helpful	profitable	useful
advent	n	appearance	approach	arrival	emergence
adventitious	adj	accidental	chance	incidental	random
adversarial	adj	antagonistic	combative	hostile	opposed
adversary	n	competitor	enemy	opponent	rival
adverse	adj	dangerous	harmful	injurious	unfavorable

adversity	n	affliction	distress	hardship	misfortune
advertise-ment	n	announce-ment	notice	poster	promotion
advertiser	n	advocate	promoter	publicist	sponsor
advertising	n	broadcasting	promotion	propaganda	publicity
advice	n	counsel	information	recommenda-tion	suggestion
advise	v	counsel	inform	notify	suggest
advocate	v	champion	defend	plead	support
advocate	n	backer	defender	patron	supporter
aegis	n	backing	protection	sponsorship	patronage
aequitas	n	conformity	equality	fairness	justice
aerial	adj	airy	atmospheric	elevated	towering
aerobics	n	callisthenic	exercise	training	workout
aesthete	n	art lover	cognoscente	connoisseur	dilettante
aesthetic	adj	appealing	artistic	beautiful	tasteful
affability	n	cordiality	friendliness	sociability	warmth
affable	adj	friendly	gentle	kind	pleasant
affect	v	alter	change	impact	influence
affectation	n	mannerism	pose	pretension	show
affected	adj	artificial	contrived	pretentious	unnatural
affidavit	n	attestation	certification	deposition	testimony
affiliate	v	ally	associate	connect	join
affiliation	n	alliance	association	connection	relationship
affinity	n	attraction	connection	fondness	kinship
affirm	v	assert	confirm	insist	support
affirmations	n	acknowledg-ments	assertions	certifications	confirmations
affix	v	attach	connect	fasten	secure
afflatus	n	epiphany	inspiration	genius	revelation
afflict	v	agonize	anguish	torment	torture
affliction	n	distress	misery	suffering	trouble
affluence	n	luxury	prosperity	riches	wealth
affluent	adj	moneyed	prosperous	rich	wealthy
affordable	adj	cheap	inexpensive	low-cost	reasonable
affray	n	brawl	disturbance	fight	fracas
affront	v	insult	mortify	offend	provoke

affront	n	indignity	offense	slight	slur
aficionado	n	devotee	enthusiast	fan	follower
afoul	adj	amiss	disgusting	distasteful	entangled
afraid	adj	cowardly	fearful	frightened	scared
aft	adj	astern	back	behind	rearward
aftermath	n	consequence	effect	outcome	result
against	pre	on	upon	anti	contra
agape	adj	ajar	open	expectant	anticipant
agency	n	bureau	instrument	means	vehicle
agenda	n	plan	program	schedule	timetable
agglomeration	n	accumulation	assemblage	cluster	collection
agglutinate	v	attach	bind	fuse	join
aggrade	v	fill	deposit	raise	sediment
aggrandize	v	exaggerate	elevate	exalt	magnify
aggrandizement	n	enlargement	elevation	expansion	greatness
aggravate	v	annoy	exacerbate	increase	worsen
aggregate	v	accrue	accumulate	garner	gather
aggregate	n	total	collect	amount	sum
aggregation	n	accumulation	assemblage	collection	gathering
aggression	n	assault	attack	offensive	onslaught
aggressive	adj	belligerent	combative	hostile	offensive
aggressor	n	attacker	assailant	assaulter	intruder
aggrieve	v	afflict	mistreat	injure	oppress
aggrieved	adj	disgruntled	discontented	displeased	malcontent
aghast	adj	appalled	astonished	dumbfounded	shocked
agile	adj	active	nimble	quick	sprightly
agility	n	dexterity	liveliness	nimbleness	quickness
agitation	n	commotion	disturbance	excitement	turmoil
agitprop	n	catalyst	disinformation	indoctrination	propaganda
agnate	adj	akin	cognate	kindred	related
agnostic	n	heathen	infidel	pagan	skeptic
agnosticism	n	disbelief	doubt	skepticism	unbelief
agrarian	adj	farming	land	rural	agriculture
agreeable	adj	amenable	delightful	friendly	pleasant

agreement	n	accord	concord	contract	harmony
agrestic	adj	agrarian	bucolic	pastoral	rustic
agronomy	n	agriculture	cultivation	farming	husbandry
ahead	adv	before	forward	in advance	in front
ailment	n	disease	disorder	illness	sickness
air	v	broadcast	discuss	expound	ventilate
airs	n	arrogance	front	pretension	show
akin	adj	alike	cognate	related	similar
alacrity	n	eager	lively	prompt	swiftness
albatross	n	burden	encumbrance	load	weight
albeit	con	although	notwithstanding	when	while
albescent	adj	achromatic	ivory	pale	white
albino	n	blonde	no pigmentation	translucent	white
alchemical	adj	alchemic	chemical	pseudoscience	synthetic
alchemist	n	apothecary	chemist	logician	philosopher
alchemy	n	chemistry	magic	sorcery	witchcraft
alcove	n	bay	corner	niche	recess
aleatory	adj	chance	luck	uncertain	unpredictable
alert	adj	attentive	aware	vigilant	watchful
alias	n	assumed name	false name	nickname	pseudonym
alibi	n	excuse	deception	pretext	ruse
alien	adj	accidental	extraneous	external	foreign
alienate	v	distance	divide	estrange	isolate
alienation	n	breach	division	estrangement	separation
alight	v	land	perch	roost	settle
alimony	n	livelihood	living	maintenance	support
allay	v	calm	decrease	diminish	reassure
allegation	n	accusation	assertion	charge	declaration
allege	v	assert	declare	claim	contend
alleged	adj	assumed	pretended	so-called	supposed
allegiance	n	devotion	faithfulness	fidelity	loyalty
allegory	n	fable	legend	myth	symbolic
allegro	adj	fast	happy	lively	sprightly

allergy	n	aversion	disfavor	dislike	disinclination
alleviate	v	ease	lesson	reduce	relieve
alliance	n	association	league	partnership	union
allocate	v	assign	designate	earmark	distribute
allocution	n	address	lecture	oration	speech
allot	v	allocate	apportion	assign	distribute
allotment	n	apportion-ment	portion	quota	share
allotted	v	allocate	allow	apportion	assign
allow	v	admit	concede	permit	sanction
alloy	n	amalgam	blend	combination	compound
allude	v	hint	imply	refer	suggest
allure	n	appeal	attractiveness	charm	enchantment
allurement	n	attraction	charisma	enticement	temptation
alluring	adj	attractive	charming	enticing	fascinating
allusion	n	hint	mention	reference	suggestion
allusive	adj	indirect	indicative	significant	suggestive
alluvial	adj	deposit	sedimentary	silty	soil
ally	v	associate	coalesce	conjoin	cooperate
ally	n	backer	confederate	supporter	sympathizer
almanac	n	annual	calendar	journal	yearbook
alms	n	charity	contribution	donation	gift
aloof	adj	arrogant	removed	standoffish	withdrawn
alopecia	n	baldness	hair loss	hairlessness	loss of hair
alpine	adj	highland	lofty	mountainous	towering
alpinism	n	ascension	climbing	mountain climbing	mountaineer-ing
already	adv	before	earlier	formerly	previously
altar	n	holy table	chancel table	sanctuary	shrine
altercation	n	argument	disagreement	dispute	quarrel
alternative	n	choice	discretion	preference	selection
altitude	n	elevation	height	eminence	loftiness
altogether	adj	completely	entirely	totally	wholly
altruism	n	benevolence	generosity	selflessness	unselfish
altruist	n	benefactor	bestower	contributor	humanitarian
altruistic	adj	charitable	compassion-ate	kind	selfless

amalgam	n	alloy	blend	combination	mixture
amalgamate	v	combine	consolidate	intermingle	unite
amalgamation	n	mixture	fusion	compound	blend
amass	v	accumulate	assemble	collect	gather
amateur	n	beginner	nonprofessional	novice	unskilled
ambagious	adj	indirect	meandering	rambling	roundabout
ambient	n	atmosphere	climate	environment	surrounding
ambient	adj	current	environmental	moving	surrounding
ambiguous	adj	confusing	doubtful	uncertain	unclear
ambit	n	circuit	circumference	range	scope
ambitious	adj	difficult	eager	serious	weighty
ambivalence	n	doubt	indecisiveness	mixed feelings	uncertainty
ambivalent	adj	conflicted	doubtful	indecisive	uncertain
amble	v	hike	perambulate	ramble	tromp
amble	n	constitutional	saunter	stroll	walk
ambrosia	n	dainty	delicacy	dessert	nectar
ambulate	v	pace	step	tread	walk
ambulatory	adj	locomotive	mobile	moving	walking
ameliorate	v	amend	correct	improve	reform
amenable	adj	agreeable	compliant	obedient	submissive
amend	v	correct	change	improve	altar
amenities	n	comforts	conveniences	courtesies	pleasantries
amenity	n	agreeableness	helpfulness	comfort	luxury
amiable	adj	affable	amicable	cordial	friendly
amicable	adj	cooperative	cordial	friendly	harmonious
amid	pre	among	mid	midst	through
amiss	adj	awry	defective	faulty	wrong
amity	n	companionship	friendship	harmony	understanding
amnesia	n	blankness	forgetfulness	memory loss	obliviousness
amnesty	n	pardon	forgiveness	absolution	remission
among	pre	amid	amongst	between	betwixt
amoral	adj	corrupt	unethical	unprincipled	unscrupulous

amoretto	n	angel	baby	beautiful infant	seraph
amorous	adj	flirty	passionate	romantic	sexy
amorphous	adj	formless	indefinite	shapeless	vague
amortize	v	clear	liquidate	pay off	redeem
amount	n	measure	quantity	sum	volume
amphibology	n	ambiguity	double meaning	double entendre	uncertainty
amphigory	n	balderdash	claptrap	drivel	gobbledygook
amphitheater	n	auditorium	coliseum	field	oval-shaped
amphora	n	jar	pot	urn	vase
ample	adj	adequate	enough	plenty	sufficient
amplifier	n	amp	bullhorn	loudspeaker	megaphone
amplify	v	boost	expand	extend	increase
amplitude	n	fullness	magnitude	strength	range
amuck	adv	berserkly	frantically	helter-skelter	madly
amulet	n	charm	fetish	talisman	trinket
amuse	v	charm	divert	entertain	please
anabasis	n	advancement	headway	increase	progress
anachronism	n	chronological error	misdate	reversion	throwback
anachronistic	adj	chronologically off	historically wrong	obsolete	outdated
anagogic	adj	allegorical	figurative	mystical	spiritual
analgesic	n	anesthetic	anodyne	painkiller	sedative
analogical	adj	alike	comparable	parallel	similar
analogous	adj	akin	alike	comparable	similar
analogue	n	correlate	counterpart	match	parallel
analogy	n	comparison	likeness	similarity	resemblance
analysis	n	examination	inquiry	investigation	study
analytical	adj	diagnostic	investigative	logical	systematic
analyze	v	dissect	examine	investigate	study
Ananias	n	fabricator	false witness	falsifier	perjurer
anarchic	adj	chaotic	disobedient	disorderly	lawless
anarchism	n	chaos	disorder	disarray	turmoil
anarchist	n	insurgent	mutineer	rebel	revolutionary
anarchy	n	chaos	disorder	lawlessness	mayhem

14

anathema	n	abhorrence	abomination	curse	disgrace
anatomical	adj	biological	bodily	physical	structural
anatomy	n	build	form	physique	structure
anchor	v	fasten	fix	moor	secure
anchorite	n	ascetic	hermit	monk	recluse
ancilla	n	assistant	attendant	helper	servant
ancillary	adj	additional	extra	supplementary	supportive
androgynous	adj	bisexual	genderless	sexless	unisex
anecdote	n	fable	fiction	story	tale
anfractuous	adj	complex	intricate	labyrinthine	sinuous
angle	n	aspect	facet	perspective	view
angst	n	anxiety	distress	dread	worry
anguish	n	affliction	agony	distress	sorrow
angularities	n	corners	forking	sharp	zig zag
anhydrous	adj	without water	dry	arid	dehydrated
anile	adj	decrepit	infirm	old	senile
anima	n	mind	psyche	soul	spirit
animadversion	n	accusation	criticism	censure	stricture
animadvert	v	criticize	remark	observe	regard
animate	v	arouse	excite	stimulate	stir
animated	adj	energetic	excited	lively	spirited
animation	n	energy	liveliness	spirit	vitality
animosity	n	dislike	hatred	hostility	malice
animus	n	antagonism	antipathy	hatred	malice
annals	n	chronicle	historical records	list	register
anneal	v	harden	strengthen	temper	toughen
annex	v	add	affix	append	attach
annihilate	v	destroy	eradicate	extinguish	obliterate
annihilation	n	destruction	eradication	extinction	extermination
annotate	v	comment	edit	expound	interpret
annotated	v	commented	explained	interpreted	notated
announcement	n	advertisement	declaration	notice	proclamation
annually	adj	each year	every year	per annum	yearly

annuity	n	allowance	income	investment	pension
annul	v	cancel	nullify	quash	rescind
annular	adj	circular	ring shaped	round	spherical
annulet	n	bandelet	circlet	ring	roundel
anodize	v	bronze	electroplate	galvanize	plate
anodyne	adj	benign	harmless	hurtles	innocent
anoint	adj	bless	consecrate	hallow	sanctify
anomalous	adj	abnormal	irregular	peculiar	strange
anomaly	n	aberration	abnormality	irregularity	oddity
anomie	n	alienation	anarchy	detachment	disorder
anonymity	n	inconspicu-ousness	invisibility	namelessness	obscurity
anonymous	adj	nameless	obscure	unidentified	unknown
anserine	adj	dopy	foolish	goosy	jerky
antagonism	n	friction	hostility	opposition	rivalry
antagonist	n	adversary	enemy	foe	opponent
antagonistic	adj	contrary	hostile	opposed	unfriendly
antagonize	v	annoy	counteract	harass	irritate
antecedent	n	ancestor	forerunner	precursor	predecessor
antechamber	n	foyer	lobby	vestibule	waiting room
antedate	v	antecede	backdate	precede	predate
antediluvian	adj	ancient	antiquated	obsolete	old
anterior	adj	antecedent	former	front	prior
anthem	n	carol	chant	hymn	psalm
anthology	n	album	collection	compilation	miscellany
anthropoid	adj	ape	humanoid	manlike	primate
anthropo-morphize	v	ascribe	humanize	personalize	personify
anthropoph-agy	n	cannibalism	eater	flesh-eating	man-eating
antic	n	caper	practical joke	prank	trick
anticipate	v	await	expect	foresee	predict
anticlimax	n	comedown	decline	disappoint-ment	letdown
antidote	n	antitoxin	countermea-sure	cure	remedy
antigen	n	active immu-nity	allergen	immunogen	serum

antihistamine	n	counter histamine	drug	medicament	remedy
antimacassar	n	chair protector	cloth	cover	doily
antipathy	n	dislike	hatred	hostility	repulsion
antipodal	adj	antithetical	diametric	contrary	opposite
antipodes	n	antithesis	converse	opposite	reverse
antiquarian	adj	ancient	antique	archaeological	archaic
antiquated	adj	ancient	antique	obsolete	outdated
antiquity	n	ancientness	antique	artifact	relic
antiseptic	adj	clean	germ free	pure	sterile
antithesis	n	contradiction	contrast	reverse	opposite
antithetical	adj	contrary	counter	opposing	opposite
antitoxin	n	antibiotic	antidote	antiserum	antivenin
anxiety	n	apprehension	distress	fear	worry
anxious	adj	apprehensive	nervous	uneasy	worried
apathetic	adj	casual	indifferent	unconcerned	uninterested
apathy	n	dispassion	emotionlessness	indifference	unconcern
ape	v	copy	emulate	imitate	mimic
apercu	n	abridgment	abstract	digest	synopsis
aperture	n	gap	hole	opening	orifice
apex	n	acme	peak	summit	zenith
aphorism	n	adage	maxim	motto	proverb
aphoristic	adj	axiomatic	concise	epigrammatic	pithy
aphrodisiac	adj	amorous	erotic	lascivious	sexy
aplomb	n	assurance	composure	confidence	poise
apocalyptic	adj	ominous	doomed	revelation	discovery
apocrypha	n	disputed book	spurious book	doubtful literature	unknown literature
apocryphal	adj	counterfeit	fraudulent	illegitimate	unauthorized
apodictic	adj	certain	incontestable	proved	true
apodictically	adv	actually	absolutely	incontestably	indisputably
apologia	n	defense	explanation	justification	reason
apologist	n	advocate	justifier	proponent	vindicator
apologized	v	absolved	atoned	excused	pardoned
apologue	n	allegory	fable	parable	story

apology	n	confession	justification	regret	vindication
apoplectic	adj	angry	furious	indignant	irate
apostasy	n	abandonment	defection	disloyalty	withdrawal
apostate	n	deserter	heretic	renegade	turncoat
apostle	n	disciple	evangelist	follower	missionary
apothegm	n	adage	aphorism	maxim	proverb
apotheosis	n	deification	embodiment	ideal	paragon
appall	v	floor	horrify	jolt	shock
appalled	adj	aghast	alarmed	scared	shocked
appalling	adj	awful	dreadful	hideous	shocking
apparatus	n	device	equipment	gear	tool
apparent	adj	evident	manifest	obvious	plain
appeal	n	petition	plea	prayer	solicitation
appear	v	arise	arrive	emerge	show
appearance	n	aspect	figure	form	look
appease	v	assuage	disarm	pacify	soothe
appellation	n	designation	label	name	title
append	v	add	affix	annex	attach
appendage	n	adapter	accessory	appliance	attachment
applies	v	addresses	employs	refers	uses
apply	v	administer	employ	implement	utilize
applying	v	connecting	employing	referring	utilizing
appointment	n	assignment	engagement	job	position
apposite	adj	apt	appropriate	fitting	relevant
appraise	v	assess	estimate	evaluate	judge
appreciate	v	comprehend	enjoy	understand	value
apprehend	v	arrest	catch	perceive	understand
apprehension	n	anxiety	dread	fear	worry
apprehensive	adj	anxious	nervous	uneasy	worried
apprentice	n	beginner	learner	novice	student
apprise	v	advise	inform	notify	tell
approach	n	method	procedure	technique	way
approbate	v	accept	approve	authorize	sanction
approbation	n	admiration	approval	esteem	sanction
appropriate	v	commandeer	hijack	seize	thieve
approve	v	accept	agree	allow	endorse

apriorism	n	premise	presumption	supposition	thesis
apropos	adj	appropriate	apt	fitting	pertinent
apt	adj	fitting	proper	relevant	suitable
aptitude	n	ability	gift	knack	talent
aquatic	adj	marine	maritime	oceanic	watery
aquiline	adj	angular	bent	crooked	hooked
arabesque	n	agreement	approval	authorization	consent
arabesque	adj	baroque	elaborate	fancy	florid
arable	adj	cultivatable	farmable	fertile	tillable
arbiter	n	judge	mediator	negotiator	referee
arbitrament	n	adjudication	conclusion	judgment	verdict
arbitrariness	n	fickleness	flightiness	randomness	whimsy
arbitrary	adj	illogical	random	tyrannical	unreasoned
arbitrate	v	adjudicate	judge	mediate	referee
arcana	n	enigma	mystery	secret	occult
arcane	adj	ambiguous	cryptic	mysterious	obscure
arch	adj	impish	ironic	saucy	waggish
archaic	adj	ancient	antiquated	obsolete	old-fashioned
archetype	n	original	model	prototype	typical
architecture	n	building	construction	formation	structure
archive	n	chronicle	depository	record	register
arctic	adj	frigid	frosty	glacial	icy
ardent	adj	enthusiastic	fervent	passionate	zealous
ardor	n	devotion	enthusiasm	passion	zeal
arduous	adj	difficult	hard	laborious	strenuous
area	n	district	field	region	territory
argot	n	jargon	lingo	specialized vocabulary	vernacular
arguing	v	assert	contend	altercate	brawl
argument	n	altercation	disagreement	dispute	quarrel
aria	n	operatic	song	vocal	solo
arid	adj	dry	dull	boring	unimaginative
arise	v	appear	develop	emerge	originate
aristocracy	n	elite	gentry	nobility	upper-class
aristocrat	n	blue blood	lord	nobleman	patrician
aristocratic	adj	elite	genteel	noble	royal

armada	n	fleet	flotilla	naval force	ships
Armageddon	n	apocalypse	battlefield	judgment day	war
armature	n	architecture	configuration	framework	infrastructure
armistice	n	agreement	cease-fire	peace	truce
aromatic	adj	fragrant	odorous	perfumed	scented
arraign	v	accuse	charge	impeach	indict
arrangement	n	agreement	organization	structure	system
arrant	adj	absolute	complete	flagrant	utter
arras	n	drapery	curtain	tapestry	wall hanging
array	n	arrangement	assemblage	group	set
arrears	n	arrearage	debt	deficit	liability
arrive	v	flourish	prosper	succeed	thrive
arrogance	n	haughtiness	loftiness	pompousness	snootiness
arrogant	adj	boastful	conceited	haughty	proud
arrogate	v	appropriate	assume	seize	usurp
arrogation	adj	appropriation	assumption	seizure	usurpation
arroyo	n	channel	gorge	gully	ravine
arsenal	n	armory	depository	repository	storehouse
arterial	n	expressway	freeway	highway	thoroughfare
artful	adj	crafty	cunning	shrewd	sly
article	n	composition	essay	paper	theme
articulate	v	enunciate	pronounce	voice	utter
articulate	adj	eloquent	effective	fluent	well-spoken
artifact	n	antique	image	relic	ruin
artifice	n	cunning	cleverness	deceit	trickery
artisan	n	craftsman	handworker	journeyman	tradesman
artless	adj	genuine	honest	innocent	naive
artless	adj	clumsy	rude	rough	unrefined
ascend	v	arise	aspire	climb	soar
ascendancy	n	authority	dominance	sovereignty	supremacy
ascendant	adj	dominant	superior	supreme	paramount
ascertain	v	deduce	discern	discover	learn
ascetic	adj	abstinent	austere	celibate	self-denying
asceticism	n	abstinence	austerity	self-denial	severity
ascribe	v	assign	attribute	charge	impute
ascription	n	assignment	attribution	credit	imputation

asepsis	n	cleanliness	purity	sanitation	sterility
aseptic	adj	antiseptic	clean	hygienic	sterile
ashen	adj	cadaverous	pale	pasty	white
asinine	adj	absurd	foolish	idiotic	stupid
askance	adv	distrustfully	doubtfully	skeptically	suspiciously
askew	adj	awry	cockeyed	crooked	lopsided
aspect	n	angle	facet	appearance	look
asperity	n	bitterness	sharpness	harshness	severity
asperse	v	defame	malign	libel	slander
aspersion	n	defamation	disparage-ment	impingement	vilification
asphyxiate	v	choke	smother	strangle	suffocate
aspirant	n	applicant	contestant	petitioner	seeker
aspiration	n	ambition	desire	goal	hope
aspire	v	contemplate	intend	propose	yearn
aspiring	adj	ambitious	aspirant	enterprising	wishful
assail	v	assault	attack	abuse	bash
assailant	n	aggressor	attacker	assaulter	enemy
assassin	n	cutthroat	killer	manslayer	murderer
assay	n	analysis	breakdown	deconstruc-tion	dissection
assay	v	examine	prove	seek	test
assemble	v	collect	gather	meet	convene
assent	v	accept	agree	consent	sanction
assert	v	affirm	declare	maintain	state
assertion	n	affirmation	contention	declaration	statement
assess	v	appraise	estimate	evaluate	judge
asset	n	advantage	benefit	boon	help
assets	n	belongings	capital	resources	substance
asseverate	v	affirm	assert	declare	state
asseveration	n	affirmation	assertion	declaration	statement
asseveratively	v	affirmingly	assertively	declaringly	statedly
assiduity	n	attention	diligence	industry	perseverance
assiduous	adj	busy	diligent	hardworking	persistent
assiduously	adv	diligently	industriously	intently	laboriously
assignation	n	appointment	date	rendezvous	tryst
assignment	n	charge	duty	job	task

assimilate	v	absorb	adapt	comprehend	incorporate
assimilation	n	absorption	adaption	digestion	osmosis
assist	v	abet	aid	help	support
association	n	alliance	connection	league	union
assonance	n	anacrusis	blank verse	partial rhyme	vowel sounds
assonant	adj	accordant	concordant	consonant	harmonic
assuage	v	appease	pacify	relieve	satisfy
assume	v	believe	imagine	presume	suppose
assurance	v	certitude	confidence	conviction	guarantee
astral	adj	celestial	dreamy	stellar	visionary
astringent	adj	acerbic	caustic	sharp	severe
astute	adj	clever	discerning	perceptive	shrewd
asunder	adj	apart	disconnected	distant	separate
asylum	n	refuge	retreat	sanctuary	shelter
asymmetric	adj	disproportion-ate	irregular	unequal	uneven
asymmetrical	adj	crooked	irregular	lopsided	unbalanced
atavism	n	regression	relapse	reversion	throwback
atavistic	adj	ancestral	ancient	primitive	regressive
atelier	n	office	studio	workshop	workplace
atheism	n	disbelief	godlessness	heresy	impiety
atheist	n	disbeliever	heathen	infidel	pagan
athlete	n	competitor	jock	player	sportsman
athletic	adj	brawny	muscular	powerful	strong
athwart	adv	across	over	crosswise	diagonally
atmospheric	adj	aerial	airy	breezy	ethereal
atoll	n	archipelago	island	isle	reef
atomize	v	destroy	disintegrate	pulverize	vaporize
atone	v	amend	compensate	expiate	recompense
atrabilious	adj	gloomy	glum	melancholy	morose
atrocious	adj	appalling	deplorable	direful	horrible
atrophy	v	decay	degenerate	deteriorate	wither
attain	v	accomplish	achieve	gain	reach
attainable	adj	achievable	feasible	possible	workable
attend	v	accompany	follow	heed	serve
attendance	n	crowd	participation	presence	turnout

attendant	n	assistant	accessory	follower	servant
attended	v	accompanied	aided	heeded	served
attenuate	v	lessen	mitigate	reduce	weaken
attenuated	v	decreased	lowered	reduced	weakened
attenuation	n	decrease	diminution	reduction	weakness
attest	v	affirm	authenticate	certify	testify
attestations	n	certifications	confirmations	evidences	testimonies
attire	n	apparel	clothing	garment	outfit
attitude	n	disposition	manner	outlook	view
attract	v	beguile	entice	lure	tempt
attraction	n	allure	appeal	draw	magnetism
attribute	v	accredit	ascribe	assign	impute
attribute	n	characteristic	feature	trait	quality
attrition	n	abrasion	deterioration	erosion	reduction
atypical	adj	abnormal	odd	strange	unusual
audacious	adj	bold	brave	daring	fearless
audacity	n	boldness	daring	effrontery	nerve
audible	adj	detectable	discernible	hearable	perceptible
audience	n	attendance	meeting	public	spectator
audit	n	check	examination	inspection	review
audition	n	interview	test	trial	tryout
auditor	n	accountant	bookkeeper	hearer	listener
auger	n	awl	drill	gimlet	wimble
aught	n	naught	nothing	zero	zilch
augment	v	enlarge	expand	increase	supplement
augur	v	forecast	foretell	forewarn	predict
augur	n	diviner	foreseer	prophesier	visionary
augury	n	portent	presage	prognosticate	sign
august	adj	dignified	distinguished	noble	respected
aura	n	ambience	atmosphere	feeling	mood
aural	adj	acoustic	audible	audio	hearing
aureole	n	aura	corona	halo	nimbus
aurora	n	dawn	daybreak	morning	sunrise
auspice	n	patronage	portent	presage	protection
auspicious	adj	encouraging	favorable	fortunate	promising
austere	adj	harsh	serious	severe	stern

austerity	n	harshness	severity	sternness	strictness
austral	adj	Australian	meridional	southerly	southern hemisphere
autarchy	n	authoritarianism	despotism	dictatorship	tyranny
authentic	adj	bona fide	certified	genuine	real
authenticate	v	certify	confirm	validate	verify
authenticity	n	actuality	conviction	fact	truth
author	n	creator	inventor	originator	writer
authoritarian	adj	bossy	dictatorial	domineering	overbearing
authoritative	adj	important	official	powerful	valid
authority	n	command	control	power	sway
authorization	n	approval	consent	permission	sanction
authorize	v	approve	grant	permit	sanction
auto	n	car	machine	motor	vehicle
autobiography	n	diary	journal	life story	memoir
autochthon	n	aboriginal	aborigine	indigene	native
autochthonous	adj	aboriginal	domestic	indigenous	native
autocracy	n	absolutism	despotism	dictatorship	tyranny
autocrat	n	despot	dictator	oppressor	tyrant
autocratic	adj	authoritarian	despotic	dictatorial	tyrannical
autodidact	n	inquirer	learner	self-taught	trainee
automatic	adj	habitual	involuntary	mechanical	reflex
automaton	n	automatic	machine	mechanical man	robot
autonomic	adj	autonomous	free	sovereign	stand-alone
autonomies	n	choice	volition	freedom	independence
autonomous	adj	freestanding	independent	self-governing	sovereign
autonomy	n	free will	self-governance	sovereignty	volition
auxiliary	adj	accessory	ancillary	secondary	supplementary
avail	v	advantage	benefit	help	profit
avail	n	account	service	usefulness	utility
available	adj	accessible	obtainable	open	ready

avarice	n	covetousness	greed	materialism	money-grub-ber
avaricious	adj	covetous	greedy	mercenary	miserly
avatar	n	embodiment	epitome	incarnation	personifica-tion
avenge	v	redress	repay	retaliate	revenge
aver	v	affirm	assert	declare	profess
averse	adj	allergic	loath	opposed	reluctant
aversion	n	dislike	disgust	hatred	hostility
avert	v	avoid	divert	prevent	ward off
avid	adj	desirous	eager	enthusiastic	passionate
avidity	n	avarice	cupidity	eagerness	enthusiasm
avocation	n	hobby	diversion	pastime	pursuit
avoid	v	dodge	elude	evade	shun
avouch	v	attest	avow	declare	guarantee
avow	v	affirm	assert	aver	declare
avulsion	n	abruption	detachment	disruption	separation
avuncular	adj	genial	good-hearted	kindly	uncle-like
aware	adj	conscious	informed	mindful	perceptive
awesome	adj	amazing	breathtaking	impressive	splendid
awkward	adj	disturbing	embarrassing	uncomfort-able	unpleasant
awry	adj	amiss	wrong	crooked	lopsided
axiom	n	conviction	principle	self-evident	truth
aye	adv	commonly	frequently	always	eternally
azure	n	cerulean	cyan	indigo	sapphire
babel	n	bedlam	brawl	pandemoni-um	uproar
bacchanal	n	carousal	drunk	orgy	revel
bacillus	n	bacterium	germ	microbe	virus
background	n	scenery	behind	experience	training
Baconian	n	harsh	severe	strict	stringent
bacterium	n	bacillus	germ	microbe	microscopic
bade	v	invite	order	express	bid
badger	v	annoy	bother	harass	pester
badinage	n	good-natured	joking	playful	teasing
bagatelle	n	bauble	toy	trifle	trinket

bagnio	n	cathouse	bordello	brothel	whorehouse
bailiwick	n	business	field	domain	territory
baksheesh	n	consideration	gift	gratuity	tip
balance	v	adjust	equalize	compensate	symmetry
baleful	adj	hostile	menacing	threatening	unfriendly
balk	v	hesitate	refuse	frustrate	resist
balky	adj	contrary	hesitant	obstinate	stubborn
ballad	n	narrative	poem	song	story
ballast	n	anchor	counterbal-ance	load	weight
ballistics	n	archery	gunnery	trajectories	projectiles
ballyhoo	v	blow up	tout	pitch	promote
ballyhoo	n	bluster	commotion	hype	publicity
balm	n	soothing	ointment	fragrant	healing
balmy	adj	crazy	insane	mild	pleasant
bamboozle	v	deceive	dupe	hoodwink	trick
banal	adj	clichéd	commonplace	conventional	ordinary
banality	n	bromide	cliché	commonplace	platitude
banausic	adj	commonplace	ordinary	practical	utilitarian
bandy	v	agitate	argue	interchange	reciprocate
bane	n	curse	scourge	poison	toxic
baneful	adj	adverse	damaging	dangerous	destructive
banish	v	dismiss	eject	exile	expel
banister	n	balustrade	guardrail	handrail	railing
bankrupt	adj	bare	barren	destitute	devoid
bankrupt	v	break	bust	impoverish	ruin
banter	n	jesting	repartee	witticism	wordplay
baptism	n	confirmation	immersion	inauguration	initiation
barb	n	affront	dig	indignity	insult
barbarian	adj	heathen	savage	uncivilized	wild
barbaric	adj	brutal	cruel	inhuman	savage
barbarism	n	brutality	cruelty	savagery	vulgarity
barbarity	n	brutality	cruelty	inhumanity	savagery
barbarous	adj	brutal	inhuman	ruthless	savage
barbiturate	adj	anodyne	narcotic	opiate	sedative
bard	n	minstrel	poet	storyteller	troubadour

bargain	n	accord	agreement	compact	contract
bargain	v	dicker	haggle	arrange	negotiate
baroque	adj	elaborate	florid	ornate	rococo
barren	adj	bleak	desolate	harsh	inhospitable
barren	adj	infertile	sterile	unfruitful	unproductive
barrister	n	advocate	attorney	counsel	lawyer
base	adj	corrupt	despicable	mean	vile
basilica	n	church	cathedral	temple	sanctuary
basilisk	n	dragon	reptile	serpent	viper
basis	n	cause	foundation	ground	root
bask	v	lie	luxuriate	relish	sunbathe
bastille	n	brig	jail	prison	stockade
bastion	n	castle	citadel	fort	stronghold
bate	v	diminish	lessen	moderate	reduce
bathos	n	anticlimax	mushiness	sentimentality	schmaltziness
batten	v	bar	fasten	secure	tie
battery	n	assault	attack	barrage	beating
bauble	n	curio	knickknack	ornament	trinket
bawd	n	harlot	prostitute	streetwalker	whore
bawdy	adj	indecent	lewd	obscene	smutty
bay	v	howl	keen	ululate	wail
bazaar	n	emporium	exposition	fair	market
beatific	adj	blissful	divine	happy	joyful
beatify	v	bless	consecrate	glorify	sanctify
beatitude	n	blessedness	bliss	happiness	joy
beautify	v	adorn	decorate	embellish	enhance
becket	n	loop	picket	rigging	rope
beckon	v	lure	signal	summon	wave
becoming	adj	decent	fitting	proper	suitable
bedeck	v	adorn	decorate	embellish	ornament
bedizen	v	adorn	beautify	decorate	garnish
bedlam	n	chaos	pandemonium	turmoil	uproar
befit	v	agree	become	behoove	suit
beforehand	adj	advance	ahead	earlier	previously
befriend	v	aid	assist	favor	sustain

beget	v	generate	engender	procreate	produce
begrudge	v	covet	deny	envy	resent
beguile	v	charm	deceive	mislead	seduce
beguiling	adj	alluring	bewitching	captivating	enticing
behave	v	act	comport	conduct	deport
behemoth	n	colossus	dinosaur	giant	monster
behest	n	bidding	command	mandate	order
beholden	adj	grateful	indebted	obligated	thankful
behoove	v	become	befit	necessary	proper
belabor	v	assail	batter	beat	buffet
belated	adj	delayed	late	overdue	tardy
belay	v	cease	halt	quit	stop
beleaguer	v	besiege	harass	pester	worry
beleaguered	adj	besieged	embattled	oppressed	troubled
belfry	n	spire	steeple	tower	turret
belie	v	contradict	garble	misrepresent	negate
belief	n	confidence	conviction	faith	trust
believe	v	consider	deem	suppose	think
belittle	v	bad-mouth	dismiss	disparage	trivialize
belle	n	beautiful woman	enchantress	lovely	stunner
belletrist	n	author	humorist	wordsmith	writer
belletristic	adj	bookish	classical	cultured	literary
bellicose	adj	aggressive	belligerent	combative	warlike
belligerence	n	aggressive-ness	combative-ness	hostility	militancy
belligerent	n	combatant	fighter	hawk	militant
belligerent	adj	aggressive	antagonistic	hostile	threatening
bellow	v	holler	roar	shout	yell
bellwether	n	guide	forerunner	influencer	leader
belvedere	n	gazebo	lookout	observatory	watchtower
bemoan	v	bewail	lament	mourn	regret
bemuse	v	bewilder	confuse	perplex	puzzle
bemused	adj	bewildered	baffled	confused	lost
benchmark	n	criterion	measure	standard	yardstick
benedict	n	bridegroom	fiancé	husband	man
benediction	n	blessing	closing	grace	praise

benefactor	n	backer	patron	sponsor	supporter
beneficence	n	benevolence	charity	kindness	philanthropy
beneficent	adj	charitable	compassionate	humane	kindhearted
beneficently	adv	altruistically	benevolently	charitably	kindly
beneficial	adj	advantageous	good	helpful	profitable
beneficiary	n	heir	inheritor	recipient	successor
beneficiate	v	enrich	extract	prepare	process
benefit	n	advantage	gain	help	profit
benevolence	n	charity	generosity	goodwill	kindness
benevolent	adj	caring	compassionate	humane	kindhearted
benighted	adj	ignorant	illiterate	uneducated	unenlightened
benign	adj	favorable	harmless	healthful	kindly
benignant	adj	good	gracious	kind	sympathetic
bent	n	aptitude	disposition	inclination	tendency
bequeath	v	entrust	grant	transfer	will
bequest	n	endowment	gift	grant	legacy
berate	v	criticize	rebuke	reprimand	scold
bereave	v	deprive	divest	leave	rob
bereaved	adj	grieving	heartbroken	mourning	sorrowing
bereft	adj	deprived	destitute	grieving	forlorn
berm	n	bank	ledge	mound	wall
berserk	adj	crazy	frenzied	mad	wild
berth	n	dock	moor	bed	bunk
beseech	v	beg	entreat	implore	plead
beset	v	afflict	oppress	torment	trouble
besiege	v	assault	attack	storm	surround
besmirch	v	blacken	soil	slander	smear
besom	n	broom	brush	mop	rake
besot	v	amaze	befuddle	stun	stupefy
besotted	adj	cockeyed	fuddled	infatuated	tipsy
bespeak	v	attest	foreshadow	foretell	indicate
best	v	beat	better	outdo	overcome
bestial	adj	brutal	cruel	inhuman	savage
bestiality	n	barbarity	bloodlust	cruelty	savagery
bestir	v	arouse	awaken	incite	stir

bestow	v	award	endow	grant	offer
bestride	v	astride	ride	sit	stand
beta rays	n	plutonium	radium	radon	uranium
betide	v	befall	happen	occur	transpire
betoken	v	foreshadow	foretell	indicate	predict
betray	v	allure	bate	entice	seduce
betroth	v	contract	engage	espouse	promise
betrothed	v	engaged	married	pledged	promised
bevel	n	cant	edge	slant	slope
bevy	n	of beauties	crowd	flock	group
bewildered	v	astonished	baffled	confounded	perplexed
bewitch	v	captivate	enchant	enrapture	fascinate
bhang	n	cannabis	hashish	hemp	weed
bias	n	favoritism	inclination	leaning	tendency
biased	adj	one-sided	opinionated	partial	unfair
Bible	n	Good Book	Holy Writ	Scripture	Word of God
bibliography	n	authors	publications	references	sources
bibliophile	n	booklover	bookworm	editor	reader
bibulous	adj	alcoholic	boozy	drunken	inebriated
bicker	v	dispute	quarrel	squabble	wrangle
bier	n	casket	coffin	hearse	stretcher
bifurcate	v	branch	divide	fork	split
bigamy	n	deuterogamy	monogamy	polygamy	trigamy
bigot	n	doctrinaire	fanatic	intolerant	zealot
bijou	n	diamond	gem	jewel	trinket
bilateral	adj	common	joint	mutual	two-sided
bilge	n	bottom of ship	bullshit	nonsense	rubbish
bilious	adj	cantankerous	cross	ill-tempered	testy
bilk	v	cheat	defraud	swindle	trick
billingsgate	n	abuse	coarse language	cursing	foul language
biodegradable	adj	decomposable	destructible	disposable	perishable
biome	n	association	biosphere	colony	community
biometry	n	anatomy	biometrics	biostatistics	topography
bionomics	n	biology	botany	ecology	zoology

biopsy	n	diagnostics	examination	operation	test
biota	n	biology	fauna	flora	neurobiology
bisect	v	cut	divide	halve	split
bistro	n	bar	diner	eatery	restaurant
bivouac	n	camp	lodging	shelter	tent
bizarre	adj	eccentric	odd	peculiar	strange
blackbirding	n	deception	kidnapping	slavery	South Pacific
blackguard	n	rascal	scoundrel	unscrupulous	villain
blacklist	v	blackball	boycott	exclude	ostracize
blamable	adj	culpable	guilty	reprehensible	reproachable
bland	adj	boring	dull	tasteless	uninteresting
blandish	v	blarney	cajole	coax	flatter
blandishment	n	caress	coaxing	flattering	ingratiating
blanket	adj	common	generic	overall	universal
blasphemer	n	curser	heretic	profaner	curser
blasphemous	adj	irreverent	profane	sacrilegious	ungodly
blasphemy	n	defilement	irreverence	profanity	sacrilege
blatant	adj	boisterous	clamorous	loud	noisy
blather	n	chatter	foolishness	jabber	nonsense
blatherskite	n	gibberish	gossip	jabberwocky	nonsense
blazon	v	announce	broadcast	declare	publish
bleach	v	blanch	decolorize	fade	whiten
bleak	adj	dismal	dreary	gloomy	grim
blench	v	flinch	recoil	shrink	wince
blight	n	curse	decay	plague	ruin
blighted	v	destroyed	rotted	ruined	withered
bliss	n	delight	ecstasy	happiness	joy
blithe	adj	blissful	cheerful	happy	joyful
blithesome	adj	gleeful	happy	jolly	joyful
blizzard	n	snowstorm	snow squall	tempest	whiteout
bloated	adj	distended	inflated	puffy	swollen
bloc	n	coalition	federation	league	union
bloviate	v	babble	rant	rave	spout
bludgeon	v	bash	beat	club	strike
blueprint	n	diagram	design	layout	plan
bluestocking	n	academic	bookworm	female geek	lady nerd

blunt	adj	abrupt	brusque	candid	direct
blurt	v	blab	disclose	divulge	reveal
board	n	cabinet	committee	council	panel
bode	v	forecast	foretell	foreshadow	predict
bogey	n	bugaboo	ghost	hobgoblin	phantom
boggle	v	astonish	baffle	confuse	perplex
bogus	adj	counterfeit	false	fake	forged
boisterous	adj	noisy	riotous	uproarious	wild
bold	adj	audacious	brave	courageous	fearless
bolster	v	brace	prop	reinforce	support
bolt	v	dart	dash	run	skedaddle
bolus	n	capsule	pellet	pill	tablet
bombast	n	bluster	bravado	pomposity	pretentious-ness
bombastic	adj	arrogant	inflated	pompous	pretentious
bombastic	adj	inflated	overblown	pompous	pretentious
bonanza	n	extravaganza	godsend	wealth	windfall
bondage	n	captivity	enslavement	serfdom	servitude
bonhomie	n	cheerfulness	friendliness	geniality	good-natured-ness
boniface	n	host	innkeeper	landlord	proprietor
booboisie	n	ignorant	stupid	uneducated	uncultured
boom	v	bellow	roar	resound	reverberate
boon	n	benefit	blessing	godsend	windfall
boor	n	bumpkin	clodhopper	peasant	yokel
boorish	adj	crude	uncouth	rude	vulgar
boot	v	discharge	dismiss	fire	sack
bootless	adj	futile	unavailing	unprofitable	useless
booty	n	loot	plunder	prize	spoils
boreal	adj	arctic	freezing	glacial	icy
borrow	v	adopt	appropriate	obtain	take
boscage	n	brush	grove	thicket	undergrowth
bosomy	adj	busty	buxom	curvy	well-endowed
botany	n	botanical	flora	plants	vegetation
botch	v	bollix	bungle	flub	fumble
bounce	v	discharge	pink slip	terminate	sack
boundary	n	border	confines	limit	partition

32

bountiful	adj	abundant	ample	generous	plentiful
bouquet	n	aroma	fragrance	perfume	scent
bourgeois	n	middle class	populace	proletariat	public
bourse	n	bazaar	board	exchange	market
bovine	adj	dumb	slow	stupid	unintelligent
bowdlerize	v	censor	edit	purge	sanitize
boycott	v	abstain	avoid	protest	reject
brachylogy	n	brevity	conciseness	curtness	shortness
bracing	adj	brisk	invigorating	refreshing	stimulating
brackish	adj	briny	distasteful	saline	salty
braggadocio	n	arrogance	bluster	boaster	bravado
braggart	n	blowhard	boaster	show-off	windbag
braise	v	fix	form	join	solder
bran	n	farina	grain	grit	husk
brand	v	engrave	etch	imprint	infix
brandish	v	display	flaunt	shake	wave
brash	adj	bold	brazen	cheeky	impertinent
brassard	n	armband	armor	armlet	cloth
bravado	n	bravery	boast	brag	swaggering
bravura	n	brilliant	expert	mastery	virtuoso
brawn	n	might	muscle	power	strength
brawny	adj	burly	muscular	powerful	strong
brazen	adj	bold	impertinent	impudent	insolent
brazenly	adv	boldly	impolitely	openly	rudely
breach	n	break	crack	rupture	split
breadth	n	amplitude	extent	scope	width
breviary	n	book of liturgy	book of service	missal	prayer book
brevity	n	briefness	conciseness	shortness	succinctness
brief	n	abstract	outline	summary	synopsis
brigade	n	detachment	squad	team	troop
brigand	n	bandit	robber	thief	outlaw
brink	n	edge	margin	threshold	verge
bristle	v	anger	fume	rage	storm
broach	v	bring up	introduce	mention	raise
Brobdingnagian	adj	colossal	immense	massive	tremendous

bromide	n	banality	cliché	groaner	platitude
bromidic	adj	commonplace	corny	trite	unoriginal
brood	v	fret	ponder	sulk	worry
brook	v	abide	endure	suffer	tolerate
browbeat	v	bully	harass	intimidate	threaten
bruit	v	circulate	rumor	spread	whisper
brummagem	adj	cheap	gaudy	tacky	tawdry
brusque	adj	abrupt	curt	gruff	short
brutality	n	barbarity	cruelty	heartlessness	savageness
bucolic	adj	agrarian	pastoral	rural	rustic
buff	n	devotee	enthusiast	fan	freak
buffer	n	cushion	defense	safeguard	shield
buffet	v	batter	lash	pound	strike
buffoon	n	clown	fool	jester	harlequin
bugaboo	n	bogey	hobgoblin	ogre	specter
bugbear	n	aversion	hate	irritant	vexation
bulbous	adj	bulging	rotund	round	spherical
bulwark	n	embankment	fortification	protection	safeguard
bumble	v	mumble	murmur	hesitate	stumble
bumptious	adj	aggressive	arrogant	assertive	offensive
bumptious-ness	n	arrogance	cockiness	forwardness	pushiness
buncombe	n	bullshit	crap	hogwash	nonsense
bungle	v	botch	butcher	flub	fumble
bunk	n	bullshit	hogwash	nonsense	rubbish
buoyant	adj	cheerful	gay	happy	merry
burble	n	babble	drivel	gibberish	jabber
burden	n	cargo	freight	lading	payload
burdensome	adj	arduous	difficult	hard	tough
bureaucracy	n	establishment	formalities	government	officialism
bureaucrat	n	administrator	diplomat	official	politician
burgeon	v	develop	grow	flourish	sprout
burgeoning	adj	budding	flowering	flourishing	growing
burglary	n	pilferage	robbery	stealing	theft
burin	n	graver	point	style	tool
burlesque	n	caricature	lampoon	parody	spoof

burly	adj	brawny	hefty	husky	muscular
burnish	v	buff	polish	shine	rub
bury	v	entomb	inhume	inter	lay
bushing	n	facing	inlay	lining	padding
bustle	n	activity	commotion	flurry	tumult
butte	n	hill	knoll	mound	mount
buttress	n	brace	prop	reinforcement	support
buxom	adj	busty	curvaceous	plump	shapely
Byzantine	adj	complex	complicated	elaborate	intricate
cabal	n	conspiracy	intrigue	plot	scheme
cabaret	n	bar	entertainment	floor show	nightclub
cache	n	hoard	store	reserve	supply
cachet	n	distinction	peculiarity	prestige	quality
cachexia	n	chronic	malnutrition	wasting	weakness
cachinnate	v	convulsive	hysterical	loud	laughter
cacodemon	n	devil	evil spirit	fiend	ghoul
cacoethes	n	desire	mania	rage	urge
cacography	n	bad spelling	bad writing	scrawl	scribble
cacophonous	adj	discordant	dissonant	harsh	raucous
cacophony	n	discord	disharmony	noise	racket
cadaver	n	body	carcass	corpse	deceased
cadaverous	adj	emaciated	gaunt	haggard	pale
cadence	n	beat	meter	rhythm	tempo
cadenza	n	flourish	passage	riff	solo
cadet	n	midshipman	plebe	recruit	trainee
cadge	v	bum	mooch	scrounge	sponge
cadre	n	core	center	nucleus	group
caesura	n	break	gap	interval	pause
cagey	adj	clever	shrewd	slick	tricky
cairn	n	beacon	marker	memorial	monument
cajole	v	coax	encourage	persuade	sweet-talk
calamitous	adj	catastrophic	destructive	disastrous	fatal
calamity	n	catastrophe	disaster	misfortune	tragedy
calcify	v	fossilize	harden	ossify	petrify
calculate	v	cipher	compute	estimate	factor
calculating	adj	crafty	scheming	shrewd	sly

caldera	n	bowl	cavity	hole	volcanic crater
calendar	n	agenda	diary	docket	schedule
calf	n	baby bovine	fawn	heifer	kid
caliber	n	class	diameter	grade	quality
calibrate	v	adjust	fix	scale	set
caliph	n	emir	shah	sultan	tsar
calk	v	seal	stop up	tighten	waterproof
calligraphic	adj	graphic	handwritten	penned	written
calligraphy	n	handwriting	penmanship	script	writing
callipygian	adj	buxom	fair	goddess-like	shapely
callosity	n	hardness	insensibility	thickness	unfeelingness
callous	adj	compassion-less	cruel	insensitive	heartless
callousness	n	cruelty	hardness	indifference	unfeelingness
callow	adj	immature	inexperienced	naive	unsophisti-cated
calumniate	v	defame	malign	slander	smear
calumny	n	accusation	defamation	lie	slander
camaraderie	n	community	brotherhood	fellowship	fraternity
Camelot	n	ideal	beautiful	enlightened	peaceful
camouflage	n	cloak	disguise	hide	mask
campy	adj	comic	effeminate	farcical	theatrical
canaille	n	mob	rabble	riffraff	scum
canard	n	fiction	hoax	story	tale
candid	adj	direct	frank	honest	outspoken
candidate	n	applicant	aspirant	competitor	nominee
candor	n	forthrightness	frankness	openness	sincere
canny	adj	clever	discerning	shrewd	smart
canon	n	law	rule	regulation	tenet
canonical	adj	authoritative	official	orthodox	sanctioned
Canonically	adj	basically	commonly	lawfully	legitimately
canonize	v	beatify	consecrate	hallow	sanctify
canoodle	v	caress	cuddle	fondle	smooch
cant	n	idiom	jargon	slang	speech
cant	v	list	roll	slant	tilt
cantankerous	adj	argumentative	contentious	disagreeable	malicious
canter	n	gait	gallop	pace	trot

canvass	v	survey	campaign	solicit	poll
capacious	adj	broad	comprehensive	roomy	spacious
capillary	n	blood vessel	hairlike	narrow	thin tube
capital	n	means	money	wealth	wherewithal
capitalism	n	competition	free enterprise	free trade	private sector
capitol	n	legislative hall	meetinghouse	political building	statehouse
capitulate	v	concede	relent	surrender	yield
caprice	n	fickleness	impulsiveness	quirk	whim
capricious	adj	changeable	fickle	flighty	impulsive
caption	n	heading	inscription	legend	title
captious	adj	critical	faultfinding	judgmental	querulous
captivate	v	bewitch	charm	enchant	fascinate
captive	n	convict	detainee	hostage	prisoner
carafe	n	bottle	decanter	flask	jug
carapace	n	armor	case	shell	shield
caravanserai	n	court	hotel	inn	lodging
carbine	n	blunderbuss	gun	musket	rifle
carbohydrate	n	dextrose	fructose	sucrose	sugar
carcinoma	n	cancer	malignant	sarcoma	tumor
cardinal	n	chief	main	primary	principal
careen	v	sway	swerve	tilt	tip
caricature	n	burlesque	comic	exaggerated	parody
caricaturing	v	burlesquing	insulting	ridiculing	scoffing
carminative	n	analgesic	antibiotic	antifungal	antitoxin
carnage	n	butchery	genocide	massacre	slaughter
carnal	adj	bodily	flesh	physical	sensual
carnivorous	adj	flesh-eating	meat-eating	predatory	raptorial
carom	v	bounce	rebound	ricochet	skip
carp	v	find fault	complain	criticize	quibble
carping	adj	critical	faultfinding	judgmental	querulous
carrier	n	bearer	conveyor	messenger	transporter
carrion	n	cadaver	carcass	corpse	decaying flesh
Carthaginian	adj	city-state	perfidious	Punic	treacherous
cartographer	n	mapmaker	plotter	surveyor	topographer

cartoon	n	animation	caricature	parody	sketch
cascade	n	cataract	falls	rapids	waterfall
cashier	v	discharge	pink slip	sack	terminate
cast	v	hurl	throw	form	shape
caste	n	class	order	position	rank
castigate	v	criticize	punish	rebuke	reprimand
casual	adj	easygoing	informal	random	relaxed
casuistry	n	deception	hypocrisy	sophistry	unsound reasoning
cat's cradle	n	complex	elaborateness	entanglement	intricateness
cataclysm	n	calamity	catastrophe	disaster	tragedy
catacombs	n	cemeteries	crypts	graves	tombs
catalog	v	index	list	record	register
catalyst	n	accelerator	incentive	increaser	stimulus
catapult	v	hurl	launch	shoot	sling
cataract	n	cascade	downpour	flood	torrent
catastrophe	n	calamity	disaster	misfortune	tragedy
catastrophic	adj	damning	destructive	disastrous	ruinous
catechetical	adj	analytic	instruction	teaching	pedagogy
catechism	n	belief	creed	examination	question
catechizing	v	interrogating	inquiring	probing	questioning
catechumen	n	beginner	convert	disciple	novice
categorical	adj	absolute	certain	explicit	unqualified
cater	v	feed	provide	serve	supply
caterwaul	v	bellow	howl	screech	yowl
catharsis	n	emotion	purification	release	relief
cathartic	adj	cleansing	medical	purgative	purifying
catholic	adj	comprehen-sive	open-minded	universal	worldly
Catonically	adv	basically	commonly	lawfully	legitimately
caucus	n	conference	congress	convention	meeting
caudillo	n	captain	director	employer	leader
caulk	v	coat	fill	mend	seal
caustic	adj	acidic	corrosive	sarcastic	scathing
cauterize	v	burn	char	sear	singe
caution	v	admonish	advise	alert	forewarn
cautious	adj	careful	prudent	wary	watchful

cavalier	adj	arrogant	contemptuous	haughty	nonchalant
caveat	n	admonition	caution	notice	warning
cavil	v	carp	criticize	nitpick	quibble
cavort	v	dance	frolic	romp	skip
cede	v	give up	relinquish	surrender	yield
ceiling	n	boundary	cap	extent	limit
celebrate	v	commemo-rate	honor	memorialize	praise
celebrity	n	fame	prominence	renown	stardom
celerity	n	quickness	rapidity	speed	swiftness
celestial	adj	divine	ethereal	heavenly	holy
cemetery	n	burial ground	catacomb	graveyard	necropolis
cenotaph	n	empty tomb	memorial	monument	tombstone
censor	v	blue-pencil	delete	edit	suppress
censorious	adj	condemna-tory	disapproving	fault-finding	hypercritical
censure	n	denunciation	disapproval	rebuke	reprimand
censure	v	condemn	criticize	denounce	scold
central	adj	main	middle	primary	vital
centripetal	adj	centralizing	converging	receptive	unifying
centripetal-ization	n	amalgamation	centralization	concentration	joining
ceramic	n	clay	earthenware	porcelain	pottery
cerebral	adj	brainy	cognitive	intellectual	mental
certitude	n	assuredness	confidence	conviction	doubtlessness
cessation	n	closure	discontinua-tion	shutdown	termination
chafe	v	fret	gall	irritate	vex
chaff	n	debris	husk	refuse	waste
chagrin	n	annoyance	embarrass-ment	humiliation	vexation
chagrined	adj	annoyed	offended	unhappy	upset
chain	v	bind	fetter	handcuff	shackle
chalice	n	beaker	cup	goblet	mug
challenge	n	contest	dare	dispute	question
champion	v	advocate	defend	promote	support
changeable	adj	fickle	inconstant	unstable	variable

changing	adj	erratic	fluctuating	irregular	varying
chaos	n	confusion	disorder	mayhem	turmoil
chaotic	adj	confused	disorderly	disorganized	wild
chaperon	v	accompany	companion	escort	usher
character	n	nature	personality	quality	spirit
characteristic	n	attribute	feature	hallmark	quality
characterize	v	define	depict	portray	represent
charade	n	disguise	mockery	parody	pretense
charge	n	complaint	indictment	assignment	mission
charisma	n	allure	charm	fascination	magnetism
charlatan	n	fraud	hoaxer	impostor	sham
chary	adj	careful	cautious	guarded	wary
chasm	n	abyss	break	deep	gulf
chaste	adj	nonsexual	pure	virgin	virtuous
chasten	v	castigate	discipline	correct	punish
chastise	v	correct	punish	reprimand	scold
chatoyant	adj	changeable	iridescent	luster	opalescent
chattel	n	belongings	goods	possession	property
chauvinism	n	devotion	nationalism	patriotism	sectarianism
chauvinist	n	bigot	extremist	jingo	supremacist
cheap	adj	affordable	economical	inexpensive	low-cost
check	v	curb	control	restrain	stop
cheeky	adj	brash	bold	brazen	irreverent
cheerful	adj	glad	happy	joyful	merry
cherish	v	adore	prize	treasure	value
cherub	n	angel	cupid	seraph	winged child
cherubic	adj	adorable	angelic	cute	sweet
chesterfield	n	couch	davenport	lounge	settee
chevron	n	crest	insignia	stripe	inverted V
chiaroscuro	n	contrast	light	shade	shadow
chicanery	n	deception	deviousness	trickery	underhanded-ness
chide	v	chastise	rebuke	reprimand	scold
chiding	n	rebuke	reprimand	scolding	tongue-lash-ing
chimera	n	delusion	dream	fantasy	illusion
chimerical	adj	fictitious	imaginary	make-believe	mythical

chivalrous	adj	gentlemanly	honorable	knightly	noble
chivalry	n	courage	gallantry	heroism	valor
choice	adj	elite	excellent	select	superior
choleric	adj	angry	bad-tempered	grumpy	irritable
chorale	n	anthem	canticle	hymn	spiritual
chore	n	duty	errand	job	task
chortle	v	chuckle	giggle	laugh	snicker
chrestomathy	n	anthology	canon	collection	library
chroma	n	color	intensity	purity	saturation
chromatic	adj	colorful	multihued	rainbow	variegated
chronic	adj	ceaseless	continual	persistent	unending
chronicle	v	chart	document	record	report
chronicler	n	annalist	biographer	historian	recorder
chronology	n	calendar	journal	timeline	history
chrysalis	n	cocoon	larva	nymph	pupa
chthonic	adj	diabolical	hellish	infernal	subterranean
churl	n	bumpkin	niggard	peasant	yokel
churlish	adj	crude	gross	raw	rough
chutzpah	n	audacity	gall	impudence	nerve
cicatrix	n	blemish	disfigurement	mark	scar
cicerone	n	conductor	leader	guide	pilot
Ciceronian	adj	antithesis	eloquent	long sentences	polished
cicisbeo	n	attendant	lover	paramour	suitor
Cimmerian	adj	dark	cloudy	gloomy	obscure
cipher	n	code	cryptogram	cryptograph	secret
circa	pre	about	around	approximately	roughly
circuitous	adj	circular	indirect	meandering	roundabout
circumference	n	border	boundary	perimeter	periphery
circumlocution	n	long-windedness	redundancy	verbiage	wordiness
circumlocutory	adj	indirect	roundabout	verbose	wordy
circumnavigate	v	avoid	bypass	detour	skirt
circumscribe	v	confine	hem	limit	restrict

circumspect	adj	careful	cautious	discreet	wary
circumstance	n	incident	occurrence	setting	situation
circumvent	v	avoid	bypass	evade	dodge
citadel	n	bastion	castle	fortress	stronghold
citation	n	summons	subpoena	ticket	writ
cite	v	mention	name	quote	refer
citrus	n	grapefruit	lemon	lime	orange
civility	n	consideration	courtesy	decorum	politeness
claim	v	assert	declare	demand	state
clairvoyant	adj	discerning	perceptive	psychic	telepathic
clamor	v	cry	demand	exclaim	shout
clamor	n	commotion	noise	racket	uproar
clamorous	adj	boisterous	loud	noisy	uproarious
clan	n	family	kin	lineage	tribe
clandestine	adj	concealed	covert	private	secret
claptrap	n	balderdash	bunk	drivel	nonsense
clarify	v	demonstrate	explain	illustrate	simplify
clarion	adj	clear	cloudless	fair	fine
classicism	n	dignity	elegance	refinement	purity
classified	adj	confidential	hush-hush	restricted	secret
cleave	v	divide	split	adhere	cling
cleft	n	crack	crevice	gap	split
clemency	n	empathy	forgiveness	leniency	mercy
clement	adj	calm	lenient	merciful	mild
cleric	n	clergy	minister	pastor	priest
clerisy	n	elect	elite	intellectuals	learned
client	n	buyer	customer	patron	purchaser
clientele	n	business	customer	patronage	trade
climacteric	adj	acute	critical	crucial	dire
climactic	adj	crowning	highest	peak	supreme
climatic	adj	atmospheric	meteorological	seasonable	weather
clique	n	circle	faction	gang	group
clod	n	lump	nugget	dolt	oaf
cloister	n	abbey	monastery	hideaway	refuge
clone	n	copy	double	duplicate	twin

clout	n	influence	leverage	power	sway
cloven	adj	cleft	cracked	divided	split
cloy	v	excess	glut	gorge	oversupply
cloying	adj	saccharine	sentimental	sweet	syrupy
co-opt	v	absorb	assimilate	adopt	divert
coadjutor	n	ally	assistant	associate	helper
coagulate	v	clot	congeal	solidify	thicken
coalesce	v	combine	connect	merge	unite
coalition	n	alliance	association	league	union
cockle	n	crease	crimp	fold	wrinkle
coddle	v	baby	indulge	pamper	spoil
code	n	cannon	law	rules	principles
codicil	n	addition	appendix	postscript	supplement
codify	v	categorize	classify	organize	systematize
coerce	v	compel	force	make	oblige
coercion	n	compulsion	constraint	oppression	pressure
coeval	adj	contemporary	concurrent	simultaneous	synchronous
coffer	n	box	case	chest	trunk
cogency	n	effectiveness	forcefulness	persuasive-ness	validity
cogent	adj	believable	convincing	effective	persuasive
cogitate	v	meditate	ponder	reflect	think
cognate	adj	akin	kindred	like	related
cognition	n	comprehen-sion	knowledge	perception	understanding
cognizable	adj	discernable	knowable	perceivable	perceptible
cognizance	n	awareness	consciousness	knowledge	perception
cognizant	adj	aware	conscious	informed	knowing
cohere	v	adhere	bind	cling	stick
coherence	n	cohesiveness	connection	continuity	integrity
coherent	adj	logical	rational	reasonable	sound
cohesive	adj	integrated	strong	unified	united
cohort	n	ally	associate	companion	comrade
coin	v	create	conceive	invent	originate
coinage	n	cash	currency	mintage	money
coincide	v	accord	agree	concur	correspond
coincidental	adj	accidental	casual	coinciding	concurrent

colander	n	filter	screen	sieve	strainer
collaborate	v	cooperate	league	team	work together
collaboration	n	concert	cooperation	partnership	teamwork
collaborative	adj	collective	cooperative	joint	mutual
collage	n	assortment	composite	miscellany	potpourri
collar	v	apprehend	arrest	nab	seize
collate	v	accumulate	assemble	collect	gather
collateral	n	bond	guarantee	pledge	security
collation	n	comparison	likeness	relationship	resemblance
collection	n	accumulation	assemblage	group	set
collective	adj	common	communal	joint	united
college	n	academy	institute	school	university
colloquial	adj	casual	conversational	everyday	informal
colloquium	n	conference	meeting	seminar	symposium
colloquy	n	conference	conversation	dialogue	discussion
collusion	n	complicity	connivance	conspiracy	plot
colonic	adj	abdominal	gastric	intestinal	rectal
colonnade	n	series of columns	arcade	corridor	gallery
colony	n	community	settlement	territory	village
colophon	n	brand	emblem	logo	mark
colossal	adj	astronomical	gigantic	huge	immense
colporteur	n	hawker	huckster	peddler	vendor
coltish	adj	flirty	frisky	lively	playful
comatose	adj	lethargic	senseless	sluggish	unconscious
combat	v	attack	battle	fight	tackle
combatant	n	champion	defender	fighter	warrior
combine	v	blend	join	merge	unite
combustible	adj	burnable	explosive	fiery	flammable
comedo	n	blackhead	blemish	pimple	whitehead
comedy	n	farce	funniness	humor	slapstick
comely	adj	beautiful	lovely	fair	pretty
comestible	adj	eatable	edible	esculent	safe to eat
comestibles	n	chow	edibles	foodstuffs	provisions
comfort	v	assure	console	reassure	soothe
comfortable	adj	agreeable	cozy	pleasant	relaxed

coming	n	advent	appearance	approach	arrival
comity	n	civility	courtesy	politeness	respectfulness
commandeer	v	appropriate	confiscate	seize	take
commemorate	v	celebrate	honor	memorialize	observe
commend	v	commit	delegate	deliver	entrust
commend	v	applaud	compliment	congratulate	praise
commendable	adj	admirable	good	laudable	praiseworthy
commensurate	adj	comparable	equal	equivalent	proportionate
commercialism	n	business	capitalism	commerce	mercantilism
commination	n	condemnation	denunciation	rebuke	reprimand
commingle	v	blend	combine	mix	unite
commiserate	v	condole	empathize	pity	sympathize
commissary	n	agent	delegate	envoy	representative
commission	n	assignment	mission	task	undertaking
commissioner	n	agent	deputy	magistrate	representative
commitment	n	dedication	devotion	responsibility	obligation
commodious	adj	ample	convenient	roomy	spacious
commodity	n	article	goods	product	ware
commodore	n	naval officer	admiral	captain	commander
common	adj	customary	normal	ordinary	usual
commonplace	adj	average	everyday	ordinary	usual
commonweal	n	country	domain	nation	state
commonwealth	n	independent	sovereignty	democracy	republic
communal	adj	community	popular	public	shared
commune	v	bond	click	interface	relate
communion	n	affinity	fellowship	kinship	rapport
communism	n	Leninism	Marxism	socialism	Stalinism
Communists	n	Bolsheviks	collectivist	leftist	subversive
commutation	n	barter	dicker	exchange	quid pro quo
commute	v	exchange	swap	switch	trade
commuter	n	explorer	passenger	tourist	traveler
compact	n	agreement	contract	covenant	pact

company	n	band	group	party	team
comparative	adj	analogous	metaphorical	proportionate	relative
compare	v	equate	liken	match	parallel
compassion	n	charity	kindness	pity	sympathy
compatible	adj	agreeable	harmonious	united	well-matched
compatriot	n	associate	companion	comrade	countryman
compel	v	coerce	force	oblige	require
compelling	adj	credible	convincing	irresistible	persuasive
compendium	n	abridgment	condensation	digest	summary
compensate	v	offset	reimburse	repay	reward
compensatory	adj	compensative	redeeming	remunerative	offsetting
competence	n	ability	capability	expertise	skillfulness
competent	adj	able	capable	proficient	qualified
competition	n	contest	match	race	rivalry
competitor	n	adversary	antagonist	contestant	opponent
compile	v	accumulate	collect	compose	gather
complacency	n	comfort	contentment	satisfaction	smugness
complacent	adj	apathetic	self-satisfied	smug	uninterested
complaisance	n	courtesy	compliance	helpfulness	obedience
complaisant	adj	courteous	gracious	agreeable	pleasing
complement	n	allowance	amount	capacity	quota
complementary	adj	correlative	corresponding	equivalent	reciprocal
complex	adj	difficult	elaborate	intricate	involved
complexity	n	complication	difficulty	intricacy	sophistication
compliant	adj	accommodating	cooperative	obedient	submissive
complicated	adj	complex	difficult	intricate	involved
complicity	n	accomplice	collaboration	connivance	conspiracy
compliment	n	accolade	commendation	congratulation	tribute
comply	v	agree	conform	obey	yield
component	n	element	ingredient	part	piece
comport	v	act	bear	behave	conduct
composed	adj	calm	cool	serene	tranquil
composite	adj	complex	compound	intricate	mixture

composure	n	calmness	collectedness	self-control	serenity
compound	v	aggravate	intensify	increase	worsen
comprehend	v	grasp	know	perceive	understand
comprehensible	adj	clear	intelligible	plain	understandable
comprehensive	adj	all-inclusive	complete	exhaustive	thorough
compresent	adj	associate	conscious	same	together
compress	v	compact	constrict	contract	squeeze
comprise	v	contain	comprehend	include	incorporate
compromise	v	endanger	hazard	jeopardize	risk
compulsion	n	coercion	force	obsession	pressure
compulsive	adj	compelling	driven	fanatic	obsessive
compulsory	adj	mandatory	necessary	required	obligatory
compunction	n	guilt	misgiving	regret	remorse
concatenate	v	chain	connect	join	link
concatenation	n	chain	sequence	series	succession
concave	adj	cupped	depressed	dished	sunken
concede	v	allow	admit	grant	yield
conceit	n	arrogance	pride	self-love	vanity
conceivable	adj	credible	imaginable	likely	possible
concentrate	v	condense	consolidate	focus	reduce
concentric	adj	arcs	circles	central	coaxial
concept	n	idea	image	notion	thought
concern	n	business	company	establishment	interest
concert	v	arrange	conclude	coordinate	negotiate
concerted	adj	combined	cooperative	harmonious	united
concierge	n	custodian	doorkeeper	porter	representative
conciliate	v	appease	mollify	pacify	reconcile
conciliatory	adj	disarming	pacifying	peacemaking	reconciling
concinnity	n	balance	elegance	harmony	symmetry
concise	adj	brief	compact	summary	thumbnail
conclave	n	assembly	conference	council	summit
conclusive	adj	compelling	convincing	decisive	persuasive
concoct	v	cook up	create	devise	invent
concoction	n	brew	mixture	fabrication	invention

concomitant	adj	accompanying	attendant	coincident	concurrent
concord	n	accord	agreement	harmony	peace
concordance	n	accord	agreement	consensus	harmony
concordat	n	agreement	compact	contract	covenant
concourse	n	assemblage	congregation	convergence	multitude
concubine	n	courtesan	kept women	mistress	paramour
concupiscent	adj	carnal	lascivious	lustful	sexy
concur	v	accept	agree	coincide	coexist
concurrent	adj	coinciding	parallel	simultaneous	synchronous
condemn	v	blame	criticize	rebuke	reprimand
condensation	n	abbreviation	concentration	digest	summary
condenser	n	capacitor	compressor	concentrator	prism
condescend	v	descend	patronize	stoop	submit
condescend-ing	adj	arrogant	haughty	lofty	patronizing
condescen-sion	n	haughtiness	patronage	pride	smugness
condign	adj	deserved	due	just	right
condiment	n	relish	sauce	seasoning	spice
condition	v	acclimate	prepare	temper	treat
condolence	n	comfort	compassion	solace	sympathy
condone	v	accept	excuse	forgive	overlook
conduce	v	conspire	contribute	lead	tend
conducive	adj	advantageous	beneficial	helpful	useful
conduct	v	direct	guide	lead	manage
conduit	n	duct	channel	pipe	tube
confabulate	v	advise	confer	consult	discuss
confection	n	candy	dessert	pastry	sweet
confederacy	n	alliance	coalition	league	union
confer	v	award	bestow	advise	consult
conference	n	convention	discussion	meeting	talk
confidant	n	buddy	companion	comrade	friend
confide	v	disclose	divulge	impart	reveal
confidence	n	certitude	conviction	reliance	sureness
confirm	v	affirm	certify	corroborate	substantiate
confiscate	v	commandeer	impound	seize	take
conflagration	n	blaze	firestorm	inferno	wildfire

conflate	v	blend	combine	commingle	mix
confluence	n	convergence	gathering	junction	meeting
conform	v	agree	comply	correspond	fit
conformist	n	die-hard	formalist	stuffed shirt	traditionalist
conformity	n	accordance	adherence	compliance	obedience
confound	v	amaze	astonish	baffle	surprise
confounding	adj	astonishing	breathtaking	overwhelming	surprising
confront	v	challenge	defy	encounter	oppose
confuse	v	bewilder	confound	disturb	upset
confusion	n	chaos	disorder	mess	turmoil
confutation	n	contradiction	denial	refutation	rebuttal
confute	v	contradict	disprove	refute	rebut
congeal	v	coagulate	jell	set	solidify
congelation	n	chilling	cooling	freezing	refrigeration
congenial	adj	agreeable	friendly	pleasant	suitable
congeniality	n	cordiality	friendliness	harmony	sociability
congenital	adj	hereditary	inborn	inbred	inherent
congeries	n	accumulation	heap	collection	pile
congregate	v	assemble	collect	gather	meet
congruence	n	conformity	connectivity	correspon-dence	harmony
congruent	adj	coincident	consistent	harmonious	uniform
congruity	n	commonality	parallel	resemblance	similarity
conifer	n	cedar	fir	pine	yew
coniferous	adj	cone-bearing	evergreen	nee-dle-shaped	piney
conjecture	n	guesswork	hypothesis	speculation	theory
conjoin	v	associate	link	marry	unite
conjugal	adj	connubial	marital	nuptial	spousal
conjugate	adj	conjoin	couple	marry	unite
conjunction	n	association	combination	meeting	union
conjure	v	bewitch	evoke	implore	summon
connive	v	conspire	plot	scheme	intrigue
connoisseur	n	authority	expert	guru	specialist
connotation	n	implication	indication	meaning	sense
connote	v	imply	indicate	mean	signify
connubial	adj	conjugal	marital	nuptial	wedded

conquest	n	overthrow	triumph	victory	win
consanguin-eous	adj	akin	cognate	kindred	related
consanguinity	n	affinity	connection	family	lineage
conscience	n	heart	mind	morals	scruples
conscience-less	adj	excessive	extravagant	outrageous	unprincipled
conscientious	adj	careful	honorable	thorough	upright
conscious	adj	alert	attentive	awake	aware
conscript	v	draft	enlist	enroll	induct
conscription	n	enlistment	induction	muster	recruitment
consecrate	v	bless	dedicate	hallow	sanctify
consecutive	adj	continuous	sequential	serial	successive
consensus	n	agreement	harmony	solidarity	unanimity
consequence	n	conclusion	effect	outcome	result
consequent	adj	accompanying	associated	related	resultant
consequential	adj	important	momentous	significant	weighty
conserva-tionist	n	environmen-talist	keeper	preservation-ist	rescuer
conservative	adj	modest	orthodox	traditional	unpretentious
conservator	n	curator	custodian	guardian	keeper
conservatory	n	glasshouse	greenhouse	hothouse	nursery
consider	v	contemplate	ponder	regard	think
considerably	adv	greatly	quite	significantly	well
considered	adj	calculated	reasoned	planned	studied
consign	v	assign	deliver	send	transfer
consistency	n	conformity	harmony	regularity	uniformity
consistent	adj	constant	regular	steady	uniform
consolation	n	comfort	relief	solace	sympathy
consolidate	v	combine	join	merge	unite
consonant	adj	agreeable	compatible	consistent	harmonious
consort	n	associate	companion	partner	spouse
consorted	v	associated	companioned	mated	partnered
consortium	n	association	league	society	syndicate
conspectus	n	digest	epitome	outline	synopsis
conspicuous	adj	clear	noticeable	obvious	visible
conspiracy	n	intrigue	plot	scheme	trick

conspiratorial	adj	covert	hidden	secretive	sneaky
conspire	v	collude	connive	plot	scheme
constant	adj	perpetual	persistent	stable	steady
constantly	adv	continuously	forever	invariably	perpetually
constellation	n	configuration	galaxy	pattern	star
consternation	n	amazement	anxiety	dismay	distress
constituents	n	electorate	elements	components	parts
constitute	v	compose	establish	form	make
constitutional	adj	inherent	innate	intrinsic	organic
constrained	adj	bound	compelled	confined	restrained
constraint	n	coercion	duress	pressure	restraint
constrict	v	compress	contract	narrow	squeeze
construct	v	build	create	fabricate	make
construe	v	clarify	explain	interpret	understand
consult	v	advise	confer	discuss	talk
consume	v	deplete	exhaust	expend	utilize
consuming	adj	absorbing	biting	exhausting	intense
consummate	v	achieve	complete	finish	perfect
consummate	adj	accomplished	perfect	superior	supreme
consumptive	adj	destructive	devastating	harmful	wasteful
contagion	n	contamination	disease	infection	virus
contemn	v	despise	disdain	hate	scorn
contemplate	v	consider	meditate	ponder	study
contempla-tive	adj	meditative	pensive	reflective	thoughtful
contempora-neity	n	modernism	modernity	modernness	present
contempora-neous	adj	coexistent	concurrent	simultaneous	synchronous
contempo-rary	n	companion	counterpart	equivalent	peer
contempo-rary	adj	current	modern	new	present-day
contempt	n	hatred	disgust	disrespect	scorn
contemptu-ous	adj	defiant	haughty	insulting	scornful
contemptu-ously	adv	arrogantly	disrespectfully	insultingly	scornfully

contend	v	argue	dispute	fight	struggle
contention	n	argument	conflict	disagreement	strife
contentious	adj	argumentative	belligerent	combative	quarrelsome
contentment	n	fulfillment	happiness	pleasure	satisfaction
conterminous	adj	abutting	adjacent	adjoining	neighboring
context	n	background	circumstance	setting	situation
contiguous	adj	abutting	adjacent	adjoining	close
continence	adj	celibacy	chastity	purity	self-control
continent	adj	abstemious	pure	sober	temperate
contingencies	n	accidents	chances	eventualities	possibilities
contingency	n	chance	event	incident	possibility
contingent	adj	accidental	chance	conditional	possible
continual	adj	constant	incessant	perpetual	unceasing
continue	v	endure	persist	proceed	remain
continuity	n	coherence	cohesion	flow	integrity
continuous	adj	constant	perpetual	unceasing	uninterrupted
continuum	n	permanence	progression	sequence	spectrum
contort	v	deform	distort	twist	warp
contraband	n	banned	forbidden	illegal	illicit
contraction	n	abbreviation	compression	reduction	shrinkage
contractual	adj	agreement	bond	covenant	legal
contradict	v	contravene	deny	dispute	oppose
contradiction	n	denial	inconsistency	negation	rebuttal
contrariety	n	antagonism	antithesis	discrepancy	opposition
contrary	adj	conflicting	contradictory	incompatible	opposing
contrast	n	difference	disparity	dissimilarity	distinction
contravene	v	contradict	defy	infringe	oppose
contretemps	n	awkward	embarrassing	mishap	unexpected
contribute	v	donate	give	provide	supply
contrite	adj	ashamed	apologetic	regretful	sorry
contrition	n	guilt	regret	repentance	shame
contrivance	n	apparatus	device	gadget	mechanism
contrive	v	arrange	devise	invent	plan
contriving	adj	calculating	designing	plotting	scheming
control	v	command	govern	manage	rule
controlled	adj	calm	composed	disciplined	restrained

controversial	adj	arguable	contentious	disputable	questionable
controversy	n	argument	debate	disagreement	dispute
controvert	v	deny	dispute	contradict	refute
contumacious	adj	contrary	disobedient	rebellious	stubborn
contumacy	n	contempt	defiance	disobedience	stubbornness
contumelious	adj	abusive	insulting	outrageous	scornful
contumely	n	abuse	contempt	insult	scorn
contusion	n	bruise	cut	injury	wound
conundrum	n	mystery	problem	puzzle	riddle
convalesce	v	improve	mend	recover	recuperate
convene	v	assemble	collect	gather	muster
convenience	n	benefit	ease	fitness	utility
convenient	adj	available	handy	opportune	suitable
convention	n	assembly	conference	gathering	meeting
conventional	adj	customary	normal	standard	traditional
converge	v	gather	join	meet	unite
convergence	n	concentration	confluence	junction	meeting
conversant	adj	acquainted	familiar	knowledge-able	well-informed
converse	adj	contrary	inverse	opposite	reverse
convex	adj	arched	bulging	curved	protuberant
convey	v	carry	communicate	transfer	transmit
conviction	n	assuredness	belief	confidence	reliance
convince	v	assure	coax	persuade	sway
convivial	adj	festive	jovial	merry	sociable
conviviality	n	celebration	friendliness	gaiety	merrymaking
convocation	n	assembly	conference	convention	meeting
convoke	v	assemble	convene	muster	summon
convoluted	adj	complex	complicated	intricate	twisted
cooptation	n	adoption	alternative	choice	option
coordinate	v	arrange	harmonize	organize	synchronize
cope	v	deal	handle	manage	survive
copious	adj	abundant	ample	bountiful	plentiful
coquetry	n	dallying	flirting	toying	tease
coquette	n	flirt	minx	tease	vamp
coquettish	adj	coy	flirty	kittenish	sexy

cordial	adj	cheerful	friendly	kindly	sociable
cordillera	n	mountain chain	mountain system	belt	range
cordon	n	barrier	chain	circle	line
cordon	n	barricade	barrier	obstacle	obstruction
cordon sanitaire	n	barrier	buffer	quarantine	separation
cornice	n	crown	frame	molding	valance
cornucopia	n	abundance	fruit	horn	plentitude
corollary	n	conclusion	consequence	deduction	result
corona	n	circle	crown	halo	ring
coronary	adj	genuine	intimate	sincere	warm
coronation	n	ceremony	enthronement	inauguration	installation
corporeal	adj	bodily	carnal	fleshly	physical
corps	n	company	group	team	troop
corpulence	n	obesity	overweight	plumpness	stoutness
corpulent	adj	chubby	fat	plump	obese
corral	v	cage	confine	enclose	envelop
correlate	v	associate	compare	connect	relate
correlation	n	association	connection	relation	similarity
corridor	n	aisle	hallway	lobby	passageway
corrigendum	n	correction	error	fault	misprint
corrigible	adj	correctable	fixable	improvable	reparable
corroborate	v	authenticate	certify	confirm	verify
corroborating	adj	enduring	supporting	validating	verifying
corrode	v	consume	eat	erode	gnaw
corrosion	n	breakdown	decay	decomposition	erosion
corrosive	adj	biting	caustic	harsh	sarcastic
corrupt	v	contaminate	defile	pollute	taint
corrupt	adj	depraved	evil	immoral	wicked
corruption	n	depravity	immorality	perversion	vice
cortege	n	entourage	following	parade	procession
coruscate	v	flash	glitter	sparkle	twinkle
corybantic	adj	furious	frenzied	frantic	wild
cosmetic	adj	adorning	beautifying	decorative	embellishing
cosmopolitan	adj	global	international	universal	worldwide

cosmopoli-tanism	n	elegance	refinement	sophistication	style
cosmopolite	adj	diverse	multicultural	multiethnic	multinational
cosmos	n	creation	nature	universe	world
cosset	v	coddle	indulge	pamper	spoil
costive	adj	miserly	niggardly	parsimonious	stingy
coterie	n	clique	in-crowd	inner circle	gang
cotillion	n	ball	dance	party	prom
couch	v	express	frame	phrase	word
council	n	assembly	board	committee	panel
counsel	n	advice	guidance	recommenda-tion	suggestion
counselor	n	advocate	guide	mentor	teacher
counsel-or-at-law	n	attorney	barrister	lawyer	pleader
countenance	n	appearance	composure	face	profile
countenance	v	accept	approve	condone	tolerate
counter	v	oppose	resist	return	reverse
counterfeit	adj	bogus	fake	false	sham
countermand	v	cancel	overrule	reverse	undo
counterpoint	n	antithesis	contrast	juxtaposition	opposite
counterpoise	v	compensate	counterbal-ance	neutralize	offset
counterstrike	n	assault	attack	retaliation	revenge
countervail	v	compensate	counteract	counterbal-ance	offset
coup	n	overthrow	takeover	success	triumph
coupon	n	certificate	check	note	voucher
courageous	adj	bold	brave	daring	unafraid
courier	n	carrier	envoy	messenger	runner
court-martial	n	hearing	inquest	military trial	tribunal
courteous	adj	civil	gracious	mannerly	polite
courtesan	n	harlot	prostitute	streetwalker	whore
courtier	n	attendant	steward	apple-polisher	flatterer
covenant	n	agreement	alliance	contract	treaty
Coventry	n	banishment	blackball	exclusion	ostracism
covert	adj	concealed	hidden	secluded	secret

covet	v	crave	desire	want	yearn
coveted	v	craved	desired	wanted	yearned
covetous	adj	desirous	grasping	greedy	moneygrub-bing
cower	v	cringe	flinch	shrink	wince
cowl	n	hood	cloak	cover	monk
cozen	v	deceive	dupe	swindle	trick
cozened	n	cheated	deceived	fooled	tricked
cozy	adj	comfortable	homey	snug	warm
crabbed	adj	cramped	illegible	indecipher-able	unreadable
crag	n	bluff	cliff	escarpment	precipice
cramped	adj	close	narrow	small	tight
crampon	n	climbing iron	clamp	grappling hook	spike
crannies	n	coves	niches	nooks	recesses
crapulous	adj	drunk	inebriated	intoxicated	tipsy
crass	adj	crude	insensitive	thoughtless	uncultured
crave	v	covet	desire	lust	want
craven	adj	cowardly	fearful	gutless	spineless
craving	n	desire	hunger	longing	yearning
create	v	build	fabricate	generate	produce
credence	n	belief	confidence	faith	trust
credenza	n	buffet	cabinet	cupboard	sideboard
credible	adj	believable	plausible	reliable	trustworthy
creditable	adj	admirable	commendable	meritorious	praiseworthy
credo	n	belief	doctrine	philosophy	teaching
credulity	n	certainty	credence	gullibility	sureness
credulous	adj	gullible	naive	impres-sionable	unsuspecting
creed	n	belief	doctrine	faith	philosophy
crepitate	v	crackle	pop	rattle	snap
crepuscular	adj	dark	dim	dusky	twilight
crescendo	n	climax	culmination	peak	summit
crestfallen	adj	disappointed	discouraged	depressed	heartbroken
crevasse	n	abyss	chasm	cleft	fissure
crevice	n	cleft	crack	fissure	gap

crimp	n	crease	crinkle	furrow	wrinkle
cringe	v	cower	flinch	shrink	wince
crisis	n	calamity	catastrophe	disaster	emergency
criteria	n	benchmark	guideline	specification	standards
criterion	n	benchmark	measure	specification	standard
critical	adj	accusatory	condemning	fault-finding	judgmental
criticism	n	commentary	critique	disapproval	review
criticize	v	condemn	denounce	reprimand	scold
critique	n	analysis	commentary	criticism	review
crony	n	buddy	companion	pal	sidekick
croon	v	hum	sing	vocalize	warble
crop	v	clip	cut	lop	trim
crotchet	n	eccentric	oddity	peculiarity	quirk
crotchety	adj	crabby	cranky	grouchy	irritable
crucial	adj	critical	key	pivotal	vital
crucible	n	caldron	pot	ordeal	trial
crucifixion	n	agony	execution	martyrdom	torture
cruet	n	bottle	decanter	flask	vial
crustacean	n	crab	lobster	shrimp	barnacle
crux	n	core	essence	gist	key
cryptic	adj	dark	deep	mysterious	obscure
cryptographer	n	cipher	code	linguist	translator
cudgel	v	bash	batter	beat	club
cudgel	n	bat	club	nightstick	truncheon
cuisine	n	cooking	cookery	dishes	food
culinary	adj	cooking	edible	gastronomic	kitchen
cull	v	collect	gather	pick out	select
culminate	v	climax	crown	finish	peak
culmination	n	climax	high point	peak	summit
culpable	adj	accountable	answerable	blameworthy	guilty
culprit	n	criminal	delinquent	outlaw	perpetrator
culture	n	civilization	cultivation	elegance	refinement
culvert	n	canal	channel	conduit	ditch
cumbersome	adj	awkward	burdensome	clumsy	unwieldy
cumulative	adj	additive	increasing	heightening	summative

cunctation	n	delay	procrastination	retardation	shillyshally
cunning	adj	artful	clever	crafty	sly
cupidity	n	covetousness	desirous	greed	materialism
curable	adj	benign	correctable	recoverable	remediable
curate	n	clergyman	cleric	pastor	priest
curator	n	caretaker	conservator	custodian	guardian
curb	v	block	control	inhibit	restrain
curio	n	antique	curiosity	oddity	trinket
curiosity	n	interest	inquisitiveness	marvel	wonder
curious	adj	odd	peculiar	strange	unusual
curmudgeon	n	boor	crank	grouch	ill-tempered
current	adj	contemporary	mainstream	modern	present
currently	adv	now	presently	recently	today
curricula	n	class	lesson	study	training
curriculum	n	course	program	schedule	syllabus
curry	v	captivate	charm	flatter	ingratiate
cursive	adj	effortless	flowing	fluent	smooth
cursory	adj	hasty	hurried	quick	rapid
curt	adj	abrupt	blunt	short	rude
curtail	v	cut	diminish	reduce	shorten
cusp	n	corner	point	tip	top
customer	n	buyer	client	consumer	patron
cuticle	n	epidermis	epithelial	membrane	outer layer
cyclone	n	hurricane	storm	tornado	typhoon
cyclotron	n	accelerator	activator	catalyst	synchrotron
cynic	n	doubter	pessimist	skeptic	unbeliever
cynical	adj	distrustful	pessimistic	skeptical	suspicious
cynicism	n	disbelief	distrust	doubt	suspicion
cynosure	n	compass	direction	focus	lodestar
cytology	n	anatomy	botany	embryology	physiology
czar	n	dictator	emperor	king	tycoon
dab	v	blot	pat	press	touch
dais	n	platform	stage	stand	soapbox
dalliance	n	dawdling	flirting	toying	trifling
dally	v	delay	linger	play	procrastinate

damage	n	affliction	detriment	harm	injury
damp	adj	humid	muggy	sticky	sultry
dander	n	anger	rage	temper	wrath
dandle	v	coddle	fondle	pamper	pet
dank	adj	clammy	damp	humid	moist
dapper	n	neat	smart	spiffy	stylish
daring	adj	bold	brave	courageous	fearless
dastard	n	chicken	coward	scoundrel	sneak
dastardly	adj	cowardly	lily-livered	shameful	yellow
datum	n	detail	fact	information	particular
daub	v	paint	smear	spot	spread
daunt	v	discourage	intimidate	horrify	shock
dauntless	adj	bold	courageous	determined	fearless
deadline	n	boundary	limit	date	time frame
deadlock	n	gridlock	impasse	stalemate	standoff
deadpan	adj	blank	vacant	expressionless	unexpressive
deal	n	agreement	bargain	pact	understanding
dealt	v	dispensed	distributed	gave	rationed
dearth	n	deficiency	lack	scarcity	shortage
debacle	n	disaster	failure	fiasco	overthrow
debark	v	arrive	dismount	land	unload
debase	v	corrupt	defile	degrade	devalue
debased	adj	degenerate	degraded	depraved	reduced
debasement	n	corruption	degradation	desecration	humiliation
debauch	v	cheapen	corrupt	defile	pervert
debaucher	n	libertine	ravisher	seducer	violator
debauchery	n	corruption	degeneracy	depravity	vice
debauches	v	degrades	misuses	perverts	twists
debenture	n	bill	bond	draft	voucher
debilitate	v	exhaust	fatigue	tire	weaken
debilitating	adj	draining	enervating	exhausting	weakening
debility	n	feebleness	frailty	infirmity	weakness
debonair	adj	cultivated	cultured	sophisticated	polished
debrief	v	examine	interrogate	divulge	notify
debris	n	ashes	residue	rubble	wreckage
debt	n	arrears	due	liability	obligation

debunk	v	discredit	expose	refute	uncover
debut	n	initiation	introduction	launching	presentation
debutante	n	fashion plate	heiress	socialite	upper-class
decadence	n	corruptness	degeneration	immorality	self-indulgence
decadent	adj	degenerate	depraved	immoral	perverted
decant	v	draft	empty	ladle	pour
decanter	n	bottle	carafe	flask	jug
decapitate	v	behead	guillotine	execute	murder
deceased	adj	dead	demised	departed	expired
decedent	n	body	carcass	dead	remains
deceitful	adj	dishonest	false	fraudulent	untruthful
deceive	v	bamboozle	fool	hoodwink	trick
decelerate	v	brake	delay	retard	slow
deception	n	fraud	hoax	ruse	trickery
decided	adj	definite	determined	firm	resolute
deciduous	adj	brief	fleeting	temporary	short-lived
decimate	v	annihilate	destroy	eliminate	eradicate
decimation	n	annihilation	destruction	extermination	slaughter
decipher	v	decode	explain	interpret	solve
decision	n	conclusion	determination	resolution	verdict
decisive	adj	conclusive	critical	crucial	final
declaim	v	lecture	orate	recite	speak
declamation	n	address	lecture	sermon	speech
decline	n	decrease	devaluation	downturn	reduction
declivity	n	decline	descent	dip	slope
decommission	v	deactivate	demilitarize	disband	retire
decor	n	adornment	embellishment	furnishings	ornamentation
decorous	adj	seemly	conforming	proper	good taste
decorum	n	manners	etiquette	politeness	propriety
decree	n	command	edict	mandate	proclamation
decrepit	adj	feeble	infirm	rickety	weak
decrepitude	n	feebleness	frailty	infirmity	senility
decrescent	adj	decreasing	lessoning	subsiding	waning
decry	v	belittle	castigate	condemn	disparage

60

decrypt	v	decipher	decode	interpret	solve
dedication	n	commitment	devotion	loyalty	perseverance
deduce	v	conclude	derive	gather	infer
deduct	v	deduce	discount	reduce	subtract
deduction	n	discount	rebate	conclusion	inference
deductive	adj	analytical	inferential	logical	reasoning
deed	n	action	feat	endeavor	undertaking
deem	v	believe	consider	judge	think
deface	v	damage	disfigure	mar	vandalize
defalcate	v	abscond	embezzle	steal	rob
defamation	n	aspersion	denigration	libel	slander
defamatory	adj	abusive	derogatory	libelous	slanderous
defame	v	disparage	smear	slander	vilify
default	n	delinquency	failure	neglect	nonpayment
defeatism	n	desperation	hopelessness	pessimism	submission
defeatist	adj	despairing	fatalistic	hopeless	pessimistic
defect	n	blemish	deficiency	flaw	imperfection
defect	v	abandon	desert	forsake	leave
defendant	n	accused	appellant	litigant	suspect
defenestrate	v	dismiss	eject	expel	remove
defenestra-tion	n	discharge	ejection	expulsion	purge
defer	v	delay	postpone	suspend	yield
deference	n	homage	respect	reverence	veneration
deferential	adj	dutiful	obeisant	regardful	respectful
defiant	adj	bold	disobedient	insubordinate	rebellious
deficiency	n	deficit	insufficiency	lack	shortage
deficient	adj	inadequate	insufficient	lacking	wanting
deficit	n	deficiency	insufficiency	lack	shortage
defile	v	contaminate	taint	tarnish	pollute
define	v	delineate	describe	determine	specify
definite	adj	certain	clear	positive	sure
definitely	adv	absolutely	certainly	positively	surely
definition	n	demarcation	description	explanation	interpretation
definitive	adj	absolute	conclusive	final	ultimate
deflagrate	v	burn	combust	ignite	incinerate

deflate	v	chasten	discourage	humble	squash
deflect	v	deviate	distract	divert	sidetrack
deflower	v	defile	rape	ravish	violate
defraud	v	cheat	con	deceive	swindle
defray	v	clear	cover	discharge	settle
deft	adj	clever	dexterous	expert	skillful
defunct	adj	dead	extinct	inoperative	obsolete
defy	v	challenge	dare	oppose	resist
degenerate	adj	corrupt	depraved	immoral	wicked
deglutition	n	beverage	drink	intake	swallow
degradation	n	disgrace	dishonor	humiliation	shame
degrade	v	disgrace	humble	lower	reduce
dehisce	v	burst	crack	gape	split
dehydrate	v	desiccate	dry	evaporate	parch
deify	v	adore	exalt	idolize	worship
deign	v	concede	condescend	descend	stoop
deity	n	creator	divinity	god	goddess
delay	v	detain	hamper	hinder	impede
delectable	adj	delicious	palatable	tasty	yummy
delegate	v	appoint	assign	designate	entrust
delegate	n	agent	emissary	envoy	representative
delete	v	cancel	erase	excise	remove
deleterious	adj	destructive	detrimental	harmful	injurious
deliberate	v	consider	contemplate	debate	ponder
deliberately	adv	consciously	intentionally	knowingly	purposely
delicate	adj	dainty	fragile	frail	sensitive
Delilah	n	enchantress	femme fatale	siren	temptress
delimit	v	confine	restrict	define	demarcate
delineate	v	define	outline	describe	depict
delineation	n	outline	picture	representa-tion	sketch
delinquent	n	culprit	felon	offender	perpetrator
delinquent	adj	behind	late	overdue	tardy
deliquesce	v	dissolve	liquefy	melt	thaw
delirium	n	frenzy	hallucination	hysteria	insanity
delivery	n	articulation	conveyance	diction	enunciation

delude	v	deceive	fool	mislead	trick
deluge	n	flood	inundate	overflow	torrent
delusion	n	fantasy	hallucination	false belief	misconception
delusive	adj	deceitful	illusive	false	misleading
deluxe	adj	elegant	expensive	grand	luxurious
delve	v	dig	excavate	explore	investigate
demagogic	adj	inflammatory	orator	rabble-rousing	speechmaker
demagogue	n	agitator	inciter	instigator	rabble-rouser
demanding	adj	difficult	exacting	hard	severe
demarcate	v	circumscribe	define	delimit	restrict
demean	v	belittle	degrade	humble	humiliate
demeanor	n	attitude	bearing	behavior	conduct
demented	adj	crazy	deranged	insane	mad
dementia	n	madness	mania	insanity	senility
demerit	n	deficiency	fault	offense	shortcoming
demimonde	n	adulteress	harlot	prostitute	whore
demise	n	death	expiration	passing	termination
demobilize	v	deactivate	disarm	disband	disperse
demographic	adj	accommodating	compliant	obliging	targeted
demoniac	adj	devilish	fiendish	insane	satanic
demonstrable	adj	apparent	obvious	provable	verifiable
demonstrate	v	display	exhibit	prove	show
demonstratively	adv	affectionately	cordially	kindly	warmly
demoralization	n	corruption	depravity	degeneration	degradation
demoralize	v	corrupt	discourage	dishearten	pervert
demoralizing	adj	corrupting	degrading	discouraging	disheartening
demote	v	degrade	downgrade	lower	reduce
demotic	adj	common	ordinary	popular	vulgar
demulcent	n	cream	lotion	ointment	salve
demur	n	challenge	complaint	objection	protest
demur	v	balk	object	protest	remonstrate
demure	n	bashful	modest	shy	timid
demurral	n	challenge	difficulty	objection	protest

denature	v	alter	contaminate	corrupt	degrade
denigrate	v	bad-mouth	belittle	criticize	defame
denim	n	durable	twilled	cotton	white filling
denizen	n	dweller	inhabitant	native	resident
denominate	v	call	designate	label	name
denomination	n	designation	title	order	sect
denominator	n	divisor	factor	multiple	trait
denote	v	designate	indicate	signify	symbolize
denouement	n	conclusion	end	outcome	resolution
denounce	v	blame	condemn	criticize	discredit
denude	v	bare	expose	strip	undress
denunciation	n	condemnation	rebuke	reprimand	scolding
depart	v	exit	flee	go	leave
dependent	adj	conditional	contingent	subject	tentative
depict	v	describe	portray	represent	show
depiction	n	picture	portrayal	representation	sketch
depilate	v	depart	remove	take	withdraw
deplete	v	consume	empty	exhaust	spend
deplorable	adj	disgraceful	dishonorable	inexcusable	shameful
deplore	v	grieve	lament	mourn	regret
deploy	v	install	locate	position	station
deportment	n	bearing	behavior	conduct	demeanor
deposition	n	declaration	evidence	statement	testimony
depraved	adj	corrupt	evil	immoral	wicked
depravity	n	corruption	immorality	perversion	sinfulness
deprecate	v	despise	detest	belittle	put down
deprecation	n	blame	condemnation	criticism	disapproval
deprecatory	adj	belittling	derogatory	disparaging	slanderous
depreciate	v	belittle	diminish	disparage	reduce
depredate	v	loot	pillage	plunder	ransack
depredation	n	destruction	devastation	ravage	robbery
deprivation	n	destitution	hardship	poverty	ruin
deprive	v	deny	rob	strip	withhold
depth	n	discernment	intelligence	understanding	wisdom
deputize	v	assign	commission	delegate	designate

deracinate	v	destroy	eliminate	eradicate	uproot
deracination	n	displacement	excision	extraction	removal
derangement	n	disorder	insanity	lunacy	madness
derelict	adj	abandoned	careless	lazy	neglectful
dereliction	n	abandonment	desertion	failure	neglect
deride	v	jeer	mock	ridicule	scoff
derision	n	mockery	ridicule	sarcasm	scorn
derisive	adj	mocking	snide	sarcastic	scornful
derisory	adj	belittling	contemptuous	absurd	comical
derivative	adj	by-product	offshoot	outgrowth	secondary
derived	adj	acquired	advanced	copied	obtained
derogate	v	belittle	detract	disparage	minimize
derogation	n	degradation	denigration	detraction	disparagement
derogatory	adj	belittling	degrading	demeaning	disrespectful
derrick	n	crane	hoist	lift	winch
descend	v	decline	drop	fall	plunge
describe	v	depict	explain	portray	report
description	n	account	explanation	illustration	rendition
descry	v	detect	discern	distinguish	spot
desecrate	v	defile	degrade	dishonor	violate
desecration	n	abuse	blasphemy	misuse	sacrilege
desert	v	abandon	jilt	leave	strand
desiccate	v	dehydrate	dry	evaporate	parch
desiccated	adj	arid	dehydrated	dried	parched
desiccation	n	dehydration	drought	drying	evaporation
desideratum	n	essential	necessity	prerequisite	requirement
designate	v	appoint	indicate	label	name
desirability	n	attractiveness	allure	appeal	suitability
desirable	adj	advisable	expedient	prudent	wise
desire	n	aspiration	inclination	want	wish
desired	v	coveted	craved	needed	wanted
desist	v	cease	discontinue	quit	stop
desolate	adj	forsaken	melancholy	lonely	unhappy
desolated	v	destroyed	devastated	ravaged	wasted
desolation	n	grief	heartbreak	misery	sorrow

despair	n	depression	heartbreak	melancholy	misery
despicable	adj	contemptible	mean	vile	wretched
despise	v	abhor	detest	hate	loathe
despite	n	hatefulness	meanness	nastiness	viciousness
despoil	v	loot	pillage	plunder	ransack
despond	n	dejection	desperation	gloom	hopelessness
despondent	adj	brokenhearted	depressed	discouraged	downcast
despot	n	dictator	fuhrer	oppressor	tyrant
despotic	adj	authoritarian	autocratic	dictatorial	tyrannical
despotism	n	cruelty	injustice	oppression	tyranny
destination	n	end	goal	objective	target
destitute	adj	broke	impoverished	penniless	poor
destitution	n	impoverishment	neediness	poverty	poorness
destroy	v	annihilate	demolish	ruin	wreck
desuetude	n	discontinuance	disuse	inactivity	obsoleteness
desultorily	adv	aimlessly	haphazardly	irregularly	randomly
desultory	adj	aimless	arbitrary	haphazard	random
detached	adj	aloof	disinterested	dispassionate	removed
detail	v	describe	explain	expound	relate
detain	v	confine	hold	imprison	keep
detect	v	discern	discover	find	identify
detente	n	appeasement	easement	relaxation	truce
detention	n	confinement	custody	imprisonment	retention
deter	v	discourage	inhibit	prevent	stop
detergent	n	cleaner	cleanser	soap	solvent
deteriorate	v	decay	decline	degenerate	worsen
determinant	n	cause	factor	motive	source
determinate	adj	certain	definite	established	fixed
determine	v	conclude	decide	establish	judge
determinism	n	fatalism	imminence	passivity	predestination
deterrent	n	hindrance	impediment	obstacle	obstruction
detestation	n	antipathy	aversion	hatred	loathing
detract	v	belittle	diminish	lessen	reduce

detractor	n	attacker	critic	depreciator	disparager
detriment	n	damage	harm	hurt	injury
detrimental	adj	damaging	dangerous	harmful	hurtful
detritus	n	debris	garbage	refuse	waste
devastate	v	demolish	destroy	ravage	ruin
devastating	adj	destructive	disastrous	deadly	ruinous
develop	v	create	evolve	grow	originate
deviant	adj	aberrant	abnormal	irregular	unusual
deviate	v	depart	diverge	turn	vary
deviation	n	aberration	difference	digression	divergence
deviationist	n	defector	deserter	heretic	renegade
device	n	apparatus	gadget	tool	trick
devil's advocate	n	agitator	arguer	debater	provocateur
devious	adj	deceitful	dishonest	underhanded	unethical
devise	v	conceive	concoct	formulate	plan
devoid	adj	barren	destitute	empty	vacant
devolution	n	decline	degeneration	degradation	downfall
devolve	v	atrophy	decay	degenerate	deteriorate
devotee	n	adherent	enthusiast	fan	follower
devout	adj	devoted	godly	pious	religious
dexterity	n	ability	expertise	proficiency	skill
dexterous	adj	agile	handy	nimble	skillful
diabolic	adj	devilish	fiendish	infernal	satanic
diabolical	adj	devilish	evil	fiendish	wicked
diadem	n	crown	halo	tiara	wreath
diagnose	v	determine	distinguish	identify	recognize
diagnosis	n	analysis	conclusion	examination	interpretation
dialect	n	idiom	language	speech	vernacular
dialectic	n	argumentation	debate	dialogue	discussion
dialectical	adj	argumentative	controversial	logical	philosophical
dialogue	n	chat	conversation	discussion	talk
diametric	adj	contrary	opposite	polar	reverse
diametrical	adj	complete	entire	opposite	polar
diapason	n	gamut	harmony	melody	range
diapasonal	adj	harmonic	octave	range	tone

diaphanous	adj	sheer	thin	translucent	transparent
diary	n	chronicle	journal	log	record
Diaspora	n	dispersal	exile	expulsion	migration
diatribe	n	assault	attack	denunciation	lambasting
dicey	adj	chancy	dangerous	risky	uncertain
dichotomy	n	contradiction	contrast	division	polarity
dictate	v	command	decree	direct	order
diction	n	enunciation	phrasing	style	wording
dictum	n	command	decree	order	proclamation
didactic	adj	edifying	educational	instructive	perceptive
diet	n	nourishment	nutrition	regimen	sustenance
difference	n	contrast	contradiction	distinction	variance
different	adj	dissimilar	diverse	distinct	various
differentiate	v	discern	discriminate	distinguish	separate
difficult	adj	hard	tough	complex	tricky
diffidence	n	humbleness	humility	modesty	timidity
diffident	adj	bashful	meek	shy	timid
diffuse	v	disperse	disseminate	distribute	spread
diffuse	adj	broadcast	distribute	scatter	spread
diffusion	n	dispersion	distribution	scattering	spread
dignifies	v	adorns	exalts	glorifies	reveres
dignity	n	distinction	honor	pride	self-respect
digress	v	deviate	ramble	stray	wander
digression	n	departure	deviation	divergence	diversion
dilapidated	adj	decayed	ramshackle	shabby	tumbledown
dilate	v	enlarge	expand	swell	widen
dilatory	adj	delaying	procrastinating	slow	tardy
dilemma	n	difficulty	plight	problem	trouble
dilettante	n	amateur	dabbler	layman	nonprofessional
diligence	n	attention	industry	perseverance	persistence
diligent	adj	careful	conscientious	hardworking	industrious
dilute	v	cut	reduce	thin	weaken
dimension	n	extent	magnitude	measure	size
diminish	v	decline	decrease	lessen	reduce
diminution	n	decline	decrease	lessening	reduction

diminutive	adj	little	petite	small	tiny
din	n	hubbub	racket	tumult	uproar
dint	n	blow	energy	force	stroke
diocese	n	bishopric	episcopate	parish	see
dipsomania	n	alcoholism	drunkenness	inebriation	intoxication
dire	adj	appalling	awful	dreadful	grievous
directive	n	decree	edict	mandate	order
directory	n	file	list	record	register
dirge	n	elegy	lament	mournful song	requiem
dirigible	n	airship	blimp	steerable	zeppelin
disabuse	v	correct	enlighten	expose	purge
disaffect	v	alienate	disunite	divide	estrange
disaffected	adj	disloyal	estranged	malcontent	unfriendly
disaffection	n	alienation	breach	disinterest	estrangement
disappoint	v	fail	foil	frustrate	sadden
disapprobation	n	condemnation	censure	objection	rejection
disarray	n	confusion	chaos	disorder	mess
disaster	n	calamity	catastrophe	misfortune	tragedy
disastrous	adj	calamitous	catastrophic	destructive	ruinous
disavow	v	deny	disown	renounce	repudiate
disband	v	dismiss	disperse	dissolve	scatter
disburse	v	distribute	expend	pay	spend
discern	v	distinguish	perceive	recognize	see
discernible	adj	detectable	evident	recognizable	visible
discerning	adj	discriminating	insightful	observant	perceptive
discernment	n	insight	perception	wisdom	understanding
disciple	n	adherent	follower	pupil	student
discipline	n	area	branch	field	specialty
disclaim	v	deny	disown	reject	renounce
disclose	v	divulge	expose	reveal	show
discombobulate	v	bewilder	confound	confuse	perplex
discomfit	v	confuse	deceive	deject	frustrate
discomfiture	n	confusion	defeat	frustration	embarrassment

discomfort	v	agitate	disturb	unsettle	upset
disconcert	v	confuse	disturb	embarrass	unsettle
disconcerting	adj	disturbing	confusing	unsettling	upsetting
disconsolate	adj	dejected	inconsolable	melancholy	sad
discontinuity	n	break	cutoff	gap	incoherence
discord	n	conflict	disharmony	friction	strife
discordant	adj	dissonant	harsh	inconsistent	inharmonious
discount	v	disregard	excuse	ignore	overlook
discountenance	v	disapprove	discourage	disfavor	dislike
discourage	v	deter	dispirit	dissuade	prevent
discourse	v	converse	lecture	orate	speak
discourse	n	dialogue	sermon	speech	talk
discredit	n	disgrace	dishonor	shame	stigmatize
discredit	v	disparage	distrust	slander	vilify
discreet	adj	careful	judicious	prudent	wise
discrepancy	n	difference	disagreement	disparity	dissimilarity
discrete	adj	different	distinct	individual	separate
discretion	n	caution	choice	discernment	prudence
discretionary	adj	elective	flexible	optional	voluntary
discriminate	v	differentiate	discern	distinguish	separate
discriminating	adj	characteristic	distinctive	discerning	differentiating
discriminatory	adj	differential	discerning	partial	selective
discursive	adj	digressive	rambling	wondering	wordy
disdain	n	contempt	despisement	despitefulness	dislike
disdain	v	slight	snub	reject	scorn
disenfranchisement	n	denial	deprivation	dispossession	disqualification
disengage	v	detach	disconnect	free	release
disestablishment	n	dissolution	resolution	solution	settlement
disfigure	v	deface	mar	ruin	spoil
disgruntled	adj	displeased	dissatisfied	resentful	unhappy
dishabille	n	bareness	disarray	nudity	scantiness
dishevel	v	disarrange	disorder	muss	tousle

disheveled	adj	disordered	messy	unkempt	untidy
disillusioned	adj	annoyed	disappointed	offended	unhappy
disillusionment	n	disappointment	disenchantment	dismay	frustration
disinclination	n	aversion	dislike	distaste	unwillingness
disingenuous	adj	crafty	deceptive	insincere	sly
disingenuousness	n	dishonesty	duplicity	falsity	insincerity
disintegrate	v	decay	decline	decompose	spoil
disinter	v	excavate	exhume	expose	unearth
disinterested	adj	detached	impartial	neutral	unbiased
disjointed	adj	confused	disconnected	disordered	incoherent
disjunction	n	detachment	disunion	partition	separation
disk	n	album	plate	record	saucer
dislocation	n	breakdown	confusion	disruption	disturbance
dismal	adj	bleak	dreary	gloomy	sad
dismantle	v	breakdown	demolish	detach	disassemble
dismay	n	anxiety	dread	fear	panic
disoblige	v	bother	disturb	inconvenience	offend
disorient	v	befuddle	bewilder	confuse	perplex
disown	v	deny	disclaim	reject	renounce
disparage	v	belittle	discredit	ridicule	scorn
disparagement	n	depreciation	derogation	shame	slander
disparate	adj	different	dissimilar	distinct	unalike
disparities	n	differences	discrepancies	inequalities	variances
disparity	n	difference	discrepancy	inconsistency	variance
dispassionate	adj	fair	impartial	objective	neutral
dispatch	v	send	mail	ship	transmit
dispel	v	banish	disperse	dissipate	scatter
dispensation	n	distribution	exemption	liberty	permission
dispense	v	allocate	apportion	distribute	supply
disperse	v	broadcast	distribute	scatter	spread
dispersion	n	diffusion	distribution	scattering	spreading
dispirit	v	discourage	dishearten	dismay	sadden
display	v	demonstrate	exhibit	reveal	show
disport	v	amuse	divert	entertain	regale

disport	n	cavort	frolic	play	sport
disposal	n	discarding	dumping	junking	scrapping
disposed	adj	arranged	discarded	inclined	placed
disposition	n	attitude	character	mindset	temperament
dispossess	v	deprive	divest	expel	strip
disputatious	adj	contentious	touchy	polemic	quarrelsome
dispute	n	conflict	debate	fight	quarrel
disquieted	adj	agitated	distressed	disturbed	upset
disquieting	adj	alarming	distressing	disturbing	troubling
disquisition	n	commentary	critique	lecture	thesis
disreputable	adj	disgraceful	dishonorable	infamous	notorious
disrepute	n	discredit	disgrace	infamy	shame
disrupt	v	breach	break	interrupt	stop
dissatisfied	adj	annoyed	complaining	displeased	frustrated
dissection	n	analysis	examination	breakdown	deconstruction
dissemble	v	conceal	deceptive	disguise	pretend
disseminate	v	broadcast	circulate	distribute	spread
disseminating	n	broadcasting	diffusing	scattering	spreading
dissemination	n	deploy	publish	release	spread
dissension	n	conflict	disagreement	dispute	strife
dissent	v	differ	disagree	clash	collide
dissenter	n	heretic	rebel	maverick	nonconformist
dissentient	adj	dissenting	dissident	negative	nonconformist
dissentious	adj	divisive	insubordinate	negative	quarrelsome
dissertation	n	discourse	essay	thesis	treatise
disservice	n	damage	injury	injustice	wrong
dissidence	n	conflict	disagreement	discord	dissension
dissident	n	insurgent	maverick	nonconformist	renegade
dissimilar	adj	different	distinct	diverse	unlike
dissimulation	n	deception	deceit	duplicity	hypocrisy
dissipate	v	disappear	dissolve	evaporate	vanish
dissipated	adj	corrupt	degenerate	degraded	perverted
dissipation	n	debauchery	dissolution	extravagance	waste

dissociate	v	detach	disconnect	separate	withdraw
dissociative	adj	cleavable	divisible	separable	severable
dissolute	adj	debauched	depraved	immoral	profligate
dissoluteness	n	debauchery	dissipation	incontinence	profligacy
dissolution	n	death	disintegration	end	extinction
dissolve	v	disband	discontinue	end	terminate
dissonance	n	disagreement	discord	disharmony	dissension
dissonant	adj	inharmonious	off-key	unmelodious	unmusical
dissuade	v	discourage	inhibit	prevent	repel
distend	v	dilate	expand	inflate	swell
distill	v	condense	extract	purify	refine
distillation	n	concentration	essence	extract	purification
distinctive	adj	characteristic	individual	peculiar	unique
distinguish	v	differentiate	discern	discriminate	separate
distort	v	falsify	misrepresent	twist	warp
distortion	n	deformity	falsification	misinterpretation	perversion
distract	v	bewilder	deflect	divert	perplex
distraction	n	amusement	diversion	entertainment	recreation
distrait	adj	absentminded	distracted	inattentive	preoccupied
distraught	adj	agitated	distressed	frantic	upset
district	n	area	quarter	region	zone
distrust	v	doubt	mistrust	question	suspect
disturb	v	bother	perturb	trouble	upset
dither	v	dillydally	hesitate	waver	wobble
dithyrambic	adj	boisterous	impassioned	hot-blooded	wild
diurnal	adj	daily	daytime	everyday	quotidian
diva	n	goddess	prima donna	queen	star
divagate	v	digress	drift	ramble	wander
diverge	v	deviate	differ	separate	vary
divergence	n	deviation	difference	discrepancy	disunion
divergent	adj	conflicting	different	dissimilar	unalike
diverse	adj	assorted	different	distinct	various
diversify	v	alter	change	modify	vary
diversion	n	amusement	distraction	entertainment	recreation
diversity	n	assortment	miscellany	mixture	variety

divert	v	alter	change	deflect	redirect
dives	v	drops	falls	pitches	plunges
divest	v	deprive	disrobe	strip	undress
divestiture	n	assignment	disposal	sale	transfer
divide	n	break	partition	share	split
dividend	n	gain	perks	portion	profit
divine	v	foretell	predict	prognosticate	prophesy
divinity	n	deity	godhead	godliness	spirit
divisive	adj	conflicting	discordant	fractious	split
divorce	v	divide	part	separate	split
divulge	v	disclose	expose	reveal	tell
docent	n	instructor	guide	lecturer	teacher
docile	adj	compliant	conformable	obedient	submissive
dock	v	berth	crop	prune	trim
doctorate	n	degree	doctoral	doctorship	doctor's degree
doctrinaire	adj	dogmatic	stubborn	obstinate	principled
doctrine	n	belief	dogma	philosophy	principle
document	v	record	register	report	verify
documentary	adj	factual	historical	newsreel	objective
documenta-tion	n	certification	corroboration	evidence	proof
dodder	v	quiver	shake	totter	tremble
doddering	adj	decrepit	feeble	senile	shaky
dogged	adj	determined	persistent	stubborn	tenacious
doggerel	adj	burlesque	comic	jingle	outlandish
dogma	n	belief	doctrine	philosophy	tenant
dogmatic	adj	emphatic	insistent	opinionated	uncompro-mising
dogmatize	v	misjudge	misunder-stand	pontificate	suppose
dogmatizer	n	bigot	doctrinaire	partisan	sectarian
doldrums	n	blues	boredom	dullness	gloom
doleful	adj	mournful	sad	sorrowful	unhappy
dolmen	n	gravestone	megalith	monument	tombstone
dolor	n	grief	heartbreak	misery	sorrow
dolorous	adj	gloomy	mournful	melancholy	sad

dolt	n	dimwit	dope	idiot	stupidness
domain	n	area	realm	region	territory
domicile	n	address	home	house	residence
dominance	n	authority	control	superiority	supremacy
dominant	adj	chief	leading	paramount	superior
dominate	v	command	control	govern	rule
dominion	n	authority	control	rule	sovereignty
don	v	assume	dress	put on	wear
donate	v	bestow	contribute	give	pledge
donee	n	beneficiary	devisee	giftee	recipient
donnybrook	n	brawl	fracas	fray	squabble
donor	n	backer	contributor	giver	supporter
doppelganger	n	copy	double	duplicate	twin
dormant	adj	asleep	idle	inactive	resting
dorsal	adj	after	back	posterior	rear
dossier	n	file	papers	record	report
dotage	n	decrepitude	feebleness	fuddy-duddy	senility
dotard	adj	faltering	floundering	tottering	senile
dote	v	adore	coddle	indulge	pamper
doting	adj	adoring	affectionate	devoted	fond
doughty	adj	resolute	unafraid	fearless	valiant
dour	adj	grim	glum	morose	sullen
dowager	n	dame	matron	widow	woman
dowdy	adj	shabby	slovenly	tacky	unfashionable
dowel	n	bolt	nail	peg	plug
dowry	n	endowment	gift	portion	trousseau
doxology	n	anthem	glory	hymn	laud
doyen	n	dean	elder	provost	senior
drab	adj	boring	dreary	dull	gloomy
draconian	adj	cruel	harsh	severe	strict
drag	n	annoyance	bother	nuisance	pest
dragoon	v	coerce	force	intimidate	make
drama	n	acting	play	stage	theatre
dramaturgical	adj	communication	histrionic	theatric	thespian
drastic	adj	excessive	extreme	radical	severe

draw	v	attract	drag	lure	pull
dray	n	cart	van	vehicle	wagon
dreadnought	n	battleship	cruiser	ironclad	warship
dredge	v	dig	drag	excavate	shovel
dregs	n	residue	sediment	slag	waste
drivel	n	gibberish	inane	nonsense	twaddle
droll	adj	amusing	humorous	ludicrous	odd
drone	v	chill	dillydally	loaf	lounge
dropped	adj	decreased	depressed	knockdown	receded
dross	n	debris	garbage	rubbish	waste
drudgery	n	grind	labor	toil	travail
dubiety	n	doubt	mistrust	suspicion	uncertainty
dubious	adj	doubtful	distrustful	questionable	suspicious
ductile	adj	flexible	malleable	pliable	pliant
ductility	n	elasticity	flexibility	pliability	resilience
dudgeon	n	huff	miff	resentment	umbrage
due	adj	deserved	justified	merited	warranted
duenna	n	au pair	chaperone	mammy	governess
duet	n	couple	duo	pair	twosome
dulcet	adj	agreeable	pleasant	pretty	sweet
dullard	n	blockhead	dolt	idiot	simpleton
duly	adv	adequately	appropriately	correctly	properly
dunce	n	blockhead	dolt	fool	idiot
dunning	v	demand	remind	pester	persist
dupe	n	chump	patsy	pushover	sucker
dupe	v	con	deceive	defraud	trick
duplicate	adj	copy	double	equal	replicate
duplicity	n	deceit	dishonesty	treachery	trickery
durable	adj	enduring	lasting	strong	sturdy
duration	n	length	period	term	time
duress	n	coercion	compulsion	constraint	pressure
during	adv	throughout	over	while	within
dutiful	adj	docile	loyal	obedient	submissive
dwindle	v	decrease	decline	diminish	fade
dwindling	v	decreasing	diminishing	lessening	shrinking
dynamic	adj	active	energetic	lively	vigorous

dynamism	n	animation	energy	force	vigor
dynamo	n	alternator	engine	go-getter	generator
dyspeptic	adj	cantankerous	grouchy	irritable	ornery
dysphasia	n	disorder	deficiency	incoherence	impediment
dysphoria	n	anxiety	dejection	depression	heartbreak
dystopia	n	Camelot	nirvana	Shangri-La	utopia
eager	adj	anxious	ardent	enthusiastic	keen
earnest	adj	ardent	eager	serious	sincere
earthly	adj	material	mundane	terrestrial	worldly
easement	n	alleviation	bondage	servitude	slavery
easily	adj	fast	quick	simple	well
easygoing	adj	carefree	even-tempered	laid-back	relaxed
eavesdrop	v	listen	overhear	snoop	spy
ebb	v	decrease	recede	retreat	subside
ebullience	n	effervescence	enthusiasm	ferment	spirit
ebullient	adj	cheerful	joyful	excitement	enthusiasm
eccentric	adj	abnormal	irregular	outlandish	unconventional
eccentricity	n	idiosyncrasy	irregularity	oddity	peculiarity
ecclesiastical	adj	church	clerical	religious	spiritual
ecdysiast	n	exotic dancer	peeler	performer	stripper
echelon	n	degree	grade	level	position
eclectic	adj	assorted	diverse	extensive	varied
eclipse	v	obscure	overshadow	outshine	surpass
eclogue	n	idyll	ode	pastoral	rondeau
ecology	n	bionomics	environment	habitat	surroundings
economic	adj	business	cost-effective	financial	saving
economical	adj	affordable	cheap	inexpensive	low-cost
ecstasy	n	bliss	happiness	joy	rapture
ecstatic	adj	blissful	happy	joyful	overjoyed
ectype	n	image	picture	portrait	representation
ecumenical	adj	catholic	cosmopolitan	universal	worldwide
eczema	n	dermatitis	rash	skin disease	tetter
edacious	adj	gluttonous	greedy	ravenous	voracious
eddy	n	spin	swirl	vortex	whirlpool

edema	n	dropsy	inflammation	puffiness	swelling
edict	n	decree	dictum	order	ordinance
edification	n	education	enlighten-ment	instruction	learning
edifice	n	building	construction	erection	structure
edify	v	enlighten	enrich	illuminate	inspire
edifying	adj	educational	enlightening	informal	instructive
editorialize	v	comment	formulate	observe	remark
educative	v	didactic	enlightening	informative	instructive
educe	v	derive	elicit	evoke	extract
efface	v	eliminate	erase	remove	obliterate
effaced	v	canceled	deleted	erased	obliterated
effacement	n	cancellation	deletion	erasure	obliteration
effect	n	consequence	result	outcome	upshot
effective	adj	actual	efficient	powerful	useful
effectual	adj	efficient	potent	operative	potent
effectuate	v	accomplish	achieve	make	perform
effeminate	adj	feminine	sissy	unmanly	womanish
effervescence	n	animation	bubble	excitement	liveliness
effervescent	adj	bubbly	buoyant	lively	sparkling
effete	adj	feeble	spent	sterile	weak
efficacious	adj	effective	efficient	powerful	productive
efficacy	n	capability	efficiency	effectiveness	validity
efficiency	n	effectiveness	capability	performance	productivity
effigy	n	image	likeness	model	representa-tion
effloresce	v	bloom	blossom	burgeon	flower
efflorescence	n	autumn	blooming	blossoming	flowering
effluent	n	drainage	outflow	sewage	wastewater
effluvia	n	emanations	essences	fumes	smells
effluvium	n	exhaust	odor	smell	stench
effrontery	n	audacity	gall	impudence	insolence
effulgence	n	brightness	brilliance	glow	radiance
effulgent	adj	beaming	brilliant	glowing	shining
effusion	n	flow	gush	outburst	outpouring
effusive	adj	gushy	emotional	extravagant	overflowing
egalitarian	adj	equal	classless	democratic	evenhanded

egalitarian	n	equal	equity	leveler	moralist
egalitarianism	n	classlessness	equality	fairness	impartiality
ego	n	conceit	narcissism	pride	self
egocentric	adj	narcissistic	self-centered	selfish	vain
egoism	n	conceit	egotism	narcissism	selfishness
egotism	n	conceit	pride	selfishness	vanity
egotist	n	boaster	braggart	cynic	narcissist
egregious	adj	awful	dreadful	shocking	terrible
egress	n	exit	outflow	outlet	way out
eider	n	duvet	eiderdown	puffin	seabird
either	adv	likewise	moreover	whatsoever	whether
ejaculate	v	climax	cum	discharge	exclaim
eke	v	augment	increase	stretch	supplement
elaborate	v	develop	expand	expound	improve
elaborate	adj	complex	detailed	involved	sophisticated
élan	n	bounce	life	panache	vigor
elapse	v	close	conclude	discontinue	end
elastic	adj	flexible	pliant	resilient	springy
elate	v	cheer	gladden	exhilarate	uplift
elated	adj	delighted	happy	joyful	jubilant
elation	n	delight	ecstasy	euphoria	exhilaration
elderly	adj	aged	decrepit	old	senior
electorate	n	balloters	constituency	people	voter
electrify	v	arouse	excite	stimulate	thrill
electronics	n	circuitry	connection	physics	radio
eleemosynary	adj	beneficent	benevolent	charitable	philanthropic
elegant	adj	classy	exquisite	fine	graceful
elegiac	adj	mournful	plaintive	sad	sorrowful
elegy	n	dirge	lament	requiem	threnody
element	n	component	item	member	part
elemental	adj	basic	elementary	essential	fundamental
elementalistic	adj	basic	elementary	essential	fundamental
elenchus	n	antilogy	cant	claptrap	refutation
elephantine	adj	enormous	gargantuan	huge	jumbo
elicit	v	coax	extract	inspire	prompt
elide	v	discount	disregard	ignore	discount

eligible	adj	acceptable	desirable	entitled	qualified
eliminate	v	destroy	eradicate	remove	terminate
elite	adj	aristocratic	champion	exclusive	supreme
elite	n	A-list	elect	nobility	upper class
elitism	n	advantage	exclusiveness	lordliness	snobbery
elixir	n	balm	medicine	remedy	potion
ellipse	n	circle	curve	orbit	oval
ellipsis	n	abbreviation	elision	omission	shortening
elliptical	adj	egg-shaped	oblong	oval	ovoid
eloquence	n	diction	expressive-ness	fluency	rhetoric
eloquent	adj	articulate	expressive	fluent	well-spoken
eloquently	adv	articulately	expressively	fluently	smoothly
elucidate	v	clarify	explain	illuminate	illustrate
elude	v	avoid	dodge	escape	evade
elusive	adj	evasive	fugitive	shifty	slippery
elysian	adj	celestial	divine	heavenly	inspired
emaciated	adj	gaunt	haggard	starved	underfed
emanate	v	arise	issue	originate	radiate
emanation	n	discharge	effusion	emission	exhalation
emancipate	v	deliver	free	liberate	release
emancipation	n	deliverance	liberation	release	rescue
emasculate	v	castrate	enervate	geld	neuter
emasculation	n	castration	gelding	neutering	vasectomy
embargo	n	ban	interdiction	prohibition	proscription
embark	v	begin	board	start	undertake
embarrass	v	disgrace	humiliate	ridicule	shame
embed	v	enroot	entrench	implant	ingrain
embellish	v	adorn	decorate	enhance	exaggerate
embellished	adj	decorated	elaborate	fancy	ornate
embezzle	v	divert	misappropri-ate	purloin	steal
embezzle-ment	n	fraud	misappropri-ation	peculation	pilferage
emblazon	v	decorate	embellish	ornament	trim
emblematic	adj	iconic	representative	symbolic	typical
embodied	adj	incarnate	included	incorporated	materialized

embody	v	incarnate	include	incorporate	personify
emboss	v	decorate	impress	imprint	stamp
embrace	v	acceptance	acquiescence	concession	consent
embrocation	n	liniment	lotion	ointment	salve
embroider	v	beautify	decorate	embellish	ornament
embroil	v	ensnare	entangle	involve	mire
embryo	n	fetus	foetus	germ	nucleus
embryology	n	anatomy	biology	cytology	genetics
embryonic	adj	immature	rudimentary	undeveloped	unformed
emend	v	correct	improve	rectify	revise
emendation	n	alternation	correction	improve	restore
emergent	adj	coming	exigent	rising	urgent
emeritus	adj	causa	distinguished	honorary	retired
emetic	adj	emesis	foul	nauseous	vomitory
emigrate	v	defect	leave	migrate	relocate
eminence	n	distinction	excellence	prestige	prominence
eminent	adj	distinguished	famous	prominent	renowned
emissary	n	agent	delegate	envoy	representative
emit	v	discharge	eject	exude	radiate
emollient	n	cream	lotion	ointment	salve
emollient	adj	demulcent	lenitive	softening	soothing
emolument	n	compensation	payment	salary	wages
emote	v	act	dramatize	overact	perform
emotive	adj	affective	emotional	stirring	touching
empathy	n	accord	compassion	sympathy	understanding
emphasize	v	accentuate	highlight	stress	underline
emphatic	adj	assertive	forceful	insistent	positive
emphatically	adv	absolutely	definitely	strongly	vigorously
empirical	adj	experiential	experimental	observed	trial
empiricism	n	experientialism	experimentalism	sensationalism	worldliness
empiricist	n	herder	mastermind	philosopher	thinker
emplace	v	install	locate	place	set
employ	v	apply	hire	use	utilize
employer	n	boss	chief	head	master
empower	v	allow	authorize	enable	permit

emulate	v	copy	follow	imitate	mimic
emulation	n	competition	contention	rivalry	simulation
emulous	adj	ambitious	competitive	jealous	rivalrous
enact	v	decree	ordain	pass	perform
enamor	v	bewitch	captivate	charm	fascinate
enamored	adj	bewitched	charmed	infatuated	smitten
encapsulate	v	abbreviate	condense	summarize	wrap
enchant	v	bewitch	captivate	charm	fascinate
enclave	n	field	outland	reservation	territory
encomiast	n	eulogist	flunkey	optimist	panegyrist
encomium	n	commenda-tion	eulogy	praise	tribute
encompass	v	cover	encircle	include	surround
encore	n	callback	reappearance	recall	repeat
encourage-ment	n	aid	incentive	stimulus	support
encroach	v	infringe	intrude	invade	trespass
enculturation	n	assimilation	cultivation	refinement	socialization
encumber	v	burden	hamper	hinder	impede
encumbrance	n	burden	hindrance	impediment	obstruction
encyclopedic	adj	broad	comprehen-sive	complete	general
encyclopedist	n	author	compiler	novelist	poet
encysted	n	acidosis	adhesion	alkalosis	pathology
endear	v	attach	attract	captivate	charm
endeavor	v	aim	seek	strive	undertake
endeavor	n	attempt	effort	try	venture
endemic	adj	domestic	local	indigenous	native
endorse	v	approve	ratify	sanction	support
endow	v	furnish	give	provide	supply
endowment	n	award	donation	gift	grant
endue	v	endow	furnish	gift	invest
endurance	n	durability	permanence	perseverance	stamina
enduring	adj	continuing	durable	lasting	persistent
energize	v	animate	excite	invigorate	stimulate
enervate	v	deplete	exhaust	fatigue	weaken
enervated	adj	debilitated	exhausted	tired	weak

enervating	adj	debilitating	draining	fatiguing	exhausting
enfetter	v	bind	chain	fetter	shackle
enfranchise	v	emancipate	free	liberate	release
engage	v	commit	hire	involve	undertake
engaging	adj	attractive	captivating	charming	enchanting
engender	v	cause	create	generate	produce
engrave	v	burn	carve	etch	inscribe
engross	v	absorb	captivate	engage	occupy
engrossed	adj	absorbed	engaged	immersed	preoccupied
engulf	v	immerse	overwhelm	submerge	swamp
enhance	v	better	improve	increase	upgrade
enigma	n	mystery	puzzle	secret	riddle
enigmatic	adj	baffling	mysterious	perplexing	puzzling
enjambment	n	bridging	crossover	running over	step over
enjoin	v	charge	command	direct	order
enlarge	v	elaborate	expand	extend	increase
enlighten	v	edify	inform	instruct	teach
enlighten-ment	n	edification	education	instruction	Nirvana
enlist	v	engage	hire	join	recruit
enliven	v	animate	inspire	invigorate	stimulate
enmity	n	animosity	antagonism	hostility	malice
ennoble	v	dignify	elevate	exalt	glorify
ennobling	adj	dignifying	exalting	honorable	royal
ennui	n	boredom	fatigue	melancholy	tiredness
enormity	n	atrocity	immensity	magnitude	outrage
enormous-ness	n	hugeness	immensity	magnitude	vastness
ensconce	adj	askew	awry	crooked	oblique
ensconced	adj	established	fixed	located	placed
enshroud	v	conceal	cover	envelop	hide
enslavement	n	bondage	serfdom	servitude	subjugation
ensnare	v	capture	catch	entangle	entrap
ensue	v	arise	follow	pursue	succeed
ensure	v	confirm	guarantee	safeguard	secure
entail	v	imply	involve	necessitate	require
enterprise	n	business	company	firm	undertaking

entertain	v	amuse	delight	divert	please
entertain-ment	n	amusement	diversion	play	recreation
enthrall	v	captivate	enslave	mesmerize	thrill
entice	v	attract	lure	seduce	tempt
entitle	v	authorize	call	empower	dub
entity	n	being	essence	existence	individual
entourage	n	cortege	followers	retinue	suite
entreat	v	beg	beseech	implore	request
entreaty	n	appeal	petition	plea	supplication
entrench	v	embed	fix	lodge	root
entrench-ment	n	consolidation	establishment	rooting	strengthening
entrepreneur	n	businessman	contractor	enterpriser	manager
entropy	n	chaos	disarray	disorder	turmoil
enumerate	v	count	itemize	list	number
enunciate	v	articulate	pronounce	utter	voice
enviable	adj	advantageous	desirable	lucky	fortunate
envious	adj	covetous	greedy	jealous	resentful
environment	n	atmosphere	conditions	habitat	surroundings
environmen-talist	n	conservation-ist	ecologist	naturalist	preservation-ist
envisage	v	anticipate	envision	foresee	imagine
envision	v	envisage	foresee	imagine	visualize
envoi	n	diplomat	emissary	envoy	stanza
envoy	n	agent	delegate	emissary	representative
ephemera	n	curiosity	exotic	oddity	rarity
ephemeral	adj	fleeting	passing	short-lived	temporary
ephemerality	n	evanescence	fleetingness	mortality	transience
epic	n	legend	narrative	saga	tale
epic	adj	heroic	gargantuan	grand	tremendous
epicene	adj	neuter	sexless	not virile	style-less
epicure	n	bon vivant	gastronome	gourmet	hedonist
Epicurean	adj	gourmet	hedonist	sybaritic	voluptuary
epicureanism	n	hedonism	indulgence	plea-sure-seeking	sensualism
epigone	n	copycat	disciple	follower	imitator

epigram	n	adage	aphorism	maxim	witticism
epigraph	n	caption	inscription	legend	motto
epilepsy	n	attack	convulsion	paroxysm	seizure
epiphany	n	discovery	inspiration	realization	revelation
episode	n	event	incident	happening	occurrence
epistle	n	communiqué	dispatch	letter	memorandum
epitaph	n	commemoration	eulogy	memorial	remembrance
epithet	n	appellation	designation	name	title
epitome	n	ideal	model	representative	summary
epitomize	v	abridge	abstract	condense	summarize
epoch	n	age	era	period	time
epochal	adj	iconic	momentous	periodic	seminal
epochs	n	ages	eras	periods	times
eponym	n	cognomen	epithet	namesake	title
epoxy	n	cement	glue	resin	rosin
equable	adj	calm	even	placid	steady
equalitarian	adj	disciplinarian	egalitarian	martinet	moralist
equalitarianism	n	democracy	doctrine	egalitarianism	philosophy
equanimity	n	calmness	composure	poise	serenity
equerry	n	groom	hostler	ostler	valet
equestrian	n	equitation	horseman	jockey	rider
equilibrium	n	balance	equipoise	poise	stability
equine	n	horse	nag	stallion	steed
equipoise	v	balance	counterbalance	offset	parallel
equitable	adj	fair	impartial	just	unbiased
equivalent	adj	equal	corresponding	same	similar
equivocal	adj	ambiguous	confusing	obscure	vague
equivocate	v	dodge	evade	hedge	lie
equivocation	n	ambiguity	deception	evasion	prevarication
equivoque	n	ambiguity	double entendre	epigram	pun
eradicate	v	abolish	destroy	eliminate	remove
eremite	n	anchorite	hermit	monk	recluse
eremitical	adj	anchoritic	hermitic	lone	religious

ergo	adv	accordingly	consequently	hence	therefore
eristic	adj	argumentative	contentious	disputatious	whiny
erode	v	corrode	diminish	reduce	undermine
erotic	adj	lascivious	lewd	sexy	sensual
err	v	blunder	sin	slip	transgress
errant	adj	sinful	rambling	vagabond	wandering
errantry	n	itinerancy	peregrination	vagrancy	wanderlust
erratic	adj	arbitrary	fickle	irregular	unpredictable
erroneous	adj	inaccurate	incorrect	false	wrong
ersatz	adj	artificial	fake	false	imitation
eructation	n	belch	burp	eruption	extravasation
erudite	adj	educated	knowledge-able	learned	scholarly
erudition	n	education	knowledge	learning	scholarship
erupt	v	break	burst	detonate	explode
eruption	n	blast	explosion	outbreak	outburst
escalate	v	heighten	increase	intensify	raise
escalation	n	growth	increase	rise	surge
escapade	n	adventure	caper	frolic	lark
escape	v	avoid	evade	flee	leave
escarp	n	bank	cliff	precipice	slope
escarpment	n	bluff	cliff	precipice	ridge
escheat	v	confiscate	deprive	forfeit	seize
eschew	v	abstain	avoid	evade	shun
escort	n	accompany	companion	convoy	guide
escritoire	n	bureau	cabinet	desk	secretary
escrow	n	deposit	guarantee	impounding	security
esoteric	adj	complex	difficult	mysterious	profound
esoterica	n	arcane	impracticality	minutiae	specialty
especially	adj	notably	particularly	specially	specifically
espionage	n	intelligence	reconnais-sance	spying	surveillance
esplanade	n	boardwalk	path	promenade	walk
espousal	n	adoption	betrothal	bridal	marriage
espouse	v	adopt	advocate	embrace	support
esprit	n	dash	life	verve	zip
essay	n	article	composition	paper	theme

essay	v	attempt	endeavor	seek	try
essence	n	core	heart	nature	substance
essential	adj	crucial	fundamental	important	vital
establish	v	build	create	determine	develop
establishmen-tarian	adj	conformist	conventional	orthodox	traditional
esteem	n	admiration	honor	regard	respect
esthetic	adj	artistic	beautiful	gorgeous	pleasing
estimable	adj	admirable	good	respectable	worthy
estimate	v	assess	calculate	evaluate	judge
estival	adj	summery	sultry	tropical	torrid
estivate	v	dormancy	doze	hibernate	torpor
estop	v	bar	preclude	prevent	prohibit
estrange	v	alienate	disaffect	disunite	separate
estuary	n	bay	creek	firth	inlet
esurient	adj	edacious	greedy	ravenous	voracious
etch	v	carve	cut	engrave	incise
eternal	adj	endless	everlasting	permanent	undying
ethereal	adj	airy	celestial	heavenly	immaterial
ethical	adj	honest	honorable	just	virtuous
ethics	n	conscience	morals	principles	standards
ethnic	adj	cultural	national	native	tribal
ethnocentric	adj	colonized	imperialistic	monocultural	xenophobic
ethnocen-trism	n	bias	genocide	partiality	racism
ethos	n	attitude	beliefs	culture	philosophy
etiolate	v	blanch	diminish	pale	weaken
etiquette	n	decorum	manners	propriety	protocol
eudemonia	n	fitness	robustness	shape	strength
eulogize	v	exalt	extol	honor	praise
eulogized	v	applauded	commended	extolled	praised
eulogy	n	commenda-tion	compliment	endorsement	tribute
eunuch	n	castrate	emasculation	gelding	guy
euphemism	n	alternative	expression	saying	substitution
euphemistic	adj	flowery	inoffensive	refined	vague
euphonic	adj	dulcet	melodious	musical	tuneful

euphonious	adj	harmonious	melodious	musical	tuneful
euphony	n	consonance	harmony	melody	tune
euphoria	n	ecstasy	elation	exaltation	happiness
euphoric	adj	ecstatic	elated	happy	overjoyed
euphuism	n	bombast	delicacy	purism	rhetoric
evade	v	avoid	dodge	elude	escape
evading	v	avoiding	dodging	ducking	shirking
evaluate	v	assess	estimate	judge	measure
evanesce	v	disappear	evaporate	fade	vanish
evanescent	adj	brief	fleeting	short-lived	temporary
evangelical	adj	apostolic	fervent	proselytizing	religious
evangelize	v	convert	preach	proselytize	sermonize
evasive	adj	elusive	deceitful	shifty	sly
eventful	adj	consequential	important	memorable	momentous
eventual	adj	concluding	final	last	ultimate
eventuate	v	befall	happen	occur	result
everyday	adj	common	daily	ordinary	routine
evict	v	eject	expel	oust	remove
evident	adj	apparent	clear	manifest	obvious
evidential	adj	demonstrated	factual	probative	proof
evince	v	demonstrate	exhibit	manifest	show
eviscerate	v	disembowel	draw	gut	weaken
evocation	n	conjuration	elicitation	invocation	summoning
evocative	adj	expressive	remindful	reminiscent	suggestive
evoke	v	arouse	elicit	provoke	raise
evolution	n	expansion	development	growth	progression
exacerbate	v	aggravate	annoy	intensify	worsen
exact	v	claim	demand	fine	require
exacting	adj	demanding	fastidious	scrupulous	strict
exactly	adv	actually	just	precisely	right
exaggerate	v	amplify	magnify	overdo	overstate
exalt	v	elevate	extol	glorify	praise
exalted	adj	elevated	grand	noble	lofty
examine	v	consider	investigate	review	study
exasperate	v	annoy	irritate	provoke	vex
exasperation	n	anger	aggravation	annoyance	irritation

exceed	v	excel	go beyond	outdo	surpass
except	v	bar	exclude	omit	save
exceptional	adj	extraordinary	singular	unique	unusual
excerpt	n	extract	passage	quote	selection
excess	n	extra	plethora	superfluity	surplus
excessive	adj	extravagant	extreme	inordinate	outrageous
exchequer	n	checkerboard	chessboard	spectrum	treasury
excise	v	amputate	cut	eradicate	remove
excision	n	ablation	amputation	extirpation	removal
excite	v	animate	arouse	stimulate	stir
exclaim	v	call	holler	scream	yell
exclude	v	ban	bar	eliminate	reject
exclusive	adj	elite	private	restricted	special
excogitation	n	conception	design	invention	rumination
excommuni-cate	v	banish	curse	exclude	expel
excommuni-cation	n	anathema	ban	exclusion	exile
excoriate	v	chafe	scalp	denounce	rebuke
excoriation	n	contempt	denunciation	hatred	odium
excretion	n	discharge	evacuation	excreta	secretion
excruciate	v	agonize	rack	torment	torture
excruciating	adj	agonizing	harrowing	painful	tormenting
exculpate	v	absolve	clear	excuse	exonerate
excursion	n	journey	outing	tour	trip
execrable	adj	abominable	atrocious	odious	vile
execrate	v	abhor	denounce	detest	loathe
execration	n	detestation	hate	loathing	odium
execute	v	accomplish	effect	implement	perform
executor	n	agent	architect	doer	proxy
exegesis	n	clarification	explanation	exposition	interpretation
exegete	n	commentator	critic	expositor	interpreter
exegetical	adj	explanatory	explicative	expository	hermeneutic
exemplar	n	example	model	paradigm	paragon
exemplary	adj	admirable	commendable	model	outstanding
exemplify	v	illustrate	represent	symbolize	typify
exempt	v	absolve	free	release	relieve

exequies	n	burial	funeral	inhumation	obsequies
exercise	v	drill	exert	practice	work
exert	v	apply	exercise	utilize	wield
exhaustive	adj	complete	comprehensive	detailed	thorough
exhibitionism	n	flashing	immodesty	showmanship	streaking
exhibitionist	n	flasher	immoralist	showboat	showoff
exhibitionistic	adj	flagrant	flashy	ostentatious	splashy
exhilaration	n	cheerfulness	delight	happiness	joy
exhort	v	advise	encourage	prompt	urge
exhume	v	disinter	excavate	unearth	uncover
exigency	n	emergency	need	pinch	urgency
exigent	adj	demanding	imperative	pressing	urgent
exiguous	adj	meager	poor	scanty	sparse
exile	v	banish	deport	expatriate	expel
exist	v	continue	live	subsist	survive
existence	n	being	life	living	presence
existent	adj	actual	existing	extant	real
existential	n	being	empirical	experiential	vital
exit	v	depart	go	leave	retreat
exodus	n	departure	exit	flight	migration
exogamy	n	endogamy	intermarriage	matrimony	outbreeding
exonerate	v	absolve	acquit	clear	excuse
exorbitant	adj	excessive	expensive	extravagant	outrageous
exorcise	v	banish	charm	conjure	expel
exoteric	adj	exterior	open	outer	public
exotic	adj	foreign	outlandish	strange	unusual
expand	v	broaden	enlarge	extend	increase
expanse	n	area	extent	range	space
expansive	adj	ample	broad	extensive	large
expatiate	v	elaborate	expound	speak	write
expatriate	v	banish	deport	exile	expel
expectorate	v	drool	hawk	spew	spit
expectoration	n	drivel	saliva	spit	sputum
expedient	adj	advantageous	convenient	opportune	useful
expedite	v	accelerate	facilitate	hasten	quicken

expeditious	adj	quick	rapid	speedy	swift
expel	v	banish	dismiss	eject	oust
expendable	adj	dispensable	disposable	insignificant	unnecessary
expenditure	n	cost	expense	spending	outlay
expensive	adj	costly	dear	pricey	valuable
experience	v	encounter	experiment	know	undergo
experiment	v	experience	research	test	trial
expert	adj	adept	master	professional	proficient
expertise	n	ability	knowledge	skill	proficiency
expiate	v	atone	compensate	redeem	redress
expiation	n	atonement	propitiation	reparation	satisfaction
expire	v	die	end	lapse	perish
explanation	n	clarification	elucidation	explication	interpretation
expletive	n	curse	cuss	oath	swearword
explicate	v	clarify	elucidate	explain	interpret
explicit	adj	clear	definite	exact	plain
explode	v	burst	detonate	discharge	erupt
exploit	n	accomplish-ment	achievement	deed	feat
exploit	v	abuse	control	manipulate	use
exploited	v	abused	explode	exploit	used
explore	v	examine	investigate	research	study
exponent	n	advocate	index	proponent	supporter
expose	v	disclose	reveal	show	uncover
exposed	adj	bared	denuded	revealed	uncovered
exposition	n	demonstra-tion	exhibition	presentation	show
expositionism	n	exhibitionist	flashing	showmanship	streaking
expository	adj	explanatory	expositive	interpretive	illustrative
expostulate	v	argue	object	protest	remonstrate
expostulation	n	complaint	objection	protest	remonstrance
expound	v	clarify	explain	elaborate	illustrate
express	v	convey	declare	reveal	utter
expropriate	v	commandeer	confiscate	dispossess	seize
expulsion	n	deportation	ejection	eviction	removal
expunge	v	cancel	delete	eradicate	erase
expurgate	v	censor	cleanse	expunge	purge

exquisite	adj	beautiful	elegant	excellent	lovely
extant	adj	alive	current	existing	present
extemporaneous	adj	impromptu	offhand	spontaneous	unrehearsed
extemporize	v	ad-lib	improvise	offhand	unpremeditated
extend	v	broaden	expand	increase	stretch
extent	n	degree	magnitude	range	scope
extenuate	v	excuse	mitigate	palliate	reduce
extinct	adj	archaic	dead	gone	obsolete
extirpate	v	abolish	destroy	eradicate	exterminate
extirpated	v	eradicated	exterminated	removed	uprooted
extol	v	commend	exalt	glorify	praise
extort	v	blackmail	extract	shakedown	wrest
extortion	n	blackmail	coercion	shakedown	squeeze
extortionate	adj	excessive	exorbitant	outrageous	steep
extract	v	pull	remove	uproot	withdraw
extracurricular	adj	adulterous	extramarital	external	outside
extradite	v	deliver	deport	exile	surrender
extraneous	adj	extra	irrelevant	unimportant	unnecessary
extrapolate	v	deduce	generalize	infer	project
extrasensory	v	conclude	deduce	gather	guess
extravagance	n	excess	luxury	prodigality	profligacy
extravagant	adj	excessive	extreme	lavish	outrageous
extravasate	v	discharge	eject	erupt	exude
extremely	adv	exceedingly	extraordinarily	highly	very
extremity	n	boundary	edge	end	limit
extricate	v	disengage	disentangle	free	liberate
extrinsic	adj	eternal	extraneous	foreign	outer
extrovert	n	backslapper	convivial	exhibitionist	mixer
extroverted	adj	expansive	forthcoming	outgoing	sociable
extrude	v	eject	emit	expel	protrude
exuberance	n	enthusiasm	exhilaration	happiness	liveliness
exuberant	adj	cheerful	enthusiastic	happy	lush
exude	v	discharge	emit	leak	ooze

exult	v	delight	gloat	rejoice	triumph
exultant	adj	delighted	elated	happy	joyful
exultation	n	elation	joy	rejoicing	triumph
eyrie	n	coop	den	hive	nest
fabricate	v	construct	make	manufacture	invent
fabrication	n	falsification	fiction	lie	manufacture
fabulist	n	fraud	impostor	liar	storyteller
fabulous	n	fantastic	marvelous	splendid	wonderful
facade	n	disguise	face	false	mask
facet	n	aspect	feature	quality	side
facetious	adj	humorous	joking	sarcastic	witty
facile	adj	easy	fluent	nimble	quick
facilitate	v	aid	assist	ease	expedite
facility	n	ability	adroitness	plant	proficiency
facsimile	n	copy	duplicate	replica	reproduction
faction	n	clique	group	party	set
factionalism	n	dissension	dissidence	friction	sectarianism
factious	adj	divisive	insurgent	rebellious	seditious
factitious	adj	artificial	false	sham	synthetic
factor	n	component	element	ingredient	part
factotum	n	broker	drudge	lackey	servant
facula	n	blaze	flame	flare	flash
faculty	n	ability	aptitude	capacity	talent
fad	n	craze	fashion	rage	trend
fagoting	n	cross-stitch	embroidery	fancywork	needlepoint
fail	v	collapse	decline	disappoint	miss
fain	adj	game	inclined	ready	willing
fakir	n	cheater	defrauder	scammer	swindler
falderal	n	absurdity	bauble	nonsense	twaddle
fallacious	adj	deceptive	erroneous	false	misleading
fallacy	n	delusion	misconception	error	mistake
fallible	adj	human	questionable	uncertain	unreliable
fallow	adj	barren	inactive	sterile	unproductive
falter	v	hesitate	stagger	stumble	waver
familiar	adj	accustomed	common	ordinary	usual

families	n	domestic	home	household	relatives
famous	adj	celebrated	famed	notorious	renowned
fanatic	n	devotee	enthusiast	extremist	fiend
fanatical	adj	enthusiastic	fervent	passionate	zealous
fanaticism	n	bigotry	enthusiasm	intolerance	zeal
fane	n	cathedral	church	shrine	temple
fanfare	n	display	flourish	hullabaloo	show
fantasia	n	daydream	fancy	fantasy	imagination
far-fetched	adj	doubtful	improbable	unbelievable	unlikely
farce	n	charade	comedy	joke	travesty
farcical	adj	absurd	funny	laughable	ridiculous
fare	n	board	food	charge	passenger
farrago	n	hodgepodge	medley	mishmash	mixture
farther	adj	away	distant	far	further
fasces	n	bale	bundle	mace	wand
fascicle	n	booklet	brochure	bundle	cluster
fascism	n	autocracy	dictatorship	nationalism	Nazism
fashion	n	form	manner	mode	style
fastidious	adj	finicky	fussy	meticulous	particular
fatal	adj	deadly	destructive	lethal	mortal
fathom	v	comprehend	grasp	see	understand
fatidic	adj	oracular	prophetic	sibylline	vatic
fatuity	n	absurdity	folly	idiocy	stupidity
fatuous	adj	asinine	foolish	silly	stupid
fault	n	blame	error	flaw	mistake
fauna	n	animal	beast	wildlife	zoology
favorite	adj	beloved	dear	favored	preferred
fawn	v	flatter	grovel	kowtow	toady
faze	v	bother	disturb	rattle	unnerve
fealty	n	allegiance	devotion	fidelity	loyalty
feasible	adj	possible	practicable	viable	workable
feat	v	accomplish-ment	achievement	deed	exploit
febrifuge	n	antipyretic	cure	medication	remedy
febrile	adj	delirious	feverish	hectic	hot
feckless	adj	incompetent	ineffectual	irresponsible	useless

feculent	adj	fecal	filthy	foul	putrid
fecund	adj	fertile	fruitful	productive	prolific
fecundity	n	abundance	fertility	fruitfulness	productivity
fee	n	charge	payment	price	salary
feebler	adj	dimmer	fainter	lamer	weaker
feign	v	counterfeit	fake	pretend	simulate
feint	n	deception	fake	ploy	trick
feisty	adj	lively	ornery	spunky	touchy
felicitate	v	commend	compliment	congratulate	praise
felicities	n	blessings	delights	ecstasies	exultations
felicitous	adj	appropriate	fitting	fortunate	opportune
felicity	n	delight	happiness	joy	pleasure
feline	adj	catlike	cunning	sly	subtle
fell	adj	barbarous	brutal	cruel	savage
felon	n	criminal	culprit	offender	outlaw
felonious	adj	corrupt	criminal	villainous	wicked
felony	n	crime	delict	misdemeanor	offense
fend	v	defend	guard	protect	shield
fenestration	n	hole	operation	surgery	windowing
feral	adj	brutal	ferocious	savage	wild
ferment	n	agitation	commotion	disturbance	turmoil
ferocious	adj	brutal	cruel	fierce	savage
ferret	v	search	seek	root	unearth
fertile	adj	fruitful	productive	abundant	plentiful
ferula	n	slat	ruler	splint	pointer
fervent	adj	ardent	passionate	vehement	zealous
fervid	adj	ardent	fervent	passionate	zealous
fervor	n	enthusiasm	excitement	intensity	passion
fester	v	decay	decompose	rankle	rot
festive	adj	cheerful	glad	happy	joyful
festoon	n	garland	garnish	ornament	wreath
fete	n	celebrate	feast	fiesta	party
fetid	adj	odorous	rancid	rank	stinking
fetish	adj	fool	kinky	lunatic	maniac
fetish	n	fantasy	fixation	obsession	passion
fetter	v	chain	handcuff	restrain	shackle

fettle	n	condition	form	health	shape
feudalism	n	bondage	captivity	servility	slavery
fewer	adj	least	lesser	lower	smaller
fey	adj	clairvoyant	eccentric	otherworldly	whimsical
fiasco	n	debacle	disaster	failure	flop
fiat	n	decree	dictum	edict	order
fickle	adj	changeable	erratic	inconstant	unpredictable
fictile	adj	flexible	moldable	plastic	pliable
fictitious	adj	false	illusory	imaginary	sham
fictive	adj	assumed	fanciful	imaginary	sham
fidelity	n	allegiance	devotion	faithfulness	loyalty
fiduciary	n	belongings	depositary	property	trustee
fiduciary	adj	believable	credible	reliable	trustworthy
fiend	n	demon	devil	freak	monster
fierce	adj	ferocious	furious	savage	violent
fiery	adj	ardent	burning	flaming	passionate
fifth column	n	infiltrators	saboteurs	Trojan horse	underground
figment	n	dream	fancy	fantasy	fiction
figurative	adj	illustrative	metaphoric	nonliteral	typical
filch	v	lift	pilfer	steal	swipe
filibuster	n	obstructionist	pirate	stall	stonewalling
filigree	n	decoration	embellish-ment	latticework	ornament
filigreed	adj	framed	interlaced	meshed	netted
fillip	n	boost	encourage-ment	incentive	stimulus
finale	n	conclusion	finish	last	termination
finally	adv	conclusively	eventually	lastly	ultimately
financially	adj	Malian	economic	economy	fiscal
financier	n	backer	banker	entrepreneur	funder
finesse	n	cunning	delicacy	skill	tact
finical	adj	fastidious	finicky	fussy	particular
finicky	adj	choosy	fussy	particular	picky
finite	adj	bounded	confined	limited	restricted
fire	v	arouse	kindle	discharge	dismiss
firebrand	n	agitator	incendiary	instigator	troublemaker
firmament	n	empyrean	heaven	sky	welkin

fiscal	n	attorney	finance	funding	taxation
fission	n	cleavage	division	scission	splitting
fissionable	adj	atomic	cleavable	fissile	scissile
fissiparous	adj	breakaway	productive	separatist	prolific
fissure	n	cleft	crack	crevice	rift
fitful	adj	erratic	intermittent	irregular	spasmodic
fitness	n	appropriate-ness	aptness	propriety	suitability
fixate	v	concentrate	fasten	focus	obsess
fixity	n	fastness	immutability	secureness	stability
fjord	n	estuary	firth	inlet	gulf
flabbergasted	adj	amassed	astonished	dumbfounded	thunderstruck
flaccid	adj	lax	limp	loose	slack
flag	v	label	languish	signal	weaken
flagellate	v	flog	lash	scourge	whip
flagitious	adj	corrupt	criminal	diabolical	wicked
flagon	n	bottle	flask	jar	jug
flagrant	adj	blatant	glaring	heinous	outrageous
flail	v	beat	lash	thrash	thresh
flamboyant	adj	extravagant	flashy	gaudy	showy
flammable	adj	burnable	combustible	ignitable	inflammable
flange	n	border	edge	projection	side
flatulent	adj	bombastic	gassy	pompous	windy
flaunt	v	display	exhibit	flourish	show off
flay	v	castigate	excoriate	lash	skin
fledge	v	feather	fledging	flight	operate
fledged	adj	entitled	mature	organic	right
fledgling	n	apprentice	beginner	novice	rookie
fleer	v	mock	ridicule	sneer	ridicule
fleeted	adj	alerted	fasted	prompted	readied
flexible	adj	compliant	pliant	soft	yielding
flippant	adj	cheeky	frivolous	impertinent	trivial
flirtatious	adj	coy	enticing	seductive	sexy
flock	n	crowd	group	herd	pack
flora	n	botany	plant	vegetation	verdure
florid	adj	flamboyant	flowery	ornate	showy

flotsam	n	driftwood	jetsam	junk	wreckage
flounce	v	prance	ruffle	strut	toss
flounder	v	blunder	falter	stagger	stumble
flourish	v	grow	prosper	succeed	thrive
flout	v	defy	disregard	mock	scorn
fluctuate	v	oscillate	vary	vacillate	waver
fluctuating	adj	capricious	vacillating	variable	wavering
fluctuation	n	change	oscillation	swing	variation
fluid	adj	flowing	fluent	liquid	unstable
flummoxed	adj	annoyed	complicated	confused	irritated
fluvial	adj	riparian	river	stream	watercourse
flux	n	flood	flow	motion	stream
focus	n	attention	core	emphasis	hub
fodder	n	feed	food	forage	provender
foe	n	adversary	antagonist	enemy	opponent
foible	n	failing	fault	flaw	weakness
foil	v	check	defeat	frustrate	thwart
foist	v	impose	inflict	insinuate	palm
fold	v	bend	crease	double	pleat
foliage	n	blade	greenery	growth	leaf
folk	n	family	people	population	public
follow	v	monitor	obey	pursue	track
foment	v	excite	incite	provoke	stimulate
font	n	fountain	source	typeface	wellspring
foolhardy	adj	daring	hasty	rash	reckless
footloose	adj	easygoing	free	unattached	uninhibited
footpad	n	bandit	highwayman	robber	thief
fop	n	coxcomb	dandy	dude	gallant
foppish	adj	conceited	dandy	mincing	vain
forage	v	feed	hunt	rummage	search
foray	v	attack	inroad	maraud	raid
forbear	n	ancestor	forefather	precursor	progenitor
forbear	v	abstain	desist	eschew	refrain
forbearance	n	long-suffering	resignation	restraint	tolerance
forbidding	adj	grim	hostile	menacing	unfriendly
forceful	adj	potent	powerful	strong	vigorous

forcible	adj	potent	powerful	strong	violent
ford	v	cross	pass over	traverse	wade
forebear	n	ancestor	precursor	predecessor	progenitor
foreboding	n	augury	premonition	presage	prognostica-tion
foreboding	adj	menacing	ominous	sinister	threatening
forecast	v	foretell	foreshadow	predict	prognosticate
foreclose	v	exclude	preclude	prevent	seize
foreign	adj	alien	external	outside	strange
foreigners	n	aliens	immigrants	outsiders	strangers
forensic	n	debate	dialectic	medical	science
foresee	v	anticipate	expect	hope	predict
foreshorten	v	abbreviate	cut	reduce	shorten
foresight	n	forecast	prediction	prognostica-tion	prudence
forestall	v	anticipate	avert	preclude	prevent
foreword	n	introduction	preamble	preface	prologue
forfeit	v	fine	lose	loss	waive
forge	v	construct	fabricate	make	shape
forgery	n	counterfeit	fake	imitation	sham
forget	v	ignore	neglect	overlook	remember
forgo	v	abandon	relinquish	renounce	waive
forlorn	v	depressed	melancholy	miserable	unhappy
form	v	build	construct	create	mold
former	adj	earlier	past	previous	prior
formerly	adj	already	before	earlier	previously
formidable	adj	fearful	frightful	intimidating	powerful
forsake	v	abandon	desert	leave	quit
forswear	v	abandon	deny	forgo	renounce
forte	n	aptitude	gift	strength	talent
forthcoming	adj	approaching	coming	future	impending
forthright	adj	candid	direct	frank	straightfor-ward
forthwith	adv	directly	immediately	promptly	straightway
fortify	v	brace	invigorate	reinforce	strengthen
fortissimo	adj	booming	deafening	loud	sonorous
fortitude	n	bravery	courage	resolution	valor

fortuitous	adj	accidental	chance	fortunate	lucky
fortuity	n	accident	chance	fluke	luck
forunate	adj	blessed	chance	happy	lucky
forward	v	advance	further	send	transmit
fossil	n	ancient	archaic	prehistoric	relic
fossilize	v	harden	indurate	ossify	petrify
foster	v	advance	encourage	promote	support
fostered	adj	developed	nourished	promoting	supported
founder	v	bomb	collapse	fail	flop
founder	n	creator	entrepreneur	inventor	originator
fox	v	delude	finagle	outwit	swindle
fracas	n	brawl	disturbance	fight	ruckus
fractious	adj	cross	irritable	testy	unruly
fragile	adj	delicate	feeble	frail	weak
fragmented	adj	broken	disconnected	divided	split
frail	adj	delicate	feeble	fragile	weak
frailty	n	debility	feebleness	infirmity	weakness
franchise	v	charter	license	permit	sanction
frangible	adj	breakable	brittle	fragile	frail
frantic	adj	excited	frenzied	mad	wild
fraternal	adj	brotherly	comradely	friendly	sibling
fraternity	n	brotherhood	fellowship	guild	association
fraught	adj	anxious	charged	filled	laden
fray	n	brawl	fight	fracas	ruckus
frenetic	adj	mad	frantic	frenzied	wild
frenzy	n	fury	passion	rage	turmoil
frequent	adj	common	often	regular	usual
frequently	adv	often	much	regularly	repeatedly
fresco	n	mural	picture	painting	panorama
fret	v	chafe	irritate	stew	worry
fretful	adj	irritable	petulant	querulous	testy
friable	adj	breakable	brittle	crumbly	fragile
friend	n	buddy	comrade	companion	pal
friendliness	n	benevolence	congeniality	cordiality	warmth
frippery	n	junk	ostentation	trifle	trinket
frisson	n	shiver	shudder	thrill	tingle

fritter	v	dissipate	misspend	squander	waste
frivolity	n	flightiness	flippancy	levity	playfulness
frivolous	adj	flighty	foolish	giddy	superficial
frizzle	v	bake	crimp	curl	fry
frolic	n	caper	gambol	play	romp
frond	n	blade	flag	leaf	thallus
froward	adj	contrary	contumacious	perverse	refractory
frugal	adj	economical	sparing	stingy	thrifty
fruitful	adj	fertile	productive	profitable	prolific
fruition	n	fulfillment	pleasure	realization	success
fruitless	adj	barren	unproductive	futile	useless
frustrate	v	foil	hinder	impede	thwart
fuchsia	adj	lilac	magenta	pink	red
fugacious	adj	ephemeral	fleeting	passing	transitory
fugue	n	elopement	flight	getaway	jailbreak
fulcrum	n	pivot	support	swivel	toehold
fulfill	v	achieve	complete	meet	perform
fuliginous	adj	muddy	murky	obscure	sooty
fulminate	v	curse	denounce	burst	detonate
fulmination	n	curse	denunciation	diatribe	explosion
fulsome	adj	disgusting	foul	offensive	obnoxious
fumarole	n	flue	funnel	pharynx	vent
fuming	adj	angry	furious	irate	mad
function	v	act	operate	serve	work
functionary	n	agent	bureaucrat	officer	official
fund	n	bottom	finance	funding	money
fund	v	back	finance	supply	support
fundamental	adj	basic	elementary	essential	primary
fundamentally	adv	basically	essentially	primarily	substantially
funereal	adj	dismal	dreary	gloomy	sad
fungible	adj	commutable	exchangeable	interchangeable	substitutable
fungus	n	fungi	mildew	mold	mushroom
furl	v	curl	fold	roll	wrap
furlough	n	holiday	leave	pass	vacation
furnace	n	heater	kiln	oven	stove

furor	n	frenzy	fury	rage	uproar
further	v	advance	again	continue	increase
furtive	adj	sly	sneaky	secretive	underhand
fury	n	fierceness	rage	vehemence	violence
fuselage	n	airframe	body	hull	trunk
fusilier	n	marksman	rifleman	shooter	soldier
fusillade	n	bombardment	burst	salvo	volley
fusion	n	amalgamation	combination	merger	mixture
fustian	adj	balderdash	bombastic	grandiloquent	pompous
futile	adj	fruitless	hopeless	ineffective	useless
futility	n	emptiness	fruitlessness	hollowness	uselessness
futurism	n	futurist	science fiction	space fiction	space odyssey
gadfly	n	annoyance	hornet	horsefly	pest
gaffe	n	blunder	error	faux pas	mistake
gaiety	n	cheer	happiness	merriment	mirth
gainful	adj	advantageous	profitable	remunerative	useful
gainsay	v	contradict	controvert	deny	oppose
galimatias	n	gibberish	humbug	nonsense	palaver
gall	n	audacity	effrontery	rancor	temerity
gall	v	annoy	irk	irritate	vex
gallantry	n	chivalry	courage	courtliness	heroism
gallimaufry	n	jumble	medley	mishmash	mixture
galling	adj	annoying	bothersome	irritating	vexatious
galvanize	v	animate	arouse	excite	stimulate
gambit	n	artifice	ploy	ruse	stratagem
gambol	v	caper	cavort	romp	skip
gamut	n	range	scale	series	spectrum
ganglion	n	cyst	knot	node	tumor
gap	n	break	crack	hole	opening
garble	v	distort	falsify	misrepresent	twist
garbled	adj	confused	disconnected	disjointed	distorted
gargantuan	adj	enormous	gigantic	huge	titanic
gargoyle	n	beast	brute	monster	spout
garish	adj	flashy	gaudy	glaring	showy
garment	n	apparel	clothes	dress	outfit
garner	v	accumulate	collect	gather	glean

garnish	v	adorn	decorate	ornament	trim
garrison	n	fort	fortification	fortress	stronghold
garrote	v	choke	strangle	suffocate	throttle
garrulity	n	loquacious-ness	talkativeness	verbosity	wordiness
garrulous	adj	chatty	gabby	rambling	talkative
gasconade	n	bluster	boast	brag	vaunt
gastronome	n	bon vivant	epicure	foodie	gourmet
gastronomy	n	cooking	cuisine	food	galley
gather	v	assemble	collect	meet	muster
gauche	adj	awkward	clumsy	crude	unpolished
gaucherie	n	blunder	faux pas	gaffe	slip
gaudy	adj	flamboyant	flashy	loud	showy
gauge	v	assess	evaluate	judge	measure
gaunt	adj	bony	scrawny	skinny	thin
gauntlet	n	armor	challenge	glove	mitten
geared	v	adapted	harnessed	rigged	tooled
gelid	adj	arctic	frigid	glacial	icy
genealogy	n	ancestry	family	lineage	pedigree
general	adj	broad	common	overall	universal
generaliza-tion	n	abstraction	expansion	mainstream-ing	spread
generic	adj	broad	common	general	universal
generosity	n	benevolence	charity	kindness	philanthropy
genesis	n	beginning	birth	creation	origin
genius	n	ability	gift	mastermind	talent
genocide	n	annihilation	extermination	holocaust	massacre
genre	n	kind	category	style	type
genteel	adj	courteous	polite	refined	sophisticated
gentle	adj	mild	nice	soft	sweet
genuflect	v	bow	curtsy	kneel	kowtow
genuine	adj	actual	authentic	real	true
geriatric	adj	ancient	elderly	hoary	old
germane	adj	appropriate	fitting	relevant	suitable
germinate	v	begin	develop	grow	sprout
gerrymander	v	circumvent	falsify	manipulate	rig
gestalt	n	figure	form	guise	shape

gestation	n	evolution	manufacture	maternity	pregnancy
gesticulate	v	beckon	gesture	motion	sign
gewgaws	n	baubles	decorations	ornamentals	trinkets
ghastly	adj	frightful	grisly	gruesome	horrible
ghoul	n	demon	devil	monster	vampire
gibbet	v	hang	lynch	noose	pillory
gibe	n	jeer	jibe	taunt	ridicule
giddy	adj	dizzy	flighty	frivolous	unsteady
gilded	adj	dorado	gold	golden	gilt
gingerly	adj	careful	cautious	circumspect	wary
gird	v	encircle	encompass	fortify	surround
girder	n	beam	joist	rafter	timber
girth	n	belt	cinch	circumference	perimeter
gist	n	core	essence	point	substance
glabrous	adj	bald	hairless	smooth	without hair
glacier	n	floe	ice	iceberg	ice field
glazier	n	glass cutter	glassmaker	glassworker	putty
glean	v	collect	gather	harvest	reap
glee	n	cheerfulness	gaiety	happiness	merriment
glen	n	dale	dell	vale	valley
glib	adj	flippant	fluent	suave	talkative
glimpse	n	glance	look	peek	sight
gloaming	n	dusk	nightfall	sunset	twilight
glorify	v	exalt	praise	revere	worship
glossolalia	n	babble	cant	gibberish	noise
glower	v	glare	frown	lower	scowl
glum	adj	depressed	gloomy	melancholy	sad
glut	v	gorge	oversupply	stuff	surfeit
glutinous	adj	adhesive	sticky	tacky	viscid
glutton	n	foodie	gourmand	hog	wolverine
gluttonous	adj	greedy	hoggish	ravenous	voracious
gnarl	v	growl	grumble	knot	snarl
gnome	n	dwarf	elf	goblin	midget
Gnostic	adj	discerning	insightful	knowing	perceptive
gnus	n	antelopes	camelopards	sheep	swine
goad	v	encourage	prod	spur	urge

goal	n	destination	objective	purpose	target
godparent	n	guarantor	sponsor	surety	underwriter
goldbrick	v	bum	laze	lounge	shirk
googol	n	count	integer	number	numeral
Gordian	adj	complex	complicated	labyrinthine	knotty
gorge	n	abyss	canyon	chasm	ravine
gorge	v	glut	satiate	stuff	surfeit
gorgon	n	battle-ax	dragon lady	hag	shrew
gormandize	v	devour	glut	gorge	stuff
gory	adj	bloody	grisly	gruesome	sanguinary
gospel	n	Christ	church	faith	truth
gossamer	adj	delicate	diaphanous	sheer	transparent
Gothic	adj	barbaric	eerie	medieval	mysterious
gouache	n	acrylic	tempera	painting	watercolor
gouge	v	overcharge	soak	sting	surcharge
gourmand	n	epicure	foodie	glutton	hedonist
gourmet	n	bon vivant	connoisseur	epicurean	gastronome
government	n	administration	authority	control	regime
governor	n	chief	director	head	manager
grabble	v	examine	fumble	feel	grope
gracile	adj	delicate	graceful	slender	willowy
gracious	adj	courteous	friendly	kind	polite
gradient	n	grade	incline	pitch	slope
gradual	adj	easy	gentle	progressive	slow
graft	n	bribery	corruption	implant	transplant
grammar	n	alphabet	language	rudiments	syntax
grandeur	n	gloriousness	magnificence	majesty	splendidness
grandilo-quence	n	bombast	grandiosity	magnilo-quence	rhetoric
grandilo-quent	adj	bombastic	grandiose	lofty	pompous
grandiose	adj	lofty	magnificent	pompous	pretentious
grandparent	n	ancestor	forebear	relative	progenitor
granitic	adj	flinty	granite	obdurate	stony
granular	adj	grainy	gritty	mealy	sandy
graphic	adj	clear	realistic	pictorial	vivid
grapple	v	clutch	grasp	struggle	wrestle

grasp	v	grab	seize	comprehend	understand
gratification	n	delight	happiness	pleasure	satisfaction
gratify	v	delight	indulge	please	satisfy
gratis	adj	compli-mentary	costless	free	freebie
gratitude	n	appreciation	gratefulness	recognition	thankfulness
gratuitous	adj	free	without charge	unjustified	unwarranted
gratuity	n	bonus	gift	reward	tip
gravamen	n	core	essence	gist	substance
grave	adj	serious	severe	solemn	weighty
gravest	adj	biggest	greatest	worse	worst
gravid	adj	expectant	expecting	pregnant	with child
gravitas	n	dignity	distinction	gravity	solemnity
gravity	n	importance	seriousness	significance	solemnity
greenhorn	n	newbie	novice	rookie	tenderfoot
greenroom	n	backstage	breakroom	lounge	waiting area
gregarious	adj	friendly	genial	outgoing	sociable
grief	n	heartbreak	misery	pain	sorrow
grievous	adj	grave	painful	sad	severe
grimace	v	frown	glare	scowl	sneer
grisette	n	harlot	prostitute	slut	temptress
grisly	adj	ghastly	gruesome	hideous	scary
grist	n	corn	grain	grinding	milling
gross	adj	coarse	foul	obscene	rude
grotesque	adj	hideous	monstrous	ugly	weird
grotesquerie	n	farce	oddity	queerness	ugliness
grotto	n	burrow	cavern	den	recess
grouse	n	beef	gripe	grumble	squawk
grovel	v	cower	crawl	creep	fawn
grudging	adj	covetous	envious	miserly	selfish
grueling	adj	arduous	backbreaking	heavy	laborious
guardian	n	defender	fighter	protector	warrior
gudgeon	n	dupe	fool	gull	victim
guffaw	n	cackle	giggle	laugh	roar
guide	v	conduct	direct	lead	steer
guild	n	association	fellowship	society	union

guile	n	craftiness	cunning	deception	trickery
guilelessly	adv	genuinely	ingenuously	simply	sincerely
guise	n	appearance	pretense	semblance	show
gulch	n	canyon	gorge	ravine	valley
gull	v	bamboozle	deceive	dupe	fool
gullible	adj	deceived	fooled	naive	simple
gustatory	adj	eating	olfactory	sensation	tasteful
gusto	n	enthusiasm	passion	zeal	zest
guttural	adj	harsh	hoarse	throaty	rough
gyrate	v	rotate	spin	twirl	whirl
habit	n	custom	practice	routine	tradition
habitat	n	environment	home	surroundings	territory
habituate	v	accustom	familiarize	inure	train
hackneyed	adj	commonplace	stock	overused	stale
haggard	adj	drawn	emaciated	gaunt	tired
haggle	v	bargain	deal	dicker	negotiate
hagiographer	n	archivist	chronologist	genealogist	historian
halcyon	adj	calm	peaceful	serene	tranquil
hale	adj	healthy	hearty	robust	vigorous
hallmark	n	characteristic	feature	quality	stamp
hallow	v	bless	consecrate	dedicate	sanctify
hallowed	adj	blessed	consecrated	sanctified	venerated
hallucinate	v	daydream	imagine	stargaze	visualize
hallucination	n	delusion	dream	illusion	vision
halt	v	cease	pause	stay	stop
hamartia	n	Achilles' heel	downfall	ruin	tragic flaw
hamper	v	block	hinder	impede	obstruct
hand	v	assist	give	help	support
handcuff	v	bind	chain	restrain	shackle
handmaiden	n	charwoman	house girl	housekeeper	servant
hap	v	befall	chance	happen	occur
haphazard	adj	chance	erratic	irregular	random
hapless	adj	miserable	unhappy	unfortunate	unlucky
happiness	n	bliss	delight	joy	pleasure
harangue	v	address	discourse	lecture	rant
harass	v	annoy	irritate	pester	torment

harbinger	n	forerunner	herald	precursor	prognostic
harbor	v	cover	haven	lodge	shelter
hardy	adj	courageous	robust	strong	tough
harking	v	attending	calling	heeding	listening
harlequin	n	buffoon	clown	jester	joker
harmonious	adj	agreeable	congenial	compatible	sympathetic
harp	v	complain	rehashing	repeat	restate
harpy	n	harridan	shrew	termagant	vixen
harridan	n	hag	shrew	vixen	witch
harrow	v	agonize	distress	rack	torture
harrowing	adj	agonizing	distressing	excruciating	painful
harry	v	annoy	harass	pester	plague
haruspex	n	augur	clairvoyant	diviner	prophet
hasten	v	hurry	race	rush	speed
haughty	adj	arrogant	conceited	proud	snobbish
hauteur	n	arrogance	disdain	haughtiness	pride
haven	n	harbor	refuge	sanctuary	shelter
havoc	n	destruction	devastation	chaos	ruin
hazardous	adj	chancy	dangerous	risky	unsafe
headlong	adj	hasty	impetuous	rash	reckless
healthful	adj	good	salubrious	salutary	wholesome
healthy	n	hearty	sound	vigorous	well
hear	v	know	learn	listen	understand
hearsay	n	gossip	grapevine	rumor	scuttlebutt
hearth	n	fireplace	fireside	home	mantel
heathen	n	agnostic	atheist	infidel	pagan
heave	v	hurl	lift	pitch	surge
hebetic	adj	bearing	breedy	fertile	proliferous
hebetude	n	dullness	lethargic	sluggish	stupidity
hector	v	bother	pester	pester	plague
hedge	v	cover	dodge	equivocate	fence
hedonism	n	debauchery	indulgence	luxury	pleasure
hedonist	n	deviant	exhibitionist	immoralist	misbehaver
hedonistic	adj	depraved	indulgent	luxurious	sensual
heed	v	follow	regard	notice	observe
heedless	adj	careless	reckless	thoughtless	unmindful

hegemonic	adj	authoritative	dominant	imperative	principal
hegemony	n	authority	command	domination	jurisdiction
hegira	n	escape	evasion	exodus	decampment
height	n	acme	peak	pinnacle	summit
heinous	adj	abominable	atrocious	evil	hideous
heir	n	beneficiary	descendant	inheritor	successor
helix	n	coil	screw	spiral	volute
Hellenism	n	classicism	Greek	Hellenic	humanist
helot	n	serf	servant	slaves	vassal
hemorrhage	v	bleed	lose blood	shed blood	phlebotomize
herald	v	announce	proclaim	foreshadow	foretell
Herculean	adj	enormous	gigantic	huge	mighty
heredity	n	genetics	heritage	inheritance	lineage
heresy	n	apostasy	blasphemy	nonconfor-mity	unorthodoxy
heretic	n	apostate	dissenter	nonconform-ist	rebel
heretical	adj	dissident	heterodox	iconoclastic	unorthodox
hermetic	adj	airtight	impervious	sealed	tight
hermetically	adv	airtightly	firmly	imperviously	tightly
hermit	n	anchorite	monk	recluse	solitary
hero	n	champion	defender	fighter	protector
heroic	adj	bold	brave	courageous	valiant
heroine	n	hero	idol	leading lady	warrior
heroism	n	bravery	courage	prowess	valor
hesitant	adj	indecisive	reluctant	uncertain	unsure
hesitate	v	doubt	falter	pause	waver
heteroclite	adj	abnormal	amorphous	anomalous	heteroge-neous
heterodox	adj	dissident	nonconform-ist	sectarian	unorthodox
heterodoxy	n	dissidence	heresy	nonconfor-mity	unorthodoxy
heteroge-neous	adj	dissimilar	diverse	mixed	varied
hew	v	carve	cut	hack	shape
heyday	n	bloom	peak	pinnacle	prime
hiatus	n	break	gap	lacuna	pause

hibernal	adj	brumal	hiemal	freezing	wintry
hibernate	v	hide	rest	sleep	winter
hidalgo	n	aristocrat	gentleman	nobleman	squire
hidebound	adj	inflexible	rigid	intolerant	narrow-minded
hideous	adj	awful	horrible	horrid	ugly
hie	v	hasten	hurry	race	rush
hierarchical	adj	gradable	pecking	pyramid	pecking
hierarchy	n	order	position	rank	scale
hieratic	adj	ecclesiastical	ministerial	pastoral	priestly
hieroglyphic	adj	indecipherable	iconographic	illustrative	pictographic
highbrow	adj	egghead	erudite	intellectual	learned
hindrance	n	barrier	obstruction	interference	restriction
hip	adj	fashionable	knowledgeable	stylish	trendy
hircine	adj	goatish	lascivious	lecherous	lewd
hire	v	employ	engage	lease	rent
hireling	n	employee	hack	mercenary	worker
hirsute	adj	bristly	furry	hairy	shaggy
hispid	adj	bristly	hairy	hirsute	spiny
historic	adj	important	momentous	significant	traditional
historical	adj	ancient	background	factual	past
histrionic	adj	affected	artificial	dramatic	theatric
histrionics	n	acting	drama	melodrama	theatrics
hoard	n	accumulation	cache	stockpile	store
hoary	adj	ancient	grey	old	venerable
hoax	n	deception	fraud	swindle	trick
Hobson's choice	n	coercion	duress	force	obligation
hodgepodge	n	jumble	mess	mishmash	mixture
holocaust	n	annihilation	destruction	genocide	massacre
homage	n	esteem	praise	respect	reverence
homely	adj	plain	simple	ugly	unattractive
homeopathic	adj	diluted	evanescent	infinitesimal	medical
Homeric	adj	august	epic	Grecian	poetic
homicide	n	assassination	killing	manslaughter	murder

homiletic	adj	didactic	preaching	sermon	teaching
homily	n	lecture	preachment	sermon	speech
homogeneity	n	agreement	conformity	consistency	uniformity
homoge-neous	adj	alike	comparable	consistent	uniform
homologous	adj	comparable	equal	equivalent	like
homunculus	n	dwarf	manikin	midget	gnome
hone	v	grind	sharpen	refine	perfect
honorable	adj	decent	noble	respectable	worthy
honorific	adj	commemora-tive	honorary	titular	voluntary
hoodwink	v	cheat	deceive	fool	trick
hoof	v	foot	pace	step	walk
hopeless	adj	despairing	desperate	forlorn	useless
hoping	v	awaiting	desiring	expecting	wishing
horary	adj	ephemeral	hourly	scheduled	transitory
horde	n	crowd	group	mob	multitude
hornswoggle	v	bamboozle	con	defraud	swindle
horrendous	adj	appalling	gruesome	hideous	horrible
hortative	adj	admonitory	didactic	encouraging	persuasive
hortatory	adj	advisory	consultative	encouraging	exhortative
horticulture	n	agriculture	farming	floriculture	gardening
hospice	n	hostel	lodging	shelter	sickbay
hostile	adj	aggressive	antagonistic	hateful	unfriendly
hotelier	n	hotelman	innkeeper	landlord	proprietor
houri	n	babe	beauty	cutie	nymph
houseboat	n	barge	canoe	cruiser	ferry
housekeeper	n	goodwife	homemaker	housewife	matron
hovel	n	dump	hut	shack	shanty
hoyden	n	dyke	lass	romp	tomboy
hubbub	n	commotion	disturbance	tumult	uproar
hubris	n	arrogance	conceit	insolence	pride
huddle	v	cluster	crowd	flock	herd
hue	n	color	shade	tint	tone
huge	n	enormous	gigantic	great	large
hull	n	body	case	husk	shell
hullabaloo	n	clamor	noise	racket	ruckus

humane	adj	benevolent	charitable	compassionate	kind
humanist	adj	discipline	doctrine	philosophy	subject
humanitarian	adj	benevolent	charitable	generous	humane
humanities	n	arts	language	literature	social sciences
humble	adj	lowly	meek	modest	submissive
humbug	n	duplicity	fraud	hypocrisy	insincerity
humbuggery	n	claptrap	deception	fraud	hogwash
humic	n	compost	dirt	humus	soil
humiliate	v	embarrass	humble	mortify	shame
humility	n	lowliness	meekness	modesty	humbleness
hummock	n	hillock	hump	knoll	mound
humor	n	comedy	comic	funniness	hilariousness
humorist	n	comedian	comic	jester	joker
humorous	adj	amusing	comical	funny	hilarious
humus	n	compost	earth	mold	soil
hurl	v	fling	launch	throw	toss
hurly-burly	n	commotion	hubbub	turmoil	uproar
hurtle	v	dart	dash	rush	speed
husband	v	conserve	economize	save	store
husbandry	n	breeding	farming	ranching	rearing
husk	n	peel	shell	shuck	skin
hyaline	adj	clear	glassy	translucent	transparent
hybrid	n	composite	compound	crossbreed	mongrel
hydra-headed	adj	beast	freak	monster	ogre
hydrate	v	dampen	humidify	moisturize	water
hygienic	adj	clean	healthful	sanitary	sterile
hymeneal	adj	conjugal	connubial	nuptial	spousal
hymn	n	anthem	carol	praise	song
hyperactive	adj	energetic	frantic	frenzied	hectic
hyperbole	n	exaggeration	extravagant	metaphor	overstatement
hypercritical	adj	captious	carping	demanding	faultfinding
hypnotize	v	bewitch	charm	fascinate	mesmerize
hypocrisy	n	deception	dissimulation	duplicity	insincerity
hypocrite	n	faker	fraud	phony	pretender
hypocritical	adj	deceitful	dishonest	false	insincere

hypostatize	v	embody	materialize	personalize	represent
hypothecate	v	conjecture	postulate	speculate	theorize
hypothesis	n	assumption	conjecture	guess	theory
hypothesize	v	assume	conjecture	imagine	theorize
hypothetical	adj	speculative	theoretical	uncertain	unproven
hysteria	n	craze	frenzy	insanity	madness
hysterical	adj	frantic	funny	mad	wild
icon	n	idol	image	picture	symbol
iconoclast	n	destroyer	extremist	radical	rebel
iconoclastic	adj	dissenting	nonconform-ist	radical	unconven-tional
id	n	mind	personality	psyche	unconscious
idea	n	concept	notion	thought	view
ideal	adj	best	excellent	model	perfect
idealism	n	high-minded-ness	optimism	perfection	romanticism
idealist	n	dreamer	optimist	romanticist	visionary
identify	v	detect	determine	find	recognize
ideological	adj	abstract	conceptual	mental	theoretical
ideology	n	belief	creed	dogma	philosophy
idiom	n	dialect	jargon	expression	phrase
idiomatic	adj	colloquial	informal	local	vernacular
idiosyncrasy	n	characteristic	distinctive	odd	peculiarity
idol	n	demigod	hero	paragon	star
idolatry	n	adoration	devotion	idolization	worship
idolize	v	admire	adore	revere	worship
idyll	n	simple	charming	scene	poem
idyllic	adj	bucolic	halcyon	pastoral	peaceful
igneous	adj	eruptive	fiery	hot	molten
ignite	v	fire	inflame	kindle	light
ignoble	adj	base	despicable	low	mean
ignominious	adj	despicable	disgraceful	disreputable	shameful
ignominy	n	disgrace	disrepute	infamy	shame
ignoramus	n	dolt	fool	idiot	simpleton
ignorant	adj	illiterate	unaware	uneducated	unknowing
ignore	v	disregard	forget	neglect	overlook
ilk	n	class	kind	species	variety

ill-conceived	adj	absurd	foolish	half-baked	misguided
ill-omened	adj	inauspicious	menacing	sinister	unlucky
illegible	adj	indecipher-able	obscure	unclear	unreadable
illicit	adj	criminal	illegal	illegitimate	unlawful
illimitable	adj	boundless	immeasurable	limitless	unlimited
illiterate	adj	ignorant	uneducated	unlettered	untaught
illuminate	v	brighten	lighten	explain	illustrate
illusion	n	fantasy	hallucination	mirage	vision
illusory	adj	fanciful	imaginary	unreal	visionary
illustrious	adj	celebrated	distinguished	famous	notable
imagery	n	imagination	picture	representa-tion	symbolism
imaginary	adj	fanciful	fictional	illusory	unreal
imagination	adj	creativity	ideation	inventiveness	originality
imagine	v	conceive	envision	ideate	visualize
imago	n	figure	form	idea	image
imbecility	n	insanity	folly	foolishness	stupidity
imbedded	adj	implanted	instilled	rooted	set
imbibe	v	drink	guzzle	quaff	swallow
imbricate	v	overlap	overlie	override	shingle
imbroglio	n	complicated	entanglement	intricate	predicament
imbue	v	infuse	instill	pervade	saturate
imbued	v	filled	permeated	saturated	soaked
immaculate	adj	clean	spotless	faultless	pure
immanent	adj	inherent	intrinsic	subjective	organic
immaterial	adj	insignificant	irrelevant	unimportant	unsubstantial
immediate	adj	direct	instant	prompt	quick
immediately	adv	directly	immediate	instantly	promptly
immense	adj	colossal	enormous	gigantic	huge
immerse	v	dunk	soak	submerge	plunge
immersion	n	dive	diving	submergence	submersion
immigrate	v	leave	arrive	settle	colonize
imminent	adj	approaching	impending	close	near
immiscible	adj	incompatible	nonhomoge-neous	nonmiscible	unmixable
immobile	adj	fixed	motionless	stationary	still

immodest	adj	improper	indecent	obscene	shameless
immolate	v	assassinate	kill	sacrifice	victimize
immortality	n	afterlife	deathlessness	eternity	hereafter
immovable	adj	firm	fixed	inflexible	stubborn
immune	adj	persistent	resistant	stable	strong
immunity	n	exemption	freedom	impunity	liberty
immure	v	confine	imprison	incarcerate	jail
immurement	n	captivity	detention	imprisonment	incarceration
immutable	adj	constant	fixed	permanent	unchangeable
impact	n	affect	consequences	effect	influence
impair	v	damage	harm	mar	undermine
impale	v	pierce	spear	stab	stick
impalpable	adj	imperceptible	intangible	unreal	vague
impart	v	bestow	give	convey	reveal
impartial	adj	disinterested	fair	neutral	unbiased
impasse	n	deadlock	predicament	standstill	stalemate
impassioned	adj	ardent	fervent	fervid	fiery
impassive	adj	calm	cool	unconcerned	unemotional
impassivity	n	apathy	detachment	disregard	indifference
impeach	v	accuse	blame	charge	incriminate
impeccable	adj	faultless	flawless	immaculate	perfect
impecunious	adj	destitute	impoverished	penniless	poor
impede	v	block	hinder	obstruct	stop
impediment	n	barrier	hindrance	obstacle	obstruction
impel	v	drive	move	push	urge
impelled	v	driven	motivated	pushed	stimulated
impending	adj	approaching	coming	close	forthcoming
impenitent	adj	remorseless	shameless	unremorseful	unrepentant
imperative	adj	essential	necessary	pressing	vital
imperceptible	adj	impalpable	indiscernible	invisible	indistinct
imperfect	adj	defective	faulty	flawed	incomplete
imperialism	n	colonialism	expansionism	jingoism	militarism
imperil	v	endanger	hazard	jeopardize	risk
imperious	adj	arrogant	dictatorial	domineering	overbearing
impermeable	adj	impenetrable	impervious	compact	tight
impertinent	adj	bold	brazen	disrespectful	rude

imperturb-ability	n	composure	coolness	equanimity	patience
imperturb-able	adj	calm	composed	cool	serene
impervious	adj	impassable	impenetrable	impermeable	resistant
impetration	n	demand	entreaty	petition	supplication
impetuosity	n	haste	impulsiveness	rashness	vehemence
impetuous	adj	hasty	impulsive	overeager	rash
impetus	n	impulse	incentive	spark	stimulus
impiety	n	irreverence	profanity	sacrilege	ungodliness
impinge	v	infringe	intrude	invade	touch
impious	adj	irreligious	profane	sinful	ungodly
implacable	adj	inexorable	inflexible	relentless	unrelenting
implant	v	embed	establish	graft	inculcate
implausible	adj	improbable	inconceivable	unbelievable	unlikely
implement	v	achieve	apply	carry out	execute
implicate	v	concern	entangle	incriminate	involve
implication	n	connotation	indication	meaning	significance
implicit	adj	implied	understood	unexpressed	unspoken
implore	v	beg	beseech	entreat	plead
implosion	n	breakdown	collapse	failure	fiasco
imply	v	hint	indicate	mean	suggest
impolite	adj	ill-mannered	discourteous	rude	uncivil
impolitic	adj	imprudent	injudicious	undiplomatic	unwise
imponderable	adj	elusive	immaterial	impalpable	intangible
import	n	drift	meaning	purport	significance
importunate	adj	insistent	obtrusive	persistent	urgent
importune	v	beg	demand	request	urge
impose	v	charge	demand	enforce	require
imposing	adj	grand	impressive	intimidating	majestic
imposition	n	assessment	duty	levy	tax
impossible	adj	hopeless	inconceivable	unbearable	unthinkable
imposture	n	deception	fraud	hoax	masquerade
impotence	n	feebleness	impotency	powerless-ness	weakness
impotent	adj	feeble	ineffective	powerless	weak
impound	v	cage	confiscate	imprison	seize

impoverish	v	deplete	deprive	drain	ruin
impoverished	adj	broke	destitute	needy	poor
impracticable	adj	impossible	unattainable	unfeasible	unworkable
impractical	adj	idealistic	unrealistic	unreasonable	unworkable
imprecate	v	blaspheme	curse	cuss	swear
imprecation	n	anathema	curse	execration	malediction
impregnable	adj	firm	hard	invincible	strong
impresario	n	agent	entrepreneur	manager	producer
impress	v	affect	imprint	move	stamp
impres-sionable	adj	receptive	responsive	sensitive	susceptible
Impressionist	n	copycat	imitator	impersonator	mimic
imprimatur	n	approval	authorization	permission	sanction
improbable	adj	doubtful	incredible	questionable	unlikely
impromptu	adj	improvise	offhand	spontaneous	unprepared
improper	adj	indecent	inappropriate	unseemly	unsuitable
impropriety	n	improperness	indecency	mistake	unfitness
improvident	adj	imprudent	reckless	thoughtless	wasteful
improvisation	n	ad-lib	extemporiza-tion	improvisa-tional	winging it
improvise	v	contrive	devise	fabricate	invent
imprudence	n	carelessness	indiscretion	rashness	recklessness
imprudent	adj	careless	rash	reckless	thoughtless
impudent	adj	brazen	impertinent	insolent	rude
impudicity	n	bawdry	immodesty	obscenity	shameless-ness
impugn	v	attack	challenge	criticize	denounce
impulse	n	impetus	momentum	stimulus	urge
impulsive	adj	hasty	rash	reckless	spontaneous
impunity	n	exemption	immunity	indemnity	rescue
imputation	n	accusation	allegation	charge	indictment
impute	v	ascribe	assign	attribute	charge
inability	n	inadequacy	incapability	incompetence	inefficiency
inactive	adj	idle	motionless	passive	sluggish
inadequate	adj	deficient	incompetent	insufficient	unsatisfactory
inadvertent	adj	careless	inattentive	negligent	thoughtless
inadvisable	adj	imprudent	inexpedient	undesirable	unwise

inalienable	adj	impre-scriptible	indefeasible	inherent	inviolable
inamorata	n	lover	mistress	paramour	sweetheart
inane	adj	absurd	foolish	silly	stupid
inanimate	adj	dead	inactive	inert	lifeless
inanition	n	exhaustion	lassitude	lethargy	starvation
inanity	n	absurdity	folly	insanity	silliness
inaudible	adj	faint	imperceptible	quiet	unhearable
inaugurate	v	begin	initiate	introduce	start
inauspicious	adj	ominous	unfavorable	unfortunate	unpropitious
inborn	adj	congenital	ingrained	inherent	innate
incalculable	adj	boundless	infinite	immeasurable	measureless
incalculably	adj	endlessly	immeasurably	infinitely	innumerably
incandes-cence	n	glow	light	radiance	shine
incandescent	adj	brilliant	glowing	luminous	radiant
incantation	n	chant	charm	magic	spell
incapable	adj	incompetent	inefficient	unfit	unqualified
incapacitate	v	disable	cripple	maim	paralyze
incarcerate	v	confine	detain	imprison	jail
incarnadine	adj	crimson	red	ruddy	pink
incarnate	v	embody	epitomize	substantiate	personify
incendiary	n	arsonist	firebomb	firebrand	firebug
incense	v	anger	enrage	infuriate	madden
incentive	n	incitement	inducement	motivation	stimulus
inception	n	beginning	initiation	introduction	start
incertitude	n	doubt	insecurity	suspense	uncertainty
incessant	adj	constant	continuous	relentless	unceasing
inchoate	adj	elementary	imperfect	incomplete	undeveloped
incident	n	accident	happening	event	occurrence
incidental	adj	accidental	casual	chance	fortuitous
incidentally	adv	accidently	casually	coincidentally	parentheti-cally
incinerate	v	blaze	burn	fire	sear
incipient	adj	beginning	embryonic	initial	introductory
incise	v	carve	cut	engrave	score
incision	n	cut	gash	slash	slit

incisive	adj	keen	penetrating	perceptive	sharp
incite	v	arouse	encourage	provoke	stimulate
incivility	n	discourtesy	disrespect	impoliteness	rudeness
inclement	adj	bitter	cruel	harsh	severe
inclination	n	bent	leaning	liking	tendency
inclusive	adj	broad	comprehensive	general	universal
incognito	adj	anonymous	concealed	disguised	unknown
incoherent	adj	confused	disconnected	disjointed	rambling
incombustible	adj	fireproof	flameproof	inflammable	noncombustible
incommensurate	adj	disproportionate	inadequate	insufficient	unequal
incommodious	adj	awkward	cumbersome	inconvenient	uncomfortable
incommunicado	adj	hidden	isolated	secluded	secrecy
incomparable	adj	inimitable	peerless	unequalled	unique
incompatibility	n	conflict	incongruity	inconsistency	opposition
incompetent	adj	inadequate	incapable	ineffective	inefficient
incomprehensible	adj	mysterious	obscure	unfathomable	unintelligible
inconceivable	adj	impossible	incredible	unimaginable	unthinkable
inconclusive	adj	indecisive	indeterminate	uncertain	weak
incongruous	adj	improper	inappropriate	incompatible	unsuitable
inconsiderate	adj	careless	insensitive	thoughtless	unsympathetic
inconspicuous	adj	faint	insignificant	obscure	unobtrusive
incontinence	n	dissoluteness	incontinency	indulgence	unrestraint
incontrovertible	adj	incontestable	indisputable	undeniable	unquestionable
incorporate	v	combine	include	integrate	mainstream
incorporeal	adj	disembodied	ethereal	immaterial	intangible
incorrigible	adj	incurable	stubborn	uncontrollable	unruly
incorruptible	adj	imperishable	indestructible	just	moral
incredible	adj	amazing	extraordinary	fantastic	unbelievable
incredulity	n	disbelief	distrust	doubt	skepticism

incredulous	adj	disbelieving	distrustful	skeptical	suspicious
increment	n	augmentation	growth	increase	rise
incriminate	v	accuse	blame	charge	inculpate
incubus	n	banshee	bogeyman	fiend	ghoul
inculcate	v	indoctrinate	infuse	instill	teach
inculcation	n	discipline	indoctrination	instilling	implantation
inculpate	v	accuse	blame	charge	incriminate
incumbent	n	licensee	occupant	officeholder	operator
incur	v	acquire	attract	catch	contract
incursion	n	assault	inroad	invasion	raid
indecent	adj	dirty	improper	lewd	obscene
indecision	n	doubt	fluctuation	hesitation	uncertainty
indecorous	adj	indecent	improper	unbecoming	unseemly
indefatiga-bility	n	perseverance	persistence	stamina	tenacity
indefatigable	adj	determined	persistent	steadfast	untiring
indefeasible	adj	inalienable	inherent	irrevocable	sure
indelible	adj	indestructible	lasting	permanent	unerasable
indelicate	adj	coarse	crude	improper	rude
indemnify	v	compensate	recompense	redress	reimburse
indemnity	n	amends	compensation	redress	reparation
indepen-dence	n	autonomy	freedom	liberty	sovereignty
independent	adj	autonomous	free	separate	self-sufficient
indetermin-able	adj	incalculable	indefinite	indefinable	infinite
indetermi-nate	adj	indefinite	indistinct	uncertain	vague
indetermin-ism	n	hesitation	indecision	suspense	vacillation
indicative	adj	characteristic	significant	suggestive	symbolic
indicator	n	gauge	index	indication	sign
indict	v	accuse	blame	charge	prosecute
indictment	n	accusation	allegation	arraignment	charge
indifference	n	apathy	coolness	disinterest	unconcern
indifferent	adj	apathetic	cool	neutral	unconcerned
indigence	n	destitution	need	penury	poverty

indigenous	adj	aboriginal	domestic	local	native
indigent	adj	impoverished	needy	penniless	poor
indignant	adj	angry	annoyed	furious	irritated
indignation	n	anger	displeasure	fury	resentment
indiscreet	adj	rash	reckless	thoughtless	unwise
indiscriminate	adj	blind	haphazard	promiscuous	random
indispensable	adj	essential	necessary	required	vital
indisposition	n	disease	disinclination	illness	malady
indisputable	adj	certain	incontestable	undeniable	unquestionable
indistinct	adj	blurry	unclear	indefinite	vague
indite	v	compose	inscribe	pen	write
individual	adj	particular	personal	separate	specific
individuation	n	definition	discrimination	distinction	personalization
indoctrination	n	discipline	education	instruction	training
indolence	n	idleness	inactivity	laziness	sluggishness
indolent	adj	idle	lazy	listless	sluggish
indomitable	adj	brave	determined	invincible	unconquerable
indubitable	adj	certain	sure	undeniable	unquestionable
induce	v	cause	persuade	prompt	urge
inducement	n	enticement	incentive	lure	stimulus
induction	n	inaugural	initiation	installation	investiture
inductive	adj	instinctive	intuitive	logical	reasonable
indulge	v	coddle	gratify	pamper	spoil
indulgent	adj	easygoing	kind	lenient	tolerant
indurate	v	callous	cold-blooded	compassionless	desensitized
industrious	adj	busy	diligent	energetic	hardworking
inebriated	adj	drunk	high	intoxicated	tipsy
inebriety	n	drunkenness	inebriation	insobriety	intoxication
ineffable	adj	indescribable	inexpressible	unspeakable	unutterable
ineffaceable	adj	indelible	ineradicable	indestructible	permanent
ineffectual	adj	futile	ineffective	unavailing	useless

ineluctable	adj	certain	inescapable	inevitable	unavoidable
inept	adj	awkward	clumsy	incompetent	unfit
inequitable	adj	biased	unequal	unfair	unjust
inequity	n	equality	fairness	honesty	justice
ineradicable	adj	deep-rooted	entrenched	fixed	ingrained
inert	adj	idle	inactive	sluggish	unreactive
inertia	n	inactivity	indolence	sloth	sluggishness
inestimable	adj	immeasurable	incalculable	invaluable	priceless
inevitable	adj	certain	destined	inescapable	unavoidable
inevitably	adv	inescapably	necessarily	surely	unavoidably
inexorability	n	inexorable-ness	inflexibility	relentlessness	rigidity
inexorable	adj	inflexible	merciless	relentless	unyielding
inextricable	adj	complex	difficult	intricate	involved
infallible	adj	certain	reliable	sure	unerring
infamous	adj	disreputable	notorious	scandalous	villainous
infamy	n	discredit	disgrace	scandal	shame
infantry	n	army	foot soldiers	militia	troops
infatuate	v	captivate	charm	enchant	fascinate
infatuation	n	adoration	crush	obsession	passion
infectious	adj	contagious	catching	toxic	transmissible
infelicitous	adj	improper	inappropriate	unfortunate	unsuitable
infer	v	conclude	deduce	gather	guess
inference	n	assumption	deduction	conclusion	reason
infernal	adj	diabolic	fiendish	hellish	satanic
inferno	n	abyss	fire	hellhole	underworld
inferred	adj	deduced	implied	presumed	understood
infidel	n	atheist	heathen	pagan	unbeliever
infidelity	n	adultery	disloyalty	perfidy	treachery
infiltrate	v	enter	insinuate	penetrate	permeate
infinitesimal	n	microscopic	minute	miniscule	tiny
infinity	n	boundless-ness	endlessness	eternity	forever
infirmary	n	clinic	dispensary	hospital	sick bay
infirmity	n	ailment	feebleness	frailty	weakness
inflame	v	excite	ignite	incite	provoke
inflammable	adj	burnable	combustible	explosive	flammable

inflammatory	adj	incendiary	instigative	provocative	seditious
inflexible	adj	firm	rigid	uncompro-mising	unyielding
influence	v	affect	impact	persuade	sway
influential	adj	effective	important	powerful	weighty
influx	n	affluence	inflow	inpouring	inrush
infraction	n	breach	crime	infringement	violation
infrangible	adj	absolute	inviolable	unbreakable	unyielding
infringe	v	break	disobey	transgress	violate
infuriate	v	anger	enrage	incense	irritate
infuse	v	imbue	inculcate	instill	permeate
infusion	n	extract	injection	perfusion	transfusing
ingenious	adj	clever	cunning	intelligent	inventive
ingenuity	n	ability	cleverness	skill	talent
ingenuous	adj	candid	frank	honest	straightfor-ward
ingenuous-ness	n	artlessness	frankness	innocence	sincerity
ingrate	n	beggar	knave	pariah	pilgarlic
ingratiate	v	captivate	charm	endear	flatter
ingratiating	adj	agreeable	charming	flattering	pleasing
ingratiation	n	fawning	flattery	insinuation	sycophancy
ingredient	n	component	constituent	element	part
ingress	n	access	entrance	entry	penetration
inhere	v	belong	consist	exist	reside
inherent	adj	built-in	inborn	ingrained	natural
inhibit	v	hinder	impede	prevent	stop
inhibition	n	hindrance	impediment	restraint	restriction
inimical	adj	harmful	hostile	unfriendly	unfavorable
inimitable	adj	matchless	peerless	unparalleled	unrivaled
iniquitous	adj	evil	immoral	sinful	wicked
iniquitously	adv	criminally	immorally	sinfully	villainously
iniquity	n	evil	injustice	sin	wickedness
initial	adj	first	introductory	opening	original
initiate	v	begin	commence	originate	start
initiation	n	beginning	commence-ment	opening	start

initiative	n	ambition	drive	energy	enterprise
injudicious	adj	ill-advised	imprudent	indiscreet	unwise
injunction	n	court order	instruction	mandate	prohibition
injurious	adj	damaging	destructive	detrimental	harmful
inkling	n	hint	idea	notion	suspicion
innate	adj	inborn	inherited	natural	native
innervate	v	energize	excite	inspire	stimulate
innocuous	adj	harmless	innocent	inoffensive	safe
innominate	adj	incognito	nameless	unidentified	unnamed
innovate	v	create	introduce	originate	pioneer
innovation	n	alteration	creation	invention	novelty
innovative	adj	advanced	groundbreaking	inventive	original
innuendo	n	allusion	hint	implication	insinuation
innumerable	adj	countless	incalculable	infinite	numberless
inoculate	v	infuse	inject	immunize	vaccinate
inopportune	adj	inappropriate	inconvenient	inexpedient	untimely
inordinate	adj	excessive	exorbitant	outrageous	unreasonable
inquest	n	inquiry	investigation	probe	research
inquisition	n	examination	inquest	interrogation	investigation
inquisitive	adj	curious	inquiring	nosy	questioning
insalubrity	n	contamination	noxiousness	toxicity	unhealthiness
insatiable	adj	gluttonous	ravenous	unquenchable	voracious
insatiate	adj	greedy	insatiable	ravenous	unquenchable
inscribe	v	engrave	enter	record	write
inscrutability	n	enigma	impenetrability	mystery	mystique
inscrutable	adj	inexplicable	mysterious	puzzling	unfathomable
insensate	adj	fatuous	insensible	senseless	unfeeling
insensibility	n	apathy	callousness	cruelty	indifference
insensible	adj	callous	insensitive	numb	unfeeling
insentience	n	anesthesia	deadness	dullness	numbness
insert	v	implant	include	inject	introduce
insidious	adj	cunning	deceitful	treacherous	tricky
insight	n	discernment	perception	understanding	wisdom
insignia	n	badge	crest	emblem	symbol

insignificant	adj	inconsequential	minor	trivial	unimportant
insinuate	v	hint	imply	intimate	suggest
insinuation	n	hint	suggestion	implication	slur
insipid	adj	bland	dull	tedious	uninteresting
insolence	n	audacity	gall	impertinence	impudence
insolent	adj	brazen	disrespectful	insulting	rude
insoluble	adj	inexplicable	inextricable	intractable	unsolvable
insolvent	adj	bankrupt	broke	destitute	penniless
insouciance	n	apathy	indifference	nonchalance	unconcern
insouciant	adj	casual	easygoing	nonchalant	unconcerned
inspect	v	check	examine	investigate	scrutinize
inspiration	n	creativeness	encouragement	insight	stimulus
inspire	v	encourage	motivate	prompt	stimulate
instability	n	insecurity	fluctuation	shakiness	unsteadiness
installment	n	episode	installment	payment	section
instant	adj	immediate	minute	moment	second
instauration	n	creation	institution	introduction	rehabilitation
instigate	v	incite	inspire	prompt	provoke
instinct	n	feeling	hunch	insight	intuition
instrument	n	apparatus	device	means	tool
insubordinate	adj	defiant	disobedient	rebellious	unruly
insufferable	adj	intolerable	obnoxious	unbearable	unendurable
insular	adj	isolated	local	narrow-minded	restricted
insularity	n	insularism	insulation	isolation	parochialism
insulate	v	isolate	segregate	separate	sequester
insulated	adj	divided	isolated	segregated	separate
insuperable	adj	impassable	insurmountable	unbeatable	unconquerable
insurgency	n	insurrection	rebellion	revolt	uprising
insurgent	adj	radical	rebellious	revolutionary	subversive
insurmountable	adj	impassable	indomitable	insuperable	invincible
insurrection	n	mutiny	rebellion	revolt	uprising
insurrectionary	n	insurgent	insurrectionist	rebel	revolutionary

intact	adj	entire	complete	unbroken	whole
intangible	adj	immaterial	impalpable	incorporeal	unsubstantial
integral	adj	built-in	hardwired	all-important	essential
integrate	v	combine	incorporate	unify	unite
integration	n	consolidation	combination	union	unity
integrity	n	honesty	morality	uprightness	virtue
integument	n	coat	covering	hide	skin
intellection	n	cerebration	idea	thinking	thought
intelligence	n	data	information	mind	sense
intelligent	adj	clever	sharp	smart	wise
intelligentsia	n	clerisy	elite	intellectual	literati
intemperance	n	alcoholism	drunkenness	excess	insobriety
intemperate	adj	excessive	extreme	immoderate	unrestrained
intend	v	aim	mean	plan	purpose
intensive	adj	concentrated	hard	profound	thorough
inter	v	bury	entomb	inhume	plant
interact	v	associate	connect	cooperate	engage
interaction	n	communica-tion	contact	cooperation	interplay
intercede	v	interfere	intervene	mediate	negotiate
intercept	v	arrest	block	prevent	stop
intercredal	adj	ecumenical	interfaith	interreligious	nonsectarian
interdict	v	ban	forbid	prohibit	proscribe
interdiction	n	ban	embargo	prohibition	proscription
interference	n	disturbance	hindrance	interfering	intervention
interim	n	interlude	meantime	provisional	temporary
interject	v	interpolate	interpose	interrupt	introduce
interloper	n	intruder	invader	outsider	trespasser
interlude	n	break	intermission	interval	recess
interment	n	burial	burying	entombment	funeral
interminable	adj	endless	eternal	everlasting	perpetual
intermittent	adj	irregular	periodic	spasmodic	sporadic
intern	v	confine	imprison	incarcerate	restrict
internecine	adj	deadly	destructive	internal	lethal
interpolate	v	inject	insert	interject	introduce
interpose	v	insert	intercalate	interfere	intervene

interposition	n	interference	interjection	interpolation	intervention
interpret	v	decipher	explain	translate	understand
interpretation	n	explanation	interpreting	reading	rendition
interregnum	n	intermission	interruption	interval	respite
interrogate	v	examine	interview	query	question
interrogation	n	examination	inquiry	investigation	question
interrupt	v	break	discontinue	stop	suspend
intersect	v	bisect	cross	meet	sever
intersperse	v	diffuse	distribute	infuse	scatter
interstice	n	aperture	gap	interval	space
interstitial	adj	intermediate	interstitially	intervening	opening
intervene	v	interfere	interrupt	meddle	mediate
intimate	adj	inner	internal	personal	private
intimation	n	allusion	hint	implication	insinuation
intimidate	v	browbeat	bully	frighten	threaten
intolerance	n	fanaticism	narrow-mind-edness	opinionated-ness	partiality
intonation	n	accent	inflection	modulation	tone
intone	v	chant	recite	sing	utter
intractable	adj	inflexible	stubborn	unmanage-able	unruly
intramural	adj	domestic	home	inside	interior
intransigence	n	inflexibility	intransigency	rigidity	stubbornness
intransigent	adj	inflexible	uncompro-mising	unwilling	unyielding
intrepid	adj	bold	brave	courageous	fearless
intricacy	n	complexity	difficulty	entanglement	involvement
intricate	adj	complex	complicated	difficult	involved
intrigue	v	connive	conspire	fascinate	interest
intrigue	n	conspiracy	design	plot	scheme
intrinsic	adj	inborn	inherent	ingrained	nature
intrinsically	adv	congenitally	inherently	innately	naturally
introduction	n	insertion	presentation	preamble	preface
introspection	n	self-analysis	reflection	rumination	self-examina-tion
introspective	adj	contemplative	meditative	ruminative	self-examining
introvert	adj	loner	reserved	shy	solitary

intrusion	n	encroachment	interference	invasion	trespass
intuit	v	divine	feel	perceive	sense
intuition	n	feeling	hunch	insight	instinct
intuitive	adj	innate	instinctual	natural	visceral
intumescent	adj	bloated	distended	puffy	swollen
inundate	v	flood	engulf	overflow	overwhelm
inundation	n	deluge	flood	overflow	torrent
inure	v	accustom	condition	familiarize	train
invalidate	v	cancel	disprove	revoke	void
invaluable	adj	costly	dear	precious	priceless
invective	n	accusation	defamation	denunciation	slander
inveigh	v	declaim	fulminate	rail	revile
inveigle	v	cajole	coax	entice	seduce
inventive	adj	cleaver	creative	imaginative	ingenious
inventiveness	n	cleverness	creativity	imagination	ingenuity
inventory	n	list	record	stock	store
inverse	n	contrary	converse	opposite	reverse
invert	v	overturn	reverse	transpose	turn
invest	v	expend	imbue	infuse	spend
investigative	adj	curious	inquiring	inquisitive	questioning
inveterate	adj	confirmed	chronic	deep-rooted	habitual
invidious	adj	hateful	jealous	obnoxious	offensive
invidiously	adv	hatefully	detestably	maliciously	offensively
invigorate	v	animate	energize	enliven	stimulate
invigorating	adj	energizing	enlivening	exhilarating	stimulating
invincible	adj	impenetrable	irresistible	unbeatable	unconquer-able
inviolability	n	immutability	intangibility	integrity	sanctity
inviolable	adj	incorruptible	safe	secure	untouchable
inviolate	adj	perfect	pure	unbroken	whole
invoke	v	appeal	conjure	evoke	summon
involuntary	adj	automatic	instinctive	spontaneous	unconscious
involuted	adj	serpentine	tortuous	twisted	winding
involution	n	convolution	engagement	intricacy	involvement
involve	v	engage	entail	implicate	include
iota	n	atom	bit	particle	speck

irascible	adj	cranky	irritable	testy	touchy
irate	adj	angry	furious	irritated	mad
iridescent	adj	nacreous	opalescent	pearlescent	shimmering
irk	v	annoy	bother	harass	irritate
irksome	adj	annoying	irritating	tiresome	troublesome
ironic	adj	caustic	cynical	sarcastic	wry
irony	n	mockery	ridicule	sarcasm	satire
irrational	adj	absurd	crazy	foolish	illogical
irreconcilable	adj	contrary	hostile	incompatible	opposing
irreducible	adj	fundamental	indivisible	intractable	pure
irrefragable	adj	incontrovertible	indisputable	irrefutable	undeniable
irrefutable	adj	incontestable	indisputable	undeniable	unquestionable
irrelevant	adj	immaterial	inapplicable	inappropriate	unrelated
irreparable	adj	hopeless	incurable	irredeemable	irreversible
irresistible	adj	alluring	appealing	charming	overpowering
irresolute	adj	flexible	hesitant	uncertain	weak
irresolvable	adj	atomic	fixed	indivisible	unsolvable
irreverent	adj	blasphemous	disrespectful	profane	sacrilegious
irrevocable	adj	certain	irretrievable	irreversible	unalterable
irrigate	v	flush	sprinkle	water	wet
irritable	adj	cranky	irascible	peevish	testy
irritate	v	annoy	bother	irk	vex
irruption	n	incursion	intrusion	outbreak	raid
isosceles	adj	balanced	equal-sided	equilateral	symmetric
isthmus	n	bridge	land	neck	peninsula
iterate	v	recapitulate	rehearse	renew	repeat
itinerant	adj	migratory	nomadic	vagrant	wandering
itinerary	n	course	path	route	schedule
jabber	n	babble	chatter	prate	prattle
jabberwocky	n	gibberish	gobbledygook	nonsense	prattle
Jacobin	n	Dominican	French	radical	revolution
jactation	n	bluster	boasting	conceit	self-praise
jactitation	n	jerking	restless	tossing	twitching
jaded	adj	exhausted	fatigued	spent	weary
jalousie	n	blind	curtain	louver	shutter

129

jangle	n	clash	clatter	jingle	rattle
jape	n	gag	jest	joke	prank
jargon	n	lingo	slang	pretentious	specialized
jaundiced	adj	bitter	cynical	resentful	soured
jaunt	v	journey	tour	trip	voyage
jaunty	adj	buoyant	cheerful	lively	sprightly
jeer	v	mock	ridicule	sneer	taunt
jejune	adj	barren	hungry	dull	uninteresting
jeopardize	v	compromise	endanger	risk	venture
jeopardy	n	danger	hazard	peril	risk
jeremiad	n	diatribe	harangue	philippic	tirade
jerkin	n	camisole	doublet	vest	waistcoat
jest	v	jape	joke	laugh	quip
jetsam	n	debris	flotsam	garbage	waste
jettison	v	discard	dump	reject	scrap
jetty	n	dock	pier	quay	wharf
Jezebel	n	hussy	slut	vamp	whore
jilt	v	abandon	desert	forsake	reject
jingoism	n	chauvinism	nationalism	superpatriotism	warlike
jingoistic	adj	chauvinistic	flag-waving	nationalistic	warmongering
jocose	adj	facetious	funny	humorous	jocular
jocosity	n	funniness	humorous	jollity	witty
jocular	adj	humorous	joking	merry	playful
jocularity	n	fun	joviality	levity	merriment
jocund	adj	gay	jolly	jovial	merry
join	v	combine	connect	link	unite
jolt	v	agitate	jog	shake	shock
Jonah	n	curse	hex	jinx	spell
jostle	v	elbow	push	shove	bump
journeyman	n	artificer	artisan	craftsman	worker
jovial	adj	fun-loving	jolly	merry	sociable
jubilant	adj	delighted	happy	joyful	pleased
jubilation	n	elation	gaiety	glee	merriment
jubilee	n	celebration	commemoration	feast	holiday

judicious	adj	discreet	prudent	sensible	sound
juggernaut	n	behemoth	force	overpowering	steamroller
jugular	n	neck	throat	vein	vulnerable
juncture	n	connection	joint	junction	moment
junket	v	jaunt	journey	outing	trip
Junoesque	adj	handsome	shapely	stately	statuesque
juridical	adj	justice	legal	legislative	statutory
jurisdiction	n	administration	authority	governance	regime
jurisprudence	n	judiciary	justice	law	police
justiciable	n	accused	liable	litigant	opponent
justify	v	defend	excuse	explain	warrant
jut	v	bulge	overhang	project	protrude
juvenescent	adj	adolescent	juvenile	young	youthful
juxtapose	v	close	near	proximity	side by side
Kafkaesque	adj	bizarre	illogical	nightmarish	uncanny
kaleidoscope	v	changing	diverse	succession	variegated
karma	n	destiny	fate	fortune	kismet
keen	adj	acute	sharp	eager	zealous
ken	n	grasp	range	sight	understanding
kermis	n	bazaar	carnival	fair	festival
kernel	n	core	essence	heart	nucleus
kibitz	v	advise	counsel	interfere	meddle
kilter	n	condition	fitness	order	shape
kindle	v	arouse	inspire	provoke	stimulate
kindred	adj	cognate	related	relative	similar
kinetic	adj	active	brisk	dynamic	energetic
kink	n	curl	knot	quirk	twist
kiosk	n	alcove	booth	newsstand	stall
kismet	n	destiny	fate	karma	lot
kissable	adj	beautiful	cuddly	sexy	sweet
kite	n	bloodsucker	predator	shark	vampire
kitsch	n	campy	cheesy	tacky	tastelessness
knave	n	rapscallion	rogue	scoundrel	villain
knavery	n	deception	dishonesty	fraud	trickery
knead	v	manipulate	massage	mold	shape
knell	v	bong	chime	ring	toll

knoll	n	dune	heap	hill	mound
knotty	adj	complex	complicated	difficult	intricate
knout	n	lash	scourge	thong	whip
knowledge	n	awareness	information	understanding	wisdom
knurled	adj	edge	gnarled	knobbed	ridge
kowtow	v	bootlick	bow	fawn	toady
kudos	n	acclaim	applause	distinction	praise
labefaction	n	deterioration	downfall	overthrow	weakening
labyrinth	n	maze	mystery	puzzle	riddle
labyrinthine	adj	complex	complicated	convoluted	intricate
lacerate	v	cut	mangle	rend	tear
laceration	n	cut	gash	rip	wound
lachrymal	adj	crying	tearful	watery	weepy
lachrymose	adj	melancholy	miserable	sad	tearful
lack	n	deficiency	insufficiency	scarcity	shortage
lackadaisical	adj	idle	lazy	sluggish	unconcerned
lackey	n	flunky	footman	servant	sycophant
lackluster	adj	dim	drab	dull	colorless
laconic	adj	brief	compact	curt	short
laconically	adv	briefly	curtly	shortly	tersely
lacuna	n	break	gap	hiatus	space
laden	adj	burdened	fraught	full	loaded
laggard	adj	dilatory	leisurely	slow	sluggish
lagniappe	n	bonus	extra	perks	tip
laic	adj	civil	layman	nonclerical	secular
laity	n	assembly	congregation	flock	parish
lambaste	v	attack	castigate	condemn	criticize
lambent	adj	bright	luminous	lucent	radiant
lament	v	bemoan	grieve	mourn	regret
lamentation	n	grief	mourning	complaint	regret
lamina	n	lamella	layer	plate	scale
laminate	n	coat	layer	plate	stratifying
lampoon	v	mock	parody	ridicule	satirize
landlord	n	lessor	manager	owner	proprietor
landmark	n	event	guide	milestone	monument
languid	adj	dull	inactive	lazy	sluggish

languish	v	decline	fade	deteriorate	wither
languorous	adj	languid	leaden	listless	sluggish
lanyard	n	cord	line	rope	string
Laodicean	adj	apathetic	indifferent	lukewarm	uncaring
lapidary	n	cutter	engraver	jeweler	polisher
larceny	n	robbery	stealing	theft	thievery
larder	n	buttery	cupboard	pantry	storeroom
largesse	n	bounty	charity	generosity	gift
lariat	n	lasso	noose	reata	riata
larva	n	caterpillar	maggot	naiad	nymph
lascivious	adj	lecherous	lewd	licentious	lustful
lasciviously	adv	randily	lewdly	lustfully	salaciously
lash	v	beat	flog	scourge	whip
lassitude	n	fatigue	sluggishness	tiredness	weariness
latent	adj	concealed	dormant	hidden	inactive
latently	adj	covertly	furtively	secretly	unrealized
latitude	n	freedom	margin	scope	space
latitudinari-anism	n	liberalism	permissive-ness	progressivism	tolerance
lattice	n	grid	mesh	network	trellis
laud	v	acclaim	commend	glorify	praise
laudable	adj	admirable	commendable	estimable	praiseworthy
laudatory	adj	commenda-tory	compli-mentary	encomiastic	flattering
laughingstock	n	dupe	fool	joke	mockery
laurels	n	accolade	award	distinction	honor
lave	v	clean	lap	wash	wet
lavish	adj	extravagant	luxurious	generous	liberal
lax	adj	flexible	loose	slack	yielding
laxity	n	looseness	negligence	remissness	slackness
laxness	n	looseness	permissive-ness	remissness	slackness
layman	n	amateur	dabbler	hobbyist	tinkerer
layout	n	arrangement	blueprint	design	plan
leach	v	filter	ooze	percolate	seep
learned	adj	erudite	knowledge-able	scholarly	well-read

lease	v	charter	hire	let	rent
leaven	v	ferment	flavor	imbue	raise
lecher	n	Casanova	lounge lizard	philanderer	womanizer
lectern	n	podium	pulpit	rostrum	stand
ledger	n	book	journal	record	register
leech	n	bloodsucker	freeloader	moocher	parasite
leery	adj	cautious	distrustful	suspicious	wary
legacy	n	bequest	gift	heritage	inheritance
legal	adj	allowed	authorized	lawful	legitimate
legend	n	fable	myth	story	tale
legerdemain	n	deception	magic	trickery	sleight of hand
legible	adj	clear	plain	intelligible	readable
legion	n	army	crowd	horde	host
legion	v	many	multitudinous	myriad	numerous
legislate	v	constitute	enact	establish	decree
legitimate	adj	legal	proper	true	valid
legume	n	bean	pea	pod	vegetable
leisure	n	entertainment	recreation	relaxation	rest
leisurely	adv	slow	deliberate	easy	unhurried
length	n	duration	long	period	time
lengthening	n	extension	prolongation	protraction	stretching
lenient	adj	forgiving	gentle	tolerant	yielding
lenity	n	clemency	compassion	mercy	leniency
leonine	adj	big cat	feline	lion like	renowned
lethal	adj	deadly	fatal	mortal	poisonous
lethargic	adj	drowsy	dull	inactive	sluggish
lethargy	n	drowsiness	inactivity	laziness	sluggishness
levee	n	bank	dam	dike	embankment
leverage	n	advantage	benefit	influence	lever
leviathan	n	behemoth	gargantuan	mammoth	monster
levity	n	flippancy	frivolity	lightness	silliness
levy	v	charge	collect	impose	raise
levy	n	charge	duty	tariff	tax
lewd	adj	dirty	indecent	lascivious	obscene
lexicon	n	dictionary	glossary	thesaurus	vocabulary

liability	n	accountability	debt	obligation	responsibility
liable	adj	accountable	answerable	likely	responsible
liaison	n	association	connection	linkage	relationship
libation	n	alcohol	beverage	drink	potion
libel	n	calumniation	defamation	slander	vilification
libelous	adj	calumnious	defamatory	disparaging	maligning
liberal	adj	bountiful	charitable	free	generous
liberate	v	deliver	discharge	free	release
libertarian	n	freethinker	independent	latitudinarian	liberal
libertine	adj	debauched	degenerate	depraved	dissolute
libidinous	adj	lascivious	lecherous	lustful	sexy
libido	n	desire	lust	passion	concupiscence
librettist	n	author	bard	lyricist	playwright
licentiate	n	assignee	candidate	licensee	permittee
licentious	adj	immoral	loose	lustful	sensual
licentiousness	n	debauchery	lechery	profligacy	wantonness
licit	adj	lawful	legal	legitimate	permissible
lien	n	attachment	bond	mortgage	security
lieu	n	place	position	site	stead
lieutenant	n	adjutant	aide	assistant	deputy
ligature	n	binding	fetter	shackle	tying
ligneous	adj	arboreal	timber	wooden	woody
likelihood	n	chance	odds	possibility	probability
Lilliputian	adj	diminutive	little	mini	tiny
limbo	n	abyss	nothingness	oblivion	obscurity
limn	v	delineate	depict	describe	portray
limpid	adj	clear	crystalline	lucid	transparent
linchpin	n	anchor	backbone	cornerstone	mainstay
lineage	n	ancestry	descent	family	line
lineaments	n	face	features	lines	traits
lingo	n	argot	jargon	language	slang
lionize	v	celebrate	exalt	glorify	praise
lipid	n	fat	grease	oil	wax
liquidate	v	destroy	eliminate	exterminate	kill
liquidation	n	elimination	eradication	removal	settlement

lissome	adj	agile	flexible	limber	supple
listless	adj	dull	inactive	sluggish	unconcerned
litany	n	invocation	list	petition	prayer
literal	adj	accurate	exact	precise	true
literati	n	academician	clerisy	intellectual	scholar
literature	n	letters	documentation	publications	writings
lithe	adj	flexible	limber	nimble	supple
litigate	v	debate	dispute	prosecute	sue
litigation	n	action	case	lawsuit	trial
littoral	adj	coastal	seaside	lakeside	shore
liturgy	n	ceremony	observance	ritual	sacrament
livelihood	n	living	subsistence	support	sustenance
liveliness	n	animation	energy	spirit	vivacity
livid	adj	mad	enraged	furious	irate
loath	adj	averse	indisposed	reluctant	unwilling
loathe	v	despise	detest	dislike	hate
lobby	v	pressure	push	sway	urge
lobster	n	crab	crawfish	crayfish	prawn
locution	n	diction	expression	phrase	term
lode	n	mine	quarry	seam	vein
lodestar	n	compass	direction	focus	guiding star
lodestone	n	attention	attraction	draw	magnet
lodgment	n	deposition	dwelling	habitation	housing
lofty	adj	elevated	exalted	grand	high
loge	n	balcony	booth	box seat	skybox
loggerheads	n	conflict	disagreement	dispute	odds
loggia	n	arcade	breezeway	cloister	piazza
logic	n	intelligence	rationale	reason	philosophy
logical	adj	rational	reasonable	sensible	sound
logician	n	academic	dialectician	philosopher	sophist
logistics	n	coordination	planning	preparation	supply
logo	n	brand	emblem	sign	symbol
logomachy	n	altercation	bickering	conflict	wrangle
logorrhea	n	garrulity	prolixity	verbosity	wordiness
logy	adj	dazed	groggy	lethargic	sluggish

loiter	v	dawdle	delay	drag	linger
loneliness	n	isolation	seclusion	solitariness	solitude
long	v	agonize	hanker	pine	yearn
longanimity	n	enduring	forbearance	long-suffering	patience
longevity	n	age	durability	endurance	permanence
longitude	n	distance	length	meridian	span
longueur	n	citation	locus classicus	purple passage	quotation
loom	v	emerge	impend	threaten	tower
looming	adj	imminent	impending	menacing	threatening
lope	v	canter	jog	run	trot
loquacious	adj	chatty	long-winded	talkative	wordy
loquacity	n	garrulousness	talkativeness	wordiness	verbosity
lothario	n	Casanova	Don Juan	Romeo	womanizer
lotus	n	Egyptian	flower	hibiscus	lily
louche	adj	disreputable	notorious	rakish	shady
lour	v	glower	frown	lower	scowl
lout	n	boor	bumpkin	clod	oaf
loutish	adj	boorish	coarse	rude	uncouth
loyal	adj	faithful	staunch	true	trustworthy
lozenge	n	capsule	pill	tablet	troche
lubricious	adj	lascivious	lewd	lustful	salacious
lubricity	n	lewdness	lubrication	oiliness	prurience
lucent	adj	aglow	lambent	luminous	radiant
lucid	adj	intelligible	rational	sane	understandable
lucidity	n	clarity	clearness	explicitness	plainness
lucrative	adj	fruitful	gainful	productive	profitable
lucre	n	income	money	pelf	profit
lucubrate	v	elaborate	enlarge	expatiate	exposit
lucubration	n	cogitation	meditation	study	work
Lucullan	adj	lavish	lush	luxury	plush
ludic	adj	flippant	humorous	joking	playful
ludicrous	adj	absurd	laughable	ridiculous	preposterous
lugubrious	adj	dismal	gloomy	mournful	sad
lumber	v	galumph	lurch	plod	trudge
luminescent	adj	fluorescent	glowing	light-emitting	radiant

luminous	adj	bright	brilliant	radiant	shining
lumpen	adj	common	lower-class	plebeian	proletarian
lunar	adj	celestial	moony	orbed	planetary
lunge	v	charge	jab	plunge	thrust
lurch	v	pitch	reel	stagger	stumble
lure	v	bait	decoy	entice	seduce
lurid	adj	ghastly	gruesome	sensational	vivid
luscious	adj	appetizing	delicious	tasty	scrumptious
lush	adj	delicious	drunk	exuberant	luxuriant
luster	n	brilliance	glaze	sheen	shine
lustful	adj	lascivious	lecherous	lewd	passionate
luxuriant	adj	abundant	fruitful	lavish	lush
luxurious	adj	lavish	rich	lush	grand
lynch	v	execute	hang	kill	murder
lynx	n	bobcat	catamount	feline	wildcat
lyric	adj	ballad	poem	verse	words
lyrical	adj	emotional	expressive	poetic	romantic
lyricism	n	exuberance	musicality	poetry	songfulness
macabre	adj	ghastly	grisly	gruesome	hideous
macerate	v	drench	emaciate	soak	steep
Machiavellian	adj	crafty	cunning	sly	wily
machicolation	n	battlement	bulwark	embrasure	parapet
machinate	v	conspire	contrive	plot	scheme
machination	n	contrivance	plot	ruse	scheme
macrobiosis	n	durability	lifetime	longevity	permanence
macrocosm	n	cosmos	creation	nature	universe
macroscopic	adj	gross	large	obvious	visible
maculate	v	defile	dirty	foul	soiled
maculation	n	blemish	blot	scar	spot
maelstrom	n	eddy	swirl	vortex	whirlpool
magenta	n	fuchsia	lavender	purple	red
magisterial	adj	arrogant	autocratic	dictatorial	imperious
magistracy	n	judge	judicature	judiciary	justice
magistrate	n	adjudicator	bailiff	judge	justice
magnanimity	n	benevolence	charity	generosity	philanthropy

magnanimous	adj	courageous	generous	honorable	noble
magnate	n	baron	mogul	king	tycoon
magniloquent	adj	bombastic	flowery	grandiloquent	pompous
magnitude	n	dimension	extent	mass	size
maiden	adj	first	earliest	inaugural	initial
maim	v	cripple	damage	injure	mutilate
maintain	v	hold	keep	preserve	sustain
maintenance	n	maintaining	preservation	support	upkeep
majority	adj	common	overall	popular	prevailing
maladjusted	adj	disturbed	dysfunctional	neurotic	unadapted
maladroit	adj	awkward	bungling	clumsy	unskillful
maladroitness	n	awkwardness	clumsiness	ineptitude	ineptness
malady	n	ailment	disease	illness	sickness
malaise	n	discomfort	pain	uneasiness	unrest
malapropism	n	distortion	abuse of terms	missaying	misuse
malcontent	n	discontented	disgruntled	dissatisfied	unhappy
malediction	n	ban	curse	denunciation	oath
malefaction	n	crime	felony	misdeed	sin
malefactor	n	criminal	offender	villain	wrongdoer
malefic	adj	baneful	evil	malevolent	malign
maleficence	n	balefulness	evil	malice	mischief
malevolence	n	animosity	hatred	hostility	malice
malevolent	adj	evil	hateful	malicious	spiteful
malfeasance	n	crime	misconduct	vice	wrongdoing
malice	n	animosity	hatred	ill will	malevolence
malicious	adj	hateful	mean	spiteful	vicious
malign	v	defame	slander	traduce	vilify
malignant	adj	deadly	malevolent	malicious	vicious
malignity	n	cruelty	hate	malevolence	malice
malinger	v	dodge	pretend	shirk	skulk
malingering	v	goldbricking	laying	shirking	truanting
malleable	adj	adaptable	flexible	moldable	shapeable
malnutrition	n	hunger	famine	starvation	undernourishment

malodorous	adj	foul	putrid	rank	smelly
malversation	n	diversion	malfeasance	misconduct	mismanage-ment
Mammon	n	lucre	pelf	riches	wealth
mammoth	adj	enormous	gargantuan	gigantic	huge
manacle	n	chain	fetter	handcuff	shackle
management	n	administration	control	direction	governance
mandate	n	charge	command	order	warrant
mandatory	adj	binding	compulsory	obligatory	required
maneuver	n	guide	move	plot	trick
mania	n	insanity	madness	passion	rage
manic	adj	crazy	frenzied	insane	mad
manifest	adj	clear	evident	obvious	plain
manifest	v	demonstrate	display	reveal	show
manifestly	adv	clearly	evidently	obviously	patently
manifesto	n	announce-ment	declaration	statement	proclamation
manifold	adj	diverse	multiple	numerous	varied
manipulate	v	control	handle	manage	operate
manna	n	blessing	boon	godsend	windfall
mannered	adj	affected	artificial	stiff	unnatural
manslaughter	n	assassination	homicide	killing	murder
mansuetude	n	gentleness	meekness	pliability	tameness
mantle	n	cape	capote	cloak	frock
mantle	n	burden	duty	onus	role
manual	n	guidebook	handbook	primer	textbook
manumission	n	emancipation	freedom	liberation	release
manumit	v	emancipate	free	liberate	unshackle
manuscript	n	document	essay	text	unpublished book
mar	v	damage	disfigure	ruin	spoil
maraud	v	loot	pillage	plunder	raid
marauder	n	bandit	looter	pillager	raider
marginal	adj	insignificant	minor	negligible	peripheral
marginalize	v	demote	ostracize	relegate	sideline
marionette	n	doll	dummy	manikin	puppet
maritime	adj	marine	nautical	naval	seafaring

marked	adj	distinct	noticeable	obvious	striking
maroon	v	abandon	desert	forsake	strand
marquee	n	canopy	dome	pavilion	tent
marred	v	damaged	defaced	disfigured	scarred
marriage	n	bridal	espousal	nuptial	wedding
marrow	adj	core	heart	pith	substance
marshal	v	assemble	dispose	gather	mobilize
martial	adj	belligerent	military	soldierly	warlike
martinet	n	authoritarian	disciplinarian	harsh	taskmaster
martyr	n	prey	sacrifice	sufferer	victim
masochism	n	cruelty	depravity	masochistic	sadism
masonry	n	brickwork	stonework	trade	Freemasonry
masquerade	v	disguise	impersonate	pose	pretend
masquerade	n	act	front	pretense	show
mastermind	v	devise	direct	engineer	manage
masticate	v	chew	chomp	crunch	munch
mastodonic	adj	gargantuan	gigantic	huge	mammoth
materialism	n	commercial-ism	greed	physicalism	possessive-ness
materialize	v	appear	arise	emerge	happen
maternal	adj	female	matriarchal	motherly	nurturing
matriarch	n	dame	matron	mother	queen
matricide	n	fratricide	murder	patricide	parricide
matriculate	v	enroll	enter	inscribe	register
matrix	n	mold	model	pattern	template
matron	n	dame	dowager	housekeeper	matriarch
mature	v	age	develop	grow	ripen
matutinal	adj	dawning	early	morning	waking
maudlin	adj	mushy	sappy	sentimental	weepy
maul	v	batter	beat	maltreat	manhandle
maunder	v	drivel	mumble	mutter	ramble
mausoleum	n	crypt	grave	tomb	vault
mauve	adj	lilac	pink	purple	violet
maverick	n	dissenter	insurgent	nonconform-ist	rebel
maw	n	craw	jaw	gullet	mouth
mawkish	adj	mushy	schmaltzy	sentimental	sloppy

maxim	n	aphorism	dictum	precept	proverb
maximize	v	expand	improve	magnify	optimize
mayhem	n	chaos	disorder	havoc	mess
meager	adj	lean	scanty	slight	sparse
mean	adj	despicable	nasty	stingy	vile
meander	v	ramble	roam	rove	wander
meandering	adj	roundabout	turning	twisting	winding
media	n	broadcasting	communications	news	press
mediate	v	intercede	referee	negotiate	settle
medicinal	adj	drug	medical	pharmaceutical	remedial
medicine	n	cure	drug	medication	remedy
mediocre	adj	average	fair	inferior	ordinary
mediocrity	n	average	generality	inferiority	medium
meditate	v	consider	ponder	reflect	think
medium	n	agency	substance	environment	means
medley	n	assortment	jumble	mixture	potpourri
meek	adj	humble	mild	submissive	timid
megalith	n	headstone	memorial	monument	obelisk
megalomania	n	arrogance	egotism	self-absorption	self-involvement
megalomaniac	n	conceited	egomaniac	narcissist	self-absorbed
megalopolis	n	city	conurbation	metropolis	municipality
melancholy	adj	gloomy	reflective	sad	unhappy
melee	n	brawl	fracas	fray	ruckus
meliorate	v	amend	advance	better	improve
mellifluous	adj	dulcet	harmonious	mellow	melodious
melodious	adj	dulcet	melodic	musical	tuneful
melodrama	n	farce	play	show	tragedy
melodramatic	adj	exaggerated	overdone	sensational	theatrical
membrane	n	coating	film	pellicle	skin
meme	n	caricature	comical	joke	parody
memento	n	commemorative	keepsake	memorial	souvenir
memoir	n	account	autobiography	memory	journal

memorabilia	n	keepsake	memento	remembrance	souvenir
memoran-dum	n	memo	minute	note	record
memorize	v	learn	remember	retain	study
menace	v	endanger	hazard	risk	threaten
menagerie	n	collection	museum	vivarium	zoo
mendacious	adj	deceitful	dishonest	fraudulent	untruthful
mendacity	n	deceit	falseness	lying	untruth
mendicant	n	beggar	moocher	panhandler	pauper
menhir	n	column	monolith	pillar	standing stone
menial	adj	base	humble	lowly	servile
mentor	n	guide	master	teacher	tutor
mephitic	adj	fetid	foul	miasmic	noisome
mercantile	adj	business	commercial	economic	trade
mercenary	adj	covetous	greedy	miserly	selfish
mercenary	n	avaricious	hireling	materialistic	venal
merchandise	n	commodity	goods	product	stock
merciful	adj	compassion-ate	forgiving	kind	lenient
mercurial	adj	changeable	flighty	impulsive	volatile
mere	n	lake	marsh	pond	pool
meretricious	adj	cheap	flashy	gaudy	tawdry
merger	n	blend	combination	fusion	joining
meridian	n	acme	peak	summit	top
merit	n	excellence	quality	value	worth
meritorious	adj	admirable	commendable	creditable	praiseworthy
mesa	n	butte	hill	plateau	tableland
mesmerize	v	charm	enchant	fascinate	hypnotize
metabolism	n	biotransfor-mation	catabolism	digestion	transforma-tion
metamor-phose	v	change	convert	transfigure	transform
metamor-phosis	n	alteration	change	mutation	transforma-tion
metaphorical	adj	allegorical	comparative	figurative	symbolic
metaphysical	adj	abstract	spiritual	supernatural	unearthly
metaphysics	n	cosmology	epistemology	ontology	philosophy

metastasize	v	distribute	filter	grow	spread
mete	v	allot	apportion	deal	measure
meteoric	adj	ephemeral	fleeting	speedy	swift
meter	v	assay	count	gauge	measure
methodical	adj	careful	orderly	regular	systematic
methodology	n	approach	procedure	process	technique
meticulous	adj	careful	detailed	particular	precise
metonymy	n	image	metaphor	simile	trope
metropolis	n	capital	city	downtown	municipality
mettle	n	bravery	courage	fortitude	nerve
mezzanine	n	balcony	entresol	intermediate	loft
miasma	n	fume	gas	stink	vapor
miasmic	adj	malodorous	mephitic	miasmal	putrid
microbe	n	bacterium	germ	microorganism	virus
microcosm	n	cross section	example	instance	sample
microscopic	adj	diminutive	minute	tiny	wee
midden	n	dump	dunghill	junkyard	muck
mien	n	appearance	aspect	look	presence
miff	v	irk	irritate	pique	vex
migrate	v	leave	move	relocate	travel
milieu	n	environment	medium	setting	surroundings
militant	adj	activist	aggressive	combative	radical
militate	v	advocate	campaign	discourage	prevent
militated	v	battled	combated	contended	contested
milk	v	bleed	drain	extort	sap
mime	v	copy	imitate	impersonate	mimic
mimesis	n	imitation	impersonation	mimicry	mirroring
mimetic	adj	emulative	imitative	mimic	onomatopoeic
mimic	v	copy	emulate	imitate	impersonate
mimicry	n	imitation	mimesis	mockery	parody
minatory	adj	menacing	ominous	sinister	threatening
mince	v	minimize	moderate	play down	soft-pedal
miniature	adj	diminutive	little	mini	tiny
minimize	v	decrease	diminish	mitigate	reduce
minion	n	lackey	servant	subordinate	sycophant

minstrel	n	folk singer	jongleur	poet	troubadour
minuet	n	defined	formal	stately	music
minuscule	adj	little	minute	small	tiny
minute	adj	little	microscopic	small	tiny
minutiae	n	details	particulars	trifles	trivia
mirage	n	delusion	hallucination	illusion	fantasy
mire	n	muck	mud	slime	quagmire
mirth	n	glee	hilarity	jollity	merriment
misanthrope	n	cynic	hater of mankind	man-hater	pessimist
misanthropic	adj	mistrustful	scornful	skeptical	unfriendly
misanthropy	n	abomination	antipathy	cynicism	hatred
misapprehension	n	misconception	misinterpretation	mistake	misunderstanding
misappropriation	n	dishonesty	embezzlement	misapplication	misuse
misbegotten	adj	bastard	illegitimate	natural	spurious
miscarry	v	abort	fail	flop	misfire
miscegenation	n	crossbreeding	interbreeding	intermarriage	intermingling
mischief	n	devilry	devilment	harm	rascality
miscible	adj	agreeable	compatible	congruous	mixable
misconstrue	v	misinterpret	misread	mistake	misunderstood
miscreant	n	evildoer	hoodlum	scoundrel	unscrupulous
miscreant	adj	corrupt	degenerate	evil	wicked
misdiagnose	n	blunder	err	erroneously	incorrectness
miser	n	cheapskate	skinflint	Scrooge	tightwad
misgiving	n	apprehension	fear	qualm	suspicion
mishap	n	accident	disaster	catastrophe	misfortune
misnomer	n	inapplicable	miscalling	mislabeling	misnaming
misogynist	n	bigot	cynic	sexist	woman-hater
misprision	n	crime	misdemeanor	misfeasance	offense
missal	n	breviary	prayer book	ritual	rosary
misshapen	adj	deformed	distorted	malformed	twisted
mission	n	assignment	commission	duty	task
missive	n	dispatch	letter	message	note

mistake	n	blunder	error	fault	wrong
mitigate	v	alleviate	ease	lessen	soothe
mitigated	adj	alleviated	eased	lessened	reduced
mixable	adj	blendable	combinable	compatible	miscible
mobile	n	motile	movable	portable	transferable
mobility	n	action	flexibility	motion	movability
mobilize	v	marshal	muster	raise	rally
mock	adj	artificial	counterfeit	fake	sham
mock	v	jeer	ridicule	tease	taunt
moderation	n	frugality	restraint	sobriety	temperance
moderator	n	arbitrator	discussant	judge	mediator
modest	adj	humble	shy	unassuming	unpretentious
modicum	n	fragment	particle	pittance	speck
modify	v	adjust	alter	amend	change
modish	adj	chic	fashionable	stylish	trendy
modulate	v	adjust	change	modify	tone
module	n	component	element	part	unit
mogul	n	baron	magnate	magnate	tycoon
Mohammed-anism	n	Ishmaelite	Islam	monotheistic	Muslimism
moiety	n	fraction	part	portion	section
molest	v	abuse	annoy	harass	plague
mollify	v	appease	calm	pacify	soothe
mollifying	adj	appeasing	calming	pacifying	soothing
mollycoddle	v	baby	indulge	pamper	spoil
molt	v	cast	defoliate	desquamate	shed
molten	adj	fluid	heated	melted	liquefied
momentous	adj	consequential	important	significant	weighty
momentum	n	drive	impetus	impulse	push
monarch	n	crowned head	king	sovereign	queen
monarchy	n	empire	kingdom	realm	sovereignty
monastic	adj	austere	contemplative	disciplined	regimented
monetary	adj	cash	financial	fiscal	money
monetize	v	decriminalize	legalize	legitimatize	mint
monger	n	dealer	merchant	trader	trafficker
monism	n	communalism	individualism	regionalism	separatism

monitor	v	check	oversee	supervise	watch
monitory	adj	admonitory	cautionary	exemplary	warning
monocle	n	eyeglass	goggles	lens	spectacles
monogamy	n	betrothal	engagement	espousal	pledge
monolithic	adj	large	massive	solid	uniform
monologue	n	discourse	lecture	soliloquy	speech
monomania	n	fanaticism	obsession	paranoia	possession
monopolize	v	absorb	control	corner	engross
monopoly	n	cartel	control	domination	trust
monotonous	adj	boring	dull	humdrum	uninteresting
moot	adj	arguable	debatable	disputable	questionable
morass	n	labyrinth	marsh	quagmire	swamp
morbid	adj	dismal	gloomy	gruesome	morose
mordant	adj	acid	biting	caustic	sarcastic
mores	n	custom	etiquette	morals	propriety
moribund	adj	dying	expiring	fading	near death
morose	adj	depressed	gloomy	glum	sad
morphological	adj	form	geological	structural	topographic
morsel	n	bit	bite	fragment	particle
mortification	n	chagrin	disgrace	humiliation	shame
mortified	adj	ashamed	embarrassed	humbled	humiliated
mosaic	adj	checkered	inlayed	patchwork	variegated
motif	n	design	pattern	theme	topic
motility	n	locomotion	mobility	shift	movement
motivate	v	encourage	move	prompt	stimulate
motivation	n	encouragement	impulse	incentive	stimulus
motive	n	cause	grounds	rationale	reason
mountains	n	heaps	piles	plenty	stacks
mountebank	n	charlatan	cheat	fraud	swindler
moxie	n	grit	guts	nerve	spunk
mucous	adj	clammy	slimy	sticky	viscous
mucus	n	phlegm	saliva	slime	snot
mufti	n	apparel	casuals	civilian clothes	civvies
mugwump	n	fence-sitter	independent	neutral	undecided

mulct	v	defraud	fine	penalize	swindle
muliebrity	n	femininity	feminity	womanhood	womanliness
multifarious	adj	assorted	diversified	manifold	various
multilingual	adj	bilingual	plurilingual	polyglot	trilingual
multitude	n	crowd	host	mass	mob
mummer	n	actor	clown	mime	player
mundane	adj	earthly	ordinary	terrestrial	worldly
munificence	n	charity	generosity	liberality	unselfishness
munificent	adj	bountiful	charitable	generous	philanthropic
munificently	adv	freely	generously	lavishly	liberally
murky	adj	cloudy	dark	gloomy	shadowy
murmur	v	mumble	mutter	grumble	whisper
muse	v	consider	contemplate	meditate	ponder
muse	n	minstrel	poet	rhymester	versifier
muster	v	assemble	collect	gather	rally
mutability	n	changeability	resilience	variability	volatility
mutable	adj	changeable	fickle	inconstant	unstable
mutant	adj	abnormal	distorted	freakish	malformed
mutation	n	alteration	change	modification	variation
mute	v	hush	quiet	silence	still
muted	adj	hushed	muffled	quiet	subdued
mutilate	v	damage	disfigure	maim	mangle
mutiny	n	insurrection	rebellion	revolt	uprising
mutter	v	grumble	mumble	murmur	whisper
muzzle	v	gag	muffle	restrain	silence
myopic	adj	improvident	narrow-mind-ed	nearsighted	shortsighted
myriad	n	abundance	boatload	heap	multitude
myriad	adj	countless	infinite	innumerable	numberless
myrmidon	n	henchman	follower	servant	subordinate
mysterious	adj	cryptic	enigmatic	obscure	puzzling
mystery	adj	conundrum	enigma	riddle	secret
mystic	n	oracle	philosopher	spiritualist	visionary
mystical	adj	cryptic	mysterious	spiritual	supernatural
mystique	n	aura	mystery	romance	secrecy
myth	n	fable	legend	story	tale

mythology	n	folklore	legend	stories	tradition
nabob	n	bigwig	dignitary	magnate	notable
nacreous	adj	iridescent	opalescent	opaline	pearly
nadir	adj	base	bottom	foot	lowest point
naiad	n	fairy	mermaid	nymph	sprite
naif	adj	credulous	gullible	naive	simple
naive	adj	candid	gullible	innocent	unsophisticated
naiveté	n	artlessness	ingenuousness	ignorance	innocence
nanny	n	governess	nurse	she-goat	sitter
nape	n	collar	neck	ring	scruff
napery	n	cloth	fabric	linen	tablecloth
narcissism	n	conceit	egotism	self-love	vanity
narcissist	n	boaster	braggart	egotist	egomaniac
narrate	v	recount	relate	report	tell
narrative	n	account	chronicle	story	tale
narrow	adj	limited	restricted	small	thin
nascent	adj	commencing	dawning	developing	emerging
natal	adj	indigenous	nascent	native	natural
nationalism	n	chauvinism	isolationism	jingoism	patriotism
nativity	n	birth	Christmas	cradle	yuletide
natter	v	chatter	chitchat	gab	prattle
natty	adj	dapper	dashing	smart	spruce
naturalism	n	literalism	realism	pragmatism	verisimilitude
naturalize	v	acclimate	accustom	adapt	adopt
nausea	n	aversion	disgust	queasiness	sickness
nauseate	v	disgust	offend	revolt	sicken
nauseous	adj	disgusting	loathsome	repulsive	sickening
nave	n	center	core	heart	hub
ne'er-do-well	n	idler	loafer	rogue	scoundrel
nebula	n	cloud	film	fog	haze
nebulous	adj	indistinct	obscure	unclear	vague
necessary	adj	essential	needed	required	vital
necrology	n	biography	death notice	eulogy	obituary
necromancy	n	divination	enchantment	magic	sorcery
necropolis	n	burial ground	cemetery	graveyard	potter's field

nefarious	adj	evil	vile	villainous	wicked
negate	v	cancel	contradict	deny	refute
negative	adj	adversarial	antagonistic	hostile	unfriendly
negligence	n	carelessness	dereliction	inattention	oversight
negligent	adj	careless	inattentive	remiss	thoughtless
negligible	adj	insignificant	trifling	trivial	unimportant
negotiable	adj	arguable	controvertible	debatable	disputable
negotiate	v	bargain	deal	dicker	haggle
neighbor	n	compassionate	humane	sympathetic	merciful
nemesis	n	enemy	foe	opponent	rival
Neo	adj	contemporary	modern	revived	new
neonate	n	baby	child	infant	newborn
neophyte	n	amateur	beginner	novice	tyro
neoptistically	adv	arrogantly	egocentrically	selfishly	vainly
neoteric	adj	fresh	modern	new	novel
nepenthe	n	anodyne	forgetfulness	narcotic	nirvana
nepotistically	adv	arrogantly	egocentrically	selfishly	vainly
nervous	adj	anxious	edgy	jumpy	uneasy
nervy	adj	cheeky	fresh	impudent	sassy
nescience	n	inexperience	innocence	unawareness	unfamiliarity
nescient	adj	ignorant	illiterate	uneducated	unenlightened
nether	adj	bottom	inferior	lower	under
nettle	v	annoy	harass	irritate	pester
network	n	grid	mesh	structure	system
neurasthenia	n	fatigue	emotional	exhaustion	irritability
neurosis	n	insanity	madness	paranoia	phobia
neurotic	adj	disturbed	irrational	insane	unstable
neuter	v	castrate	geld	spay	sterilize
neutral	adj	detached	impartial	objective	unbiased
neutralize	v	counteract	counterbalance	nullify	offset
nevus	n	birthmark	blemish	defect	mole
nexus	n	bond	connection	link	tie
nib	n	beak	bill	neb	tip
nicety	n	delicacy	nuance	refinement	subtlety
niche	n	alcove	corner	nook	recess

nidus	n	breeding ground	hotbed	nest	nursery
niggardly	adj	mean	miserly	parsimonious	stingy
niggle	v	carp	cavil	fuss	quibble
nihilistic	adj	cynical	defeatist	fatalistic	pessimistic
nimble	adj	agile	clever	quick	swift
nirvana	n	bliss	enlighten-ment	heaven	paradise
nix	v	negative	refuse	reject	veto
nocturnal	adj	night	nightly	nighttime	overnight
nocuous	adj	damaging	detrimental	harmful	injurious
noisome	adj	dangerous	destructive	harmful	injurious
nomad	n	rover	traveler	vagabond	wanderer
nomadic	adj	itinerant	roving	vagabond	wandering
nomenclature	n	classification	language	terminology	vocabulary
nominal	adj	formal	nominative	titular	token
nominate	v	appoint	choose	designate	name
nominative	adj	appointive	case	individual	registered
nominee	n	applicant	appointee	candidate	contestant
nonage	n	immaturity	infancy	minority	youth
nonagenarian	n	centenarian	dotard	octogenarian	sexagenarian
nonce	adj	inconstant	infrequent	intermittent	irregular
nonchalance	n	apathy	casualness	disregard	unconcern
nonchalant	adj	apathetic	casual	disinterested	unconcerned
noncommittal	adj	ambiguous	circumspect	evasive	guarded
nondescript	adj	characterless	common	dull	ordinary
nonentity	n	nobody	nothing	nullity	zero
nonesuch	n	ideal	model	nonpareil	paragon
nonfeasance	n	default	delinquency	failure	omission
nonpareil	adj	ideal	matchless	peerless	unequaled
nonpartisan	adj	fair	impartial	neutral	unbiased
nonplus	v	confound	confuse	perplex	puzzle
nook	n	angle	corner	niche	recess
nostalgia	n	homesickness	longing	sentimentality	yearning
nostalgic	adj	homesick	longing	sentimental	wistful
nostrum	n	false	panacea	quack	remedy
notable	adj	distinguished	noteworthy	outstanding	prominent

notary	n	clerk	lawyer	scrivener	solicitor
noted	adj	celebrated	famous	notorious	prominent
noteworthy	adj	extraordinary	important	outstanding	remarkable
noticeable	adj	discernible	perceivable	perceptible	visible
notify	v	advise	inform	report	tell
notoriety	n	disrepute	fame	renown	reputation
notorious	adj	disreputable	infamous	renowned	well-known
notoriously	adv	famously	flagrantly	notably	terribly
novation	n	refurbishment	renewal	renovation	substitution
novel	adj	fresh	new	original	unique
novelty	n	freshness	innovation	newness	originality
novice	n	amateur	apprentice	beginner	greenhorn
novitiate	n	amateur	apprentice	beginner	newcomer
noxious	adj	foul	harmful	poisonous	toxic
nuance	n	distinction	nicety	shade	subtlety
nuanced	adj	delicate	fine	refined	subtle
nub	n	core	crux	heart	kernel
nubile	adj	desirable	foxy	marriageable	sexy
nugatory	adj	trifling	trivial	useless	worthless
nuisance	n	annoyance	bother	irritation	pain
nullify	v	cancel	invalidate	neutralize	void
nullity	n	illegality	invalidity	nothingness	void
numinous	adj	divine	metaphysical	sacred	spiritual
nuncupative	adj	oral	spoken	unwritten	verbal
nuptial	adj	bridal	marital	spousal	wedding
nurture	v	foster	nourish	nurse	sustain
nutritive	adj	edible	healthful	nourishing	wholesome
nymph	n	fairy	goddess	maiden	mermaid
oaf	n	blockhead	clod	dolt	lout
obduracy	n	doggedness	inflexibility	obstinacy	stubbornness
obdurate	adj	determined	stubborn	uncompro-mising	unyielding
obedient	adj	amenable	compliant	docile	submissive
obeisance	n	adoration	homage	respect	reverence
obelisk	n	column	memorial	monument	tower
obese	n	corpulent	fat	heavy	overweight

obese	adj	fat	overweight	plump	rotund
obfuscate	v	bewilder	complicate	confuse	obscure
obfuscation	n	bafflement	bewilderment	mystification	puzzlement
obituary	n	announce-ment	biography	eulogy	necrology
object	v	complain	disapprove	oppose	protest
objective	n	aim	goal	purpose	target
objective	adj	fair	impartial	unbiased	unprejudiced
objectivism	n	fairness	impartiality	independence	justice
objectivity	n	detachment	fairness	impartiality	neutrality
objurgate	v	chastise	chide	scold	upbraid
objurgation	n	denounce	rebuke	reproof	scolding
oblation	n	charity	gift	offering	sacrifice
obligate	v	bind	compel	force	oblige
obligatory	adj	binding	mandatory	necessary	required
oblige	v	coerce	compel	force	require
obliging	adj	accommodat-ing	complaisant	considerate	kind
oblique	adj	devious	crooked	indirect	roundabout
obliquity	n	abnormality	ambiguity	deviation	skew
obliterate	v	delete	destroy	eliminate	erase
obliteration	n	annihilation	cancellation	eradication	erasure
oblivion	n	limbo	nothingness	obliviousness	unconscious-ness
oblivious	adj	clueless	ignorant	inattentive	unaware
oblong	adj	elliptical	elongated	oval	ovate
obloquy	n	discredit	disgrace	shame	slander
obnoxious	adj	disgusting	offensive	repulsive	revolting
obnubilate	v	cloud	fog	mist	obscure
obscenity	n	filth	indecency	lewdness	smut
obscurant	adj	clouded	hindering	indistinct	preventing
obscure	v	cloak	cloud	conceal	hide
obscure	adj	dark	dim	unclear	vague
obsecrate	v	beg	beseech	entreat	supplicate
obsequies	n	burial	funeral	last rites	wake
obsequious	adj	fawning	obedient	submissive	subservient

obsequy	n	burial	eulogy	funeral cere-mony	interment
observant	adj	alert	attentive	vigilant	watchful
observe	v	notice	regard	see	watch
obsess	v	consume	haunt	possess	preoccupy
obsession	n	compulsion	craze	mania	passion
obsessive	adj	compulsive	fanatic	fixated	passionate
obsidian	n	alabaster	ebon	mineral	lava
obsolescence	n	ageing	antiquation	datedness	disuse
obsolete	adj	ancient	antiquated	old-fashioned	outdated
obstinacy	n	perseverance	recalcitrance	stubbornness	tenacity
obstinate	adj	adamant	inflexible	stubborn	unyielding
obstreperous	adj	boisterous	disorderly	noisy	unruly
obstruct	v	block	hinder	impede	stop
obtain	v	acquire	gain	get	receive
obtrude	v	impose	interfere	intrude	meddle
obtrusive	adj	forward	intrusive	meddlesome	prominent
obtuse	adj	dense	dumb	slow	stupid
obverse	n	antithesis	contrary	opposite	reverse
obviate	v	avert	avoid	dispose	prevent
obvious	adj	apparent	clear	evident	plain
occasion	n	chance	event	opportunity	time
occlude	v	block	close	obstruct	seal
occlusion	n	blockage	closure	obstacle	obstruction
occult	adj	cryptic	obscure	mysterious	secret
occultation	n	blackout	concealment	eclipse	obscuration
occupancy	n	incumbency	possession	tenancy	residence
occur	v	appear	arise	develop	happen
occurred	v	appeared	befell	happened	transpired
occurrence	n	event	happening	incident	occasion
occurring	v	ensuing	happening	passing	transpiring
ocher	n	amber	sepia	tawny	yellow
ochlocracy	n	confusion	mob rule	rebellion	turmoil
ocular	n	eyepiece	lens	optic	visual
oculus	n	eyelike	circular	opening	window
odalisque	n	bondwoman	concubine	courtesan	paramour

ode	n	ballad	lyric	poem	sonnet
odeum	n	arena	music hall	playhouse	theater
odious	adj	despicable	hateful	objectionable	revolting
odium	n	abhorrence	blame	disgust	hatred
odoriferous	adj	aromatic	fragrant	perfumed	scented
odyssey	n	expedition	journey	trek	voyage
oeuvre	n	corpus	lifework	masterwork	opus
offal	n	garbage	refuse	rubbish	waste
offensive	adj	disgusting	foul	nasty	repulsive
offertory	n	collection	libation	oblation	sacrifice
officiate	v	conduct	function	preside	serve
officious	adj	intrusive	meddlesome	nosy	prying
offset	v	annul	compensate	counterbalance	neutralize
ogle	v	flirt	gawk	gaze	leer
ogre	n	demon	ghoul	grotesque	monster
oleaginous	adj	flattering	fulsome	gushing	insincere
oleaginous	adj	adipose	fat	greasy	oily
oligarch	n	autocrat	despot	dictator	tyrant
oligarchy	n	aristocracy	dictatorship	junta	monarchy
olio	n	jumble	medley	mess	mishmash
ombudsman	n	advocate	conciliator	intercessor	mediator
omega	n	conclusion	end	finale	last
ominous	adj	grim	menacing	sinister	threatening
omit	v	disregard	eliminate	ignore	overlook
omitted	v	abandoned	forgotten	neglected	overlooked
omnibus	adj	collection	compilation	comprehensive	inclusive
omnicompentent	adj	capable	effective	multitalented	powerful
omnipotent	adj	all-powerful	almighty	divine	unlimited
omnipresent	adj	everywhere	prevalent	ubiquitous	universal
omniscient	adj	all knowing	almighty	divine	wise
omnivorous	adj	devouring	gluttonous	ravenous	voracious
onerous	adj	burdensome	difficult	hard	oppressive
onslaught	n	attack	assault	offensive	raid
onus	n	burden	load	responsibility	weight

155

opalescent	adj	changeable	iridescent	nacreous	pearly
opaque	adj	cloudy	hazy	murky	unclear
operative	n	agent	mole	plant	spy
operose	adj	arduous	backbreaking	hard	laborious
opiate	n	anesthetic	anodyne	narcotic	soporific
opine	v	guess	imagine	suppose	think
opinion	n	belief	position	thought	view
opponent	adj	adversary	antagonist	competitor	enemy
opportune	adj	advantageous	appropriate	convenient	timely
opportunist	n	adventurer	developer	exploiter	operator
opportunity	n	chance	occasion	possibility	shot
oppose	v	counter	fight	object	resist
oppress	v	depress	harass	persecute	suppress
oppressive	adj	burdensome	cruel	severe	tough
opprobrious	adj	abusive	disgraceful	shameful	scornful
opprobrium	n	disgrace	dishonor	humiliation	shame
oppugn	v	contradict	controvert	dispute	oppose
oppugnant	adj	antagonistic	contrary	hostile	inimical
oppungnancy	n	antagonism	hostility	opposition	resistance
opt	v	choose	decide	elect	pick
optimism	n	encourage-ment	expectation	hope	sanguinity
optimum	adj	best	ideal	maximum	perfect
option	n	alternative	choice	opportunity	selection
optional	adj	discretionary	elective	optionally	voluntary
opulence	n	affluence	luxury	plenty	wealth
opulent	adj	luxurious	prosperous	rich	wealthy
oracle	n	prophet	seer	soothsayer	vision
oracular	adj	ambiguous	cryptic	prophetic	vague
oration	n	address	lecture	recitation	speech
orator	n	talker	lecturer	speaker	spokesman
oratory	n	diction	elocution	rhetoric	public speak-ing
orb	n	ball	globe	round	sphere
orbit	n	circle	circuit	compass	course
orchestrate	v	arrange	harmonize	organize	score
ordain	v	appoint	decree	enact	order

ordeal	n	distress	torment	trial	tribulation
orderly	adj	methodical	neat	organized	tidy
ordinal	adj	centesimal	consecutive	serial	successive
ordinance	n	decree	law	order	regulation
ordination	n	appointment	consecration	installation	ordering
ordnance	n	ammunition	artillery	munitions	weapon
ordure	n	dung	excrement	feces	filth
organ	n	bulletin	magazine	periodical	publication
organic	adj	basic	central	fundamental	key
organism	n	being	creature	entity	life
orgiastic	adj	debauched	frenzied	overexcited	sensual
orient	v	align	direct	guide	steer
orifice	n	aperture	hole	mouth	opening
origin	n	beginning	birth	root	source
original	adj	actual	authentic	genuine	real
originate	v	begin	create	initiate	start
orison	n	invocation	petition	prayer	rogation
ornate	adj	baroque	elaborate	fancy	rococo
orotund	adj	bombastic	declamatory	grandiloquent	sonorous
orthodox	adj	conventional	established	standard	traditional
oscillate	v	fluctuate	sway	vibrate	waver
oscitation	n	drowsiness	gaping	inattention	yawning
osculate	v	kiss	peck	smack	smooch
osmosis	n	absorption	assimilation	penetration	spread
ossified	adj	fossilized	hardened	petrified	rigid
ossify	v	harden	fossilize	petrify	stiffen
ostensible	adj	apparent	outward	seeming	specious
ostensibly	adj	apparently	outwardly	seemingly	superficially
ostentatious	adj	extravagant	gaudy	pretentious	showy
ostracism	n	banishment	exclusion	exile	expulsion
ostracize	v	banish	blackball	exclude	exile
otiose	adj	futile	idle	lazy	slothful
ottoman	n	banquette	bench	divan	footstool
ought	v	allow	endure	must	should
oust	v	eject	evict	expel	remove
ousted	v	ejected	evicted	expelled	toppled

ouster	n	ejection	eviction	expulsion	removal
outdated	adj	antiquated	obsolete	old	outmoded
outlandish	adj	bizarre	eccentric	odd	strange
outlet	n	discharge	exit	release	way out
outmoded	adj	antiquated	obsolete	old-fashioned	outdated
outrageous	adj	disgraceful	exorbitant	shameful	shocking
outset	n	beginning	commence-ment	first	start
outstanding	adj	excellent	extraordinary	great	remarkable
ovation	n	acclaim	applause	cheering	praise
overdo	v	amplify	exaggerate	overplay	overstate
overgrown	adj	crowded	dense	excessive	thick
overrule	v	annul	disallow	invalidate	reverse
overt	adj	clear	obvious	open	unconcealed
overture	n	preamble	preliminary	prelude	prologue
overview	n	outline	summary	survey	synopsis
overweening	adj	arrogant	conceited	haughty	presumptuous
overwhelm	v	crush	defeat	overcome	overpower
overwhelm-ingly	adv	largely	mainly	mostly	predomi-nantly
overwrought	adj	excited	frantic	nervous	upset
ovoid	adj	egg-shaped	elliptical	oval	ovate
ovum	n	cell	egg	macrogamete	ovule
oxymoron	n	contradiction	discrepancy	inconsistency	paradox
oxymoronic	adj	ambiguous	equivocal	inconsistent	paradoxical
pabulum	n	aliment	food	nourishment	sustenance
pace	v	step	stride	tread	walk
pachyderm	n	elephant	hippopotamus	rhinoceros	tapir
pacific	adj	calm	peaceful	quiet	tranquil
pacifism	n	dovishness	nonaggression	nonviolence	peacemaking
pacifist	n	appeaser	conciliator	peacemaker	peacenik
pacify	v	appease	calm	mollify	soothe
pact	n	agreement	compact	contact	treaty
paean	n	anthem	eulogy	hymn	praise
paean	adj	laud	ode	praise	song
pagan	adj	atheist	heathen	infidel	gentile
paganism	n	atheism	barbarism	heathenism	idolatry

page	n	attendant	courier	messenger	runner
pageant	n	cavalcade	exhibition	show	spectacle
pains	n	exertion	labor	striving	trouble
painstaking	adj	careful	conscientious	fussy	thorough
palatable	adj	agreeable	copacetic	ducky	satisfactory
palatable	adj	appetizing	delectable	delicious	tasty
palate	n	flavor	liking	preference	taste
palatial	adj	grand	luxurious	magnificent	splendid
palaver	n	chatter	chitchat	fuss	gossip
palaver	v	babble	chatter	jabber	gossip
palisade	n	barrier	fence	fortification	picket
pall	n	cloak	cloud	covering	mantle
pall	n	bier	casket	coffin	sarcophagus
pall	v	fade	tire	weary	wither
pallet	n	bed	futon	mattress	pad
palliate	v	diminish	lesson	mitigate	soften
palliative	adj	beneficial	curative	healthful	remedial
pallid	adj	ashen	bloodless	pale	sallow
pallor	n	paleness	pastiness	sallowness	whiteness
palmy	adj	booming	flourishing	prosperous	successful
palpable	adj	evident	obvious	touchable	unmistakable
palpably	adv	apparently	evidently	manifestly	obviously
palpitate	v	beat	flutter	quiver	throb
palsy	n	impasse	paralysis	stalemate	standstill
paltry	adj	insignificant	negligible	trivial	unimportant
pamper	v	baby	coddle	indulge	spoil
pan	v	censure	criticize	denounce	knock
panacea	n	antidote	cure-all	drug	remedy
panache	n	dash	flair	flamboyance	verve
pandemic	adj	global	universal	widespread	worldwide
pandemoni-um	n	chaos	commotion	tumult	uproar
pander	v	cater	fawn	flatter	kowtow
pander	n	cadet	fancy man	pimp	procurer
pander	v	fulfill	gratify	indulge	satisfy
panegyric	n	commenda-tion	eulogy	praise	tribute

pang	n	ache	pain	spasm	twinge
panicked	adj	frightened	scared	spooked	terrified
panjandrum	n	bigwig	dignitary	kahuna	mogul
panorama	n	picture	scene	view	vista
panoramic	adj	beautiful	comprehensive	scenic	wide
pant	v	blow	gasp	puff	wheeze
pantomime	n	charade	gesture	sign	signal
pantry	n	cupboard	larder	scullery	storeroom
parable	n	allegory	apologue	fable	lesson
paraclete	n	comforter	counselor	Holy Spirit	supporter
paradigm	n	example	model	pattern	standard
paradox	n	absurdity	contradiction	inconsistency	puzzle
paradoxical	adj	ambiguous	contradictory	incomprehensible	ironic
paragon	n	champion	ideal	model	standard
parallel	adj	aligned	analogous	collateral	equivalent
parallelism	n	correspondence	likeness	resemblance	similarity
paralogism	n	argument	fallacy	solecism	sophistry
parameter	n	criterion	limitation	quality	limitation
paramount	adj	chief	foremost	leading	supreme
paramour	n	boyfriend	lover	mistress	sweetheart
paranoiac	adj	delusional	disturbed	neurotic	psychotic
paranoid	adj	fearful	insane	mistrustful	suspicious
paranormal	adj	extrasensory	psychic	supernatural	unnatural
parapet	n	barrier	defense	fortification	rampart
paraphernalia	n	apparatus	equipment	gear	tackle
paraphrase	v	explain	interpret	restate	reword
parasite	n	bloodsucker	freeloader	leech	sponger
parch	v	dehydrate	desiccate	sear	toast
parchment	n	paper	papyrus	sheepskin	vellum
pare	v	clip	cut	trim	shave
parenthetical	adj	bracketed	by-the-way	incidental	supplementary
paresis	n	impasse	stalemate	palsy	paralysis
pariah	n	castaway	derelict	outcast	tramp

parish	n	assembly	church	congregation	flock
parity	n	equality	equivalence	sameness	similarity
parlance	n	idiom	jargon	lingo	vernacular
parlay	v	aggrandize	augment	gamble	wager
parley	v	confer	deliberate	negotiate	powwow
parliament	n	assembly	congress	house	legislature
parlous	adj	dangerous	hazardous	perilous	precarious
parochial	adj	limited	local	narrow	regional
parody	n	burlesque	charade	mockery	satire
parody	v	burlesque	caricature	spoof	travesty
parole	v	bail	free	liberate	release
paronomasia	n	double entendre	epigram	pun	wordplay
paroxysm	n	convulsion	fit	outburst	spasm
parrot	v	copy	emulate	imitate	mimic
parry	v	avert	block	evade	dodge
parse	v	analyze	dissect	examine	test
parsimonious	adj	miserly	money-grubbing	penny-pinching	stingy
parsimony	n	economy	frugality	stinginess	thrift
parson	n	clergyman	minister	pastor	preacher
parsonage	n	manse	presbytery	rectory	vicarage
partake	v	participate	receive	share	touch
partial	adj	biased	incomplete	one-sided	partisan
partiality	n	bias	inclination	liking	predilection
participant	n	contestant	contributor	partaker	player
particular	adj	certain	individual	special	specific
parting	adj	farewell	goodbye	leaving	valedictory
partisan	adj	adherent	backer	follower	supporter
partita	n	entourage	retinue	series	suite
partition	v	divide	separate	share	split
partner	n	associate	buddy	colleague	mate
parturition	n	birth	delivery	labor	travail
party	v	celebrate	enjoy	feast	game
parvenu	n	newcomer	uncultured	undeserving	upstart
pasquinade	n	burlesque	lampoon	parody	satire
passage	n	crossing	path	transit	transition

passed	v	approved	gone	happened	spent
passim	adv	around	everywhere	somewhere	throughout
passive	adj	idle	inactive	compliant	submissive
pastel	adj	delicate	light	pale	soft
pasteurize	v	disinfect	distill	purify	sterilize
pastiche	n	copy	imitation	medley	potpourri
pastime	n	amusement	diversion	entertainment	recreation
pastoral	adj	bucolic	country	rural	rustic
patent	adj	apparent	clear	evident	obvious
patently	adv	apparently	evidently	manifestly	obviously
paternal	adj	fatherly	parental	patriarchal	protective
paternalism	n	despotism	dictatorship	patronizing	tyranny
pathetic	adj	miserable	pitiful	poor	wretched
pathetically	adv	miserably	pitifully	sadly	woefully
pathogen	n	germ	microbe	microorganism	virus
pathogenic	adj	infective	infectious	unhealthy	unwholesome
pathos	n	emotion	feeling	pity	poignancy
patient	adj	forbearing	long-suffering	resigned	tolerant
patina	n	coating	covering	film	verdigris
patois	n	dialect	jargon	regionalism	vernacular
patriarch	n	dad	elder	father	papa
patrician	n	aristocrat	blue blood	lord	noble
patrimony	n	bequest	birthright	inheritance	legacy
patristic	adj	clergy	exegetical	system	theologian
patron	n	backer	customer	sponsor	supporter
patronize	v	condescend	frequent	promote	support
patronizing	adj	arrogant	condescending	snobbish	snooty
patter	v	babble	chatter	jabber	prattle
patulous	adj	expanded	expansive	open	outstretched
paucity	n	insufficiency	lack	scarcity	shortage
paunch	n	abdomen	belly	stomach	tummy
pauper	n	bankrupt	beggar	bum	tramp
pavilion	n	canopy	kiosk	lodge	pinna
pawn	n	hock	pledge	puppet	stooge
pax	n	kiss of peace	peace	relic	tablet

peaceable	adj	pacific	quiet	serene	tranquil
peaked	adj	ashen	pale	pallid	wan
peal	v	bong	chime	ring	toll
peccable	adj	blameworthy	culpable	frail	sinful
peccadillo	n	fault	flaw	indiscretion	offense
peccant	adj	impure	iniquitous	sinful	wicked
peckish	adj	empty	famished	hungry	starved
pectoral	n	breast	breastplate	chest	torso
peculate	v	embezzle	misappropriate	rob	steal
peculation	n	embezzlement	misappropriation	robbery	theft
peculiar	adj	odd	strange	unusual	weird
peculiarity	n	characteristic	idiosyncrasy	quality	quirk
pecuniary	adj	economic	financial	fiscal	monetary
pedagogical	adj	academic	educational	didactic	instructional
pedagogue	n	educator	instructor	professor	teacher
pedagogy	n	education	instruction	schooling	teaching
pedant	n	bookworm	formalist	perfectionist	purist
pedantic	adj	bookish	learned	ostentatious	scholarly
pedantry	n	bookishness	culture	edification	reading
peddle	v	hawk	market	sell	vend
pedestal	n	base	foundation	stand	support
pedestrian	adj	commonplace	dull	humdrum	ordinary
pedigree	n	ancestry	descent	genealogy	lineage
peer	n	counterpart	equal	equivalent	fellow
peerage	n	aristocracy	gentry	nobility	royalty
peerless	adj	excellent	incomparable	matchless	unequalled
peevish	adj	complaining	cranky	grouchy	irritable
pejoration	n	degeneration	depreciation	disparagement	worseness
pejorative	adj	belittling	derogatory	disparaging	insulting
pelage	n	coat	fleece	fur	jacket
pell-mell	adj	chaotic	cursory	disorderly	hasty
pellucid	adj	clear	crystalline	translucent	transparent
pelt	n	fur	hide	leather	skin
pen	v	author	compose	draft	write

penal	adj	punishing	punitive	oppressive	severe
penalty	n	fine	punishment	retribution	sentence
penance	n	atonement	contrition	penalty	punishment
penchant	n	inclination	fondness	leaning	liking
pend	v	await	depend	hang	hinge
pendant	n	bangle	charm	lavaliere	locket
pending	adj	awaiting	open	outstanding	undecided
penitence	n	atonement	contrition	regret	repentance
penitent	adj	sorry	regretful	remorseful	repentant
penniless	adj	bankrupt	broke	destitute	poverty-stricken
pensive	adj	contemplative	meditative	reflective	thoughtful
penultimate	adj	consequent	ensuing	eventual	second last
penumbra	n	darkness	gloom	shade	shadow
penurious	adj	miserly	niggardly	stingy	parsimonious
penury	n	destitution	need	poverty	want
peon	n	drudge	farmhand	laborer	peasant
peonage	n	bondage	serfdom	servitude	thralldom
perambulate	v	proceed	ramble	stroll	travel
perceive	v	discern	see	sense	understand
perception	n	awareness	discernment	insight	understanding
perceptive	adj	discerning	keen	sharp	wise
perceptiveness	n	acumen	discernment	insight	perception
percipient	adj	acute	discerning	keen	perceptive
percolate	v	filter	leach	ooze	permeate
perdition	n	damnation	doom	hell	inferno
perdurable	adj	durable	enduring	indestructible	lasting
peregrination	n	expedition	journey	travel	trip
peremptory	adj	autocratic	bossy	imperious	tyrannical
perennial	adj	continual	lasting	permanent	perpetual
perfect	v	complete	consummate	improve	refine
perfectionist	adj	idealist	precisionist	purist	stickler
perfervid	adj	ardent	burning	fervent	fiery
perfidious	adj	dishonest	disloyal	faithless	treacherous
perfidy	n	disloyalty	falseness	treachery	treason
perforate	v	bore	penetrate	pierce	puncture

perforce	adj	ineluctably	inescapably	inevitably	necessarily
perform	v	conduct	execute	implement	fulfill
performance	n	achievement	presentation	production	show
perfunctory	adj	careless	negligent	mechanical	routine
pericope	n	extract	passage	quotation	selection
perilous	adj	dangerous	hazardous	precarious	risky
perimeter	n	border	boundary	edge	periphery
periodic	adj	cyclical	frequent	recurrent	regular
periodically	adv	occasionally	regularly	routinely	sporadically
peripatetic	adj	nomadic	roving	wandering	wayfaring
peripeteia	n	change	juncture	reversal	twist
peripheral	adj	boundary	external	outer	outlying
periphery	n	border	boundary	edge	perimeter
periphrasis	n	circumlocution	redundancy	verbiage	wordiness
periphrastic	adj	circuitous	circumlocutory	diffuse	verbose
perish	v	croak	decease	die	expire
perishable	adj	biodegradable	decomposable	putrescible	spoilable
peristyle	n	atrium	colonnade	galleria	parvis
perjure	v	deceive	falsify	fib	lie
perjury	n	distortion	exaggeration	falsehood	lying
permanent	adj	constant	lasting	persistent	stable
permeable	adj	passable	penetrable	pervious	porous
permeate	v	fill	penetrate	saturate	soak
permit	v	allow	authorize	enable	license
permutation	n	alteration	change	modification	reordering
pernicious	adj	deadly	destructive	fatal	ruinous
peroration	adj	conclusion	end	finale	oration
perpetrate	v	commit	execute	inflict	perform
perpetual	adj	constant	endless	permanent	persistent
perpetuate	v	continue	maintain	preserve	sustain
perpetuity	n	eternity	endlessness	infinity	permanence
perplex	n	bewilder	confound	confuse	puzzle
perquisite	n	benefit	bonus	privilege	reward
persecute	v	bother	harass	oppress	pursue

persecution	n	abuse	oppression	torment	torture
perseverate	v	continue	insist	persist	pursue
persevere	v	continue	endure	last	persist
persiflage	n	badinage	banter	raillery	repartee
persist	v	continue	endure	persevere	remain
persistent	adj	consistent	firm	stable	strong
persona	n	character	part	personality	role
personable	adj	attractive	charming	handsome	lovely
personage	n	celebrity	dignitary	luminary	official
personal	adj	individual	intimate	particular	private
personifica-tion	n	embodiment	essence	impersonation	incarnation
personify	v	embody	exemplify	personate	typify
personnel	n	crew	employees	staff	workforce
perspective	n	outlook	position	standpoint	viewpoint
perspicacious	adj	discerning	keen	perceptive	wise
perspicacity	n	discernment	keenness	perception	understanding
perspicuity	n	clearness	distinctness	explicitness	plainness
perspicuous	adj	clear	intelligible	lucid	plain
persuade	v	convince	induce	influence	urge
persuasion	n	affiliation	belief	coaxing	encourage-ment
persuasive	adj	compelling	convincing	potent	powerful
pert	adj	bold	flippant	sassy	saucy
pertain	v	apply	concern	refer	relate
pertinacious	adj	dogged	stubborn	tenacious	unyielding
pertinacity	n	doggedness	perseverance	persistence	tenacity
pertinent	adj	applicable	appropriate	fitting	relevant
perturb	v	agitate	disturb	trouble	upset
perturbation	n	agitation	commotion	disturbance	fluster
peruke	n	false hair	periwig	rug	wig
perusal	n	examination	inspection	look	study
peruse	v	examine	read	scrutinize	study
pervade	v	fill	penetrate	permeate	saturate
perverse	adj	contrary	obstinate	stubborn	wayward
perversity	n	contrariness	evil	obstinacy	viciousness
pervert	v	corrupt	distort	misrepresent	warp

pesky	adj	annoying	bothersome	irritating	troublesome
pessimism	n	cynicism	despair	despondency	hopelessness
pessimist	n	cynic	doubter	gloomy	worrywart
pessimistic	adj	cynical	depressed	gloomy	negative
pestilence	n	disease	epidemic	pest	plague
petard	n	banger	explosive	firecracker	squib
petite	adj	diminutive	little	small	tiny
petition	n	appeal	application	entreaty	request
petrified	adj	afraid	horrified	paralyzed	terrified
petrify	v	calcify	shock	stun	stonelike
petrous	adj	hard	rocky	rugged	stony
pettifog	v	bicker	niggle	quibble	squabble
pettifogger	n	ambulance chaser	shyster	trickster	unethical lawyer
pettifoggery	n	bickering	spat	squabble	tiff
petty	adj	insignificant	mean	small	unimportant
petulance	n	crossness	irascibility	irritability	peevishness
petulant	adj	cranky	cross	irritable	testy
phalanx	n	army	battalion	brigade	company
phantasm	n	apparition	dream	fantasy	ghost
phantasmagoria	n	fantasy	hallucination	illusion	vision
pharisaicalness	n	cant	hypocrisy	insincerity	sanctimony
Pharisee	n	fraud	hypocrite	phony	tartuffe
phase	n	period	stage	step	time
phenomena	n	curiosities	miracles	oddities	rarities
phenomenon	n	event	marvel	unusualness	wonder
philanderer	n	flirt	lady-killer	playboy	womanizer
philanthropist	n	donor	humanitarian	patron	supporter
philanthropy	n	charity	generosity	goodwill	kindness
phile	n	affinity	enthusiast	fondness	love
philippic	n	diatribe	harangue	invective	tirade
Philistine	n	barbarian	rude	uncivilized	uncultured
philistinism	n	ignorance	illiteracy	materialism	nescience
philosophical	adj	contemplative	reflective	theoretical	thoughtful
philosophy	n	doctrine	ideology	logic	reason

phlegmatic	adj	calm	cool	sluggish	unemotional
phobia	n	aversion	dread	fear	terror
phoenix	n	idol	legend	paragon	rebirth
phonetic	adj	oral	spoken	vocal	voiced
physic	n	cathartic	drug	medicine	medication
physical	adj	bodily	material	real	tangible
physics	n	cures	medications	pharmaceuticals	remedies
physique	n	build	figure	frame	musculature
piacular	adj	compensatory	redemptive	reparative	sacrificial
picaresque	adj	corrupt	crooked	deceitful	episodic
picayune	adj	little	petty	small	trifling
pidgin	n	cant	dialect	jargon	lingo
piebald	adj	mottled	multicolored	pinto	spotted
piecemeal	adj	gradational	gradual	incremental	phased
pied	adj	mottled	multicolored	spotted	variegated
pier	n	dock	jetty	quay	wharf
piety	n	devotion	devoutness	reverence	sanctity
pilfer	v	lift	steal	rob	swipe
pilgrimage	n	excursion	expedition	journey	voyage
pillage	v	loot	maraud	plunder	ransack
pillory	v	attack	censure	condemn	criticize
pilose	adj	fleecy	furry	fuzzy	pillory
pine	v	ache	desire	languish	yearn
pinguid	adj	fatty	greasy	oily	unctuous
pinion	v	bind	immobilize	secure	shackle
pinnacle	n	crest	peak	summit	top
pioneer	v	establish	found	initiate	originate
pious	adj	devout	holy	religious	reverent
piously	adv	devotedly	devoutly	religiously	sanctimoniously
piquancy	n	pungency	spice	tang	zest
piquant	adj	pungent	sharp	spicy	tangy
pique	v	bother	irritate	provoke	sting
pique	n	indignation	resentment	umbrage	vexation
pirouette	n	gyration	spin	twirl	whirl
pitch	n	cant	gradient	incline	slope

piteous	adj	miserable	pathetic	pitiful	sorrowful
pitfall	n	catch	snag	snare	trap
pith	n	core	crux	essence	gist
pithy	adj	brief	compact	pointed	short
pitiable	adj	deplorable	miserable	pitiful	wretched
pittance	n	meager	portion	share	trifle
pivotal	adj	critical	crucial	important	momentous
pixelate	adj	blurred	foggy	fuzzy	hazy
pixilated	adj	addled	confused	eccentric	impish
placable	adj	agreeable	gentle	meek	pleasing
placard	n	billboard	notice	poster	sign
placate	v	calm	pacify	reconcile	soothe
placebo	n	alternant	antidote	blarney	inactive
placid	adj	calm	peaceful	quiet	still
placidly	adv	calmly	mildly	peacefully	quietly
plagiarism	n	copying	misappropriate	piracy	theft
plagiarist	n	copycat	imitator	parrot	pirate
plagiarize	v	copy	lift	pirate	steal
plagiary	n	appropriation	imitation	infringement	plagiarism
plainspoken	adj	candid	forthright	frank	outspoken
plaintive	adj	dolorous	melancholy	mournful	sad
plan	n	design	plot	schedule	scheme
plangent	adj	loud	resounding	reverberating	thundering
planned	adj	envisaged	expected	intended	scheduled
plastic	adj	elastic	flexible	pliable	supple
plateau	n	highland	level	plain	tableland
platitude	n	cliché	commonplace	dull	ordinary
platonic	adj	chaste	intellectual	nonsexual	pure
plaudit	n	acclaim	applause	cheer	praise
plausibility	n	credibility	likelihood	probability	reasonableness
plausible	adj	believable	credible	probable	reasonable
pleasant	adj	agreeable	enjoyable	nice	pleasing
pleasantry	n	banter	jest	persiflage	quip
plebeian	adj	common	humble	lowly	vulgar
plebiscite	n	ballot	election	referendum	vote

plenary	adj	complete	entire	full	total
plenipoten-tiary	n	agent	ambassador	commissioner	delegate
plentiful	adj	abundant	ample	bountiful	copious
plentitude	n	abundance	affluence	bountifulness	wealth
pleonasm	n	redundancy	tautology	verbiage	verbosity
plethora	n	excess	overabun-dance	oversupply	surplus
plethoric	adj	bloated	overabundant	plentiful	rife
plexiform	adj	complicated	elaborate	intricate	network
pliable	adj	flexible	pliant	supple	yielding
pliant	adj	adaptable	bending	flexible	supple
plight	n	dilemma	predicament	quandary	situation
plod	v	drag	lumber	slog	trudge
ploy	n	gambit	ruse	stratagem	trick
pluck	n	boldness	courage	nerve	determination
pluck	v	extract	pull	snatch	tear
plucky	adj	bold	brave	courageous	fearless
plumb	adj	perpendicular	straight	upright	vertical
plummet	v	dive	drop	fall	plunge
pluralism	n	cross-cultur-alism	diversity	multiplicity	multiracialism
plurality	n	multiple	multitude	range	variety
plutocracy	n	aristocracy	elite	jet set	wealthy
plutocrat	n	capitalist	magnate	millionaire	wealthy
pluvial	adj	moist	showery	rainy	wet
poach	v	bag	hunt	snare	steal
podgy	adj	chubby	fat	pudgy	tubby
podium	n	pulpit	stand	platform	stage
poetaster	n	bard	poet	rhymester	versifier
pogrom	n	carnage	genocide	massacre	slaughter
poignancy	n	pathos	pungency	sadness	sharpness
poignant	adj	biting	penetrating	piercing	sharp
poised	adj	balanced	calm	collected	composed
polar	adj	antipodal	contradictory	diametric	opposite
polarization	n	divergence	division	opposition	separation
polarize	v	diverge	divide	oppose	split

polemic	n	argument	controversy	debate	dispute
polemical	adj	argumentative	contentious	controversial	quarrelsome
polemicize	v	debate	dispute	quarrel	spar
policy	n	guidelines	politics	rule	strategy
politic	adj	diplomatic	discreet	judicious	prudent
politician	n	diplomat	lawmaker	legislator	statesman
polity	n	government	institution	organization	political system
poltroon	n	coward	craven	dastard	sissy
poltroon	adj	gutless	lily-livered	pusillanimous	spineless
polychro-matic	adj	colorful	motley	multicolor	variegated
polyhistor	n	brainiac	genius	intellectual	savant
polymath	n	genius	intellectual	renaissance man	scholar
polytheist	n	heathen	many gods	pagan	pantheist
pomposity	n	arrogance	conceit	ostentation	pretension
pompous	adj	affected	arrogant	haughty	pretentious
ponder	v	consider	contemplate	muse	reflect
ponderous	adj	bulky	heavy	massive	weighty
pontiff	n	bishop	cardinal	papacy	pope
pontifical	adj	apostolic	episcopal	papal	pompous
pontificate	v	harangue	lecture	moralize	preach
popinjay	n	coxcomb	extravagancy	fancy Dan	pretty boy
popularity	n	celebrity	fame	renown	reputation
porcine	adj	hoggish	piggish	portly	swinish
porous	adj	permeable	penetrable	pervious	spongy
porridge	n	cereal	gruel	mush	oatmeal
portal	n	archway	doorway	entrance	gateway
portend	v	augur	foreshadow	presage	signify
portent	n	indication	omen	prophecy	sign
portentous	adj	consequential	fateful	momentous	serious
portfolio	n	briefcase	case	file	folder
portico	n	colonnade	doorway	entrance	porch
portion	v	section	share	part	piece
portly	adj	fat	heavy	obese	stout
portmanteau	n	carry-on	handbag	luggage	suitcase

portray	v	depict	describe	draw	represent
poser	n	conundrum	mystery	problem	riddle
poser	n	exhibitionist	narcissist	poseur	show-off
poseur	n	copycat	exhibitionist	imitator	show-off
posit	v	postulate	submit	suppose	stipulate
position	v	place	post	site	spot
positivism	n	certainty	confidence	optimism	surety
positivist	adj	cheerful	hopeful	Pollyanna	upbeat
possess	v	enjoy	have	hold	own
possession	n	control	holding	ownership	proprietorship
possible	adj	available	feasible	likely	practicable
posterior	adj	back	behind	bottom	rear
posterity	n	issue	offspring	progeny	seed
posthaste	adv	apace	pronto	quick	swiftly
posthumous	adj	after death	postmortem	belated	delayed
postoperative	n	examination	going-over	inspection	investigation
postulate	v	conjecture	posit	proposition	suppose
postulated	v	assumed	hypothesized	presumed	supposed
potable	adj	clean	drinkable	fresh	pure
Potemkin	adj	counterfeit	facade	fake	fraudulent
potency	n	energy	power	puissance	strength
potent	adj	forceful	influential	powerful	strong
potentate	n	emperor	king	monarch	sovereign
potential	n	ability	capability	capacity	power
potentiality	n	capability	eventuality	likelihood	possibility
potion	n	brew	dose	drink	elixir
potlatch	n	celebration	ceremony	feast	potluck
potpourri	n	assortment	medley	miscellany	mixture
potter	v	fiddle	monkey	putter	tinker
practicable	adj	feasible	possible	practical	workable
practical	adj	pragmatic	realistic	sensible	useful
practice	adj	custom	habit	policy	procedure
praepostor	n	auditor	intern	monitor	scholar
pragmatic	adj	realistic	reasonable	practical	sensible
pragmatism	n	businesslike	logicality	practicality	realism
pragmatist	n	logician	practical	rationalist	realist

VOCABULARY BLASTER

prate	v	babble	chatter	jabber	prattle
prattle	v	babble	chatter	jabber	gab
prattle	n	blather	chatter	drivel	gibberish
praxis	n	practice	habitual	established	custom
preamble	n	foreword	introduction	preface	prologue
precarious	adj	dangerous	hazardous	risky	sensitive
precarious-ness	n	insecurity	instability	shakiness	unsteadiness
precede	v	antecede	direct	introduce	lead
precedence	n	preference	primacy	priority	superiority
precedent	n	example	model	pattern	prototype
precept	n	decree	law	principle	rule
precinct	n	area	district	territory	ward
preciosity	n	affectation	artificial	fastidiousness	refinement
precious	adj	dear	invaluable	treasured	valuable
precipice	n	bluff	brink	cliff	crag
precipitant	adj	headlong	impulsive	rash	reckless
precipitate	v	accelerate	cause	hasten	quicken
precipitate	adj	abrupt	hasty	rash	sudden
precipitous	adj	abrupt	hasty	sheer	steep
precise	adj	accurate	detailed	efficient	exact
preclude	v	exclude	hinder	prevent	prohibit
precocious	adj	advanced	premature	bright	intelligent
precocity	n	accurate	correct	exact	particular
preconceived	adj	biased	deliberate	intentional	premeditated
preconcep-tion	n	bias	favoritism	partiality	prejudgment
precursor	n	forerunner	harbinger	herald	predecessor
predacious	adj	carnivorous	predatory	rapacious	raptorial
predator	n	killer	marauder	pillager	raider
predatory	adj	acquisitive	exploitative	greedy	wolfish
predecessor	n	ancestor	forefather	forerunner	parent
predestine	v	augur	doom	fate	preordain
predeter-mined	adj	destined	fated	fixed	foreordained
predicament	n	difficulty	dilemma	mess	plight
predicant	n	clergyman	preacher	priest	sermonizer

173

predicate	v	affirm	assert	declare	rest
predication	n	forecasting	preaching	prediction	sermon
predict	v	anticipate	forecast	foretell	foreshadow
predictable	adj	anticipated	expected	foreseeable	likely
predilection	n	fondness	inclination	partiality	preference
predisposed	adj	inclined	prone	susceptible	willing
predomi-nance	n	bulk	majority	preponder-ance	prevalence
predominant	adj	chief	dominant	leading	superior
preeminent	adj	chief	dominant	prominent	supreme
preempt	v	arrogate	commandeer	seize	take
preemptive	adj	early	precautionary	preventive	proactive
preen	v	groom	plume	pride	primp
prefabricated	adj	built	made	manufactured	precast
prefecture	n	district	headquarters	office	residence
prefer	v	choose	elect	fancy	favor
preference	n	liking	partiality	preference	priority
preferment	n	advancement	elevation	preference	promotion
preferred	adj	choice	elect	favorite	handpicked
prehensile	adj	grabbing	grasping	grip	seizing
prejudice	n	bias	preconception	prejudgment	predisposition
prelate	n	bishop	pope	primate	priest
preliminary	adj	introductory	preceding	preparatory	prior
prelude	n	introduction	overture	preamble	preface
premeditate	v	calculate	design	intend	plan
premise	n	assumption	basis	postulate	supposition
premonition	n	prediction	prophecy	sign	warning
prenatal	adj	antenatal	before birth	expectant	pregnancy
preoccupa-tion	n	absorption	engrossment	fixation	obsession
prepare	v	develop	make	ready	train
preponder-ance	n	dominance	majority	prevalence	superiority
preponderant	adj	dominate	major	paramount	prevailing
preponderate	v	outweigh	overbalance	predominate	prevail
prepossessing	adj	appealing	attractive	charming	pleasing

preposses-sion	n	mindset	partiality	preconception	prejudgment
preposterous	adj	absurd	foolish	ridiculous	silly
prerequisite	n	essential	imperative	necessity	requirement
prerogative	n	authority	freedom	privilege	right
presage	v	forecast	foreshadow	foretell	omen
prescience	n	anticipation	foreknowl-edge	foresight	prophecy
prescient	adj	foreknowable	foresighted	prophetic	provident
prescind	v	abandon	disregard	forego	ignore
prescribe	v	decree	dictate	ordain	order
presence	n	attendance	bearing	existence	mien
present	v	gift	introduce	offer	submit
presentable	adj	acceptable	decent	respectable	satisfactory
presentiment	n	feeling	foreboding	intuition	premonition
preside	v	chair	direct	manage	govern
pressing	adj	imperative	important	pressed	urgent
prestidigi-tator	n	conjuror	illusionist	magician	trickster
prestige	n	dignity	distinction	renown	reputation
prestigious	adj	celebrated	distinguished	notable	respected
presto	adv	fast	quickly	rapidly	soon
presume	v	assume	imagine	suppose	surmise
presumption	n	assumption	effrontery	hypothetical	supposition
presumptive	adj	circumstantial	deeming	likely	probable
presumptu-ous	adj	assuming	bold	brazen	forward
presuppose	v	assume	infer	presume	surmise
presupposi-tion	n	assumption	hypothesis	premise	presumption
pretense	n	make-believe	pretending	pretext	show
pretension	n	affectation	ostentation	pride	pompous
pretentious	adj	affected	arrogant	haughty	inflated
preternatural	adj	abnormal	extraordinary	exceptional	unusual
preternatu-rally	adv	abnormally	prodigiously	supernaturally	uncannily
pretext	n	excuse	guise	motive	purpose
prevail	v	dominate	overcome	triumph	win

prevailing	adj	common	current	popular	widespread
prevalence	n	commonness	currency	frequency	incidence
prevalent	adj	common	general	usual	widespread
prevaricate	v	evade	dodge	fib	lie
prevarication	n	fabrication	falsehood	fib	untruth
prevent	v	avert	forestall	obviate	preclude
priapic	adj	erection	male	phallic	sexual
prick	v	pierce	poke	puncture	sting
priestly	adj	clerical	ministerial	pastoral	sacerdotal
prig	n	moralist	prude	puritan	snob
priggish	adj	pedantic	prim	staid	stuffy
priggishness	n	priggery	primness	prudishness	puritanism
prim	adj	demure	formal	proper	stuffy
primacy	n	precedence	priority	supremacy	superiority
primal	adj	aboriginal	fundamental	primary	primitive
primary	adj	first	main	major	principal
primate	n	ape	bishop	leader	monkey
primer	n	handbook	manual	schoolbook	textbook
primeval	adj	early	old	prehistoric	primitive
primogenitor	n	ancestor	forebear	forefather	progenitor
primordial	adj	early	original	primal	primitive
primp	v	dress	groom	preen	prink
princely	adj	grand	noble	regal	royal
principal	adj	chief	head	main	primary
principle	n	beginning	doctrine	precept	rule
priori	adj	deductive	inferred	reasoned	theoretical
priority	n	order	preference	rank	urgency
prismatic	adj	chromatic	colorful	kaleidoscopic	polychrome
pristine	adj	clean	immaculate	pure	spotless
privation	n	destitution	hardship	poverty	want
privilege	n	advantage	entitlement	prerogative	right
privy	adj	confidential	personal	private	secret
probably	adv	likely	maybe	perhaps	possibly
probation	n	bail	parole	test	trial
probative	adj	conclusive	evidential	proof	supporting
probatory	adj	conclusive	convincing	evidential	proof

probe	v	examine	explore	investigate	search
procedure	n	honesty	fairness	integrity	trustworthiness
problematic	adj	complicated	difficult	tricky	questionable
proboscis	n	beak	nose	snout	trunk
procedure	n	approach	method	operation	process
proceed	v	advance	continue	move	progress
proceeds	n	earnings	income	return	revenue
process	n	method	operation	procedure	way
proclaim	v	announce	broadcast	declare	publish
proclivity	n	inclination	liking	partiality	tendency
procrastinate	v	delay	linger	postpone	stall
procrastination	n	delay	hesitation	stall	vacillation
procrastinator	n	dawdler	lingerer	loiterer	slowpoke
procreate	v	beget	breed	generate	reproduce
procreation	n	breeding	generation	propagation	reproduction
proctor	n	agent	monitor	overseer	supervisor
procure	v	acquire	get	obtain	secure
procurer	n	cadet	fancy man	pander	pimp
prod	v	goad	poke	push	urge
prodding	n	goading	prompting	spurring	urging
prodigal	adj	extravagant	spendthrift	squanderer	wasteful
prodigality	n	extravagance	lavishness	profligacy	waste
prodigious	adj	enormous	extraordinary	immense	monumental
prodigy	n	genius	portent	presage	prognostic
productive	adj	fertile	fruitful	profitable	prolific
proem	n	foreword	introduction	preface	prologue
profanation	n	defilement	desecration	sacrilege	violation
profane	adj	blasphemous	irreverent	sacrilegious	ungodly
profaning	v	defiling	desecrating	pollute	profane
profess	v	affirm	avow	declare	maintain
profession	n	business	career	occupation	trade
professor	n	instructor	master	teacher	tutor
proffer	n	bid	offer	proposition	suggestion
proficient	adj	accomplished	competent	expert	skillful

profile	n	contour	outline	shape	silhouette
profitable	adj	advantageous	beneficial	productive	useful
profiteer	n	carpetbagger	extortionist	freeloader	sponge
profligate	adj	degenerate	depraved	extravagant	immoral
profound	adj	deep	difficult	insightful	knowledge-able
profundity	n	deepness	depth	profoundness	wisdom
profuse	adj	abundant	lavish	luxuriant	plentiful
profusion	n	abundance	excess	plenty	wealth
progenitive	adj	procreative	propagative	reproductive	sexual
progenitor	n	ancestor	forefather	precursor	predecessor
progeny	n	issue	offspring	posterity	seed
prognosis	n	forecast	prediction	projection	prophecy
prognosticate	v	forecast	foretell	predict	prophecy
program-matic	adj	imprinting	method	programma-ble	schedule
progress	n	advancement	development	growth	improvement
progressive	adj	advanced	gradual	liberal	radical
prohibit	v	ban	forbid	inhibit	prevent
prohibition	n	banning	interdiction	prohibiting	proscription
projected	adj	anticipated	estimated	expected	protruding
prolegome-non	n	foreword	preamble	preface	prologue
prolepsis	n	anachronism	foreword	introduction	overture
proletariat	n	populace	rabble	rank and file	working class
proliferate	v	increase	grow	multiply	spread
proliferation	n	expansion	growth	multiplication	spread
prolific	adj	abundant	fertile	fruitful	productive
prolix	adj	boring	long-winded	tiresome	wordy
prolixity	n	redundancy	verbiage	verbosity	wordiness
prologue	n	foreword	introduction	preface	prelude
prolong	v	extend	lengthen	protract	stretch
promenade	n	hike	saunter	stroll	walk
Promethean	adj	clever	creative	imaginative	inventive
prominent	adj	celebrated	distinguished	notable	outstanding
promiscuous	adj	immoral	indiscriminate	licentious	loose

promissory	n	banknote	cashier's check	draft	money order
promontory	n	cape	foreland	headland	hill
promote	v	advance	encourage	foster	support
prompt	v	induce	motivate	provoke	stimulate
prompter	n	autocue	prodder	provoker	reminder
promulgate	v	broadcast	disseminate	proclaim	publish
prone	adj	apt	inclined	liable	predisposed
proneness	n	predisposition	proclivity	propensity	tendency
proof	n	confirmation	evidence	testament	verification
propaganda	n	advertisement	hype	promotion	publicity
propagate	v	breed	circulate	disseminate	spread
propagating	v	breeding	multiplying	procreating	reproducing
propellant	n	fuel	kindling	petrol	thruster
propensity	n	bias	inclination	leaning	tendency
property	n	estate	land	quality	wealth
prophecy	n	augury	portent	presage	prognostication
prophet	n	diviner	oracle	prognosticator	seer
prophetic	adj	fateful	foreshadowing	predictive	telling
prophylactic	adj	deterrent	precautionary	preventive	protective
propinquity	n	nearness	proximity	kinship	similarity
propitiate	v	appease	conciliate	pacify	satisfy
propitiating	adj	beguiling	conciliatory	soothing	tranquil
propitiatory	adj	conciliatory	expiatory	pacifying	placatory
propitious	adj	advantageous	auspicious	favorable	opportune
proponent	n	advocate	champion	friend	supporter
proportionate	adj	commensurate	corresponding	equal	uniform
proposal	n	plan	proposition	scheme	suggestion
propose	v	advance	offer	present	suggest
proposition	n	motion	plan	proposal	suggestion
propound	v	advance	offer	propose	submit
propounded	v	moved	offered	proposed	suggested
proprietary	adj	exclusive	single	sole	unshared

proprieties	n	decorum	etiquette	formalities	manners
proprietor	n	holder	landlord	manager	owner
propriety	n	correctness	decency	fitness	properness
prosaic	adj	boring	dull	ordinary	uninteresting
proscenium	n	arch	foreground	platform	stage
proscribe	v	ban	forbid	outlaw	prohibit
proscription	n	ban	embargo	interdiction	prohibition
prose	adj	dull	humdrum	prosaic	unpoetic
prosecute	v	accuse	continue	pursue	trial
prosecutor	n	accuser	complainant	informer	plaintiff
proselyte	n	convert	disciple	follower	neophyte
proselytize	v	brainwash	convert	convince	sway
prospective	adj	expected	forthcoming	future	imminent
prospectus	n	outline	plan	scheme	synopsis
prosperity	n	affluence	fortune	success	wealth
prosperous	adj	affluent	flourishing	rich	wealthy
prostitute	v	abuse	misuse	pervert	profane
prostrate	adj	flat	overcome	prone	supine
protagonist	n	champion	defender	fighter	hero
protean	adj	changeable	mutable	variable	versatile
protect	v	defend	preserve	safeguard	shield
protectorate	n	colony	dependency	mandate	territory
proto	n	anterior	first	original	precursor
protocol	n	convention	decorum	etiquette	treaty
prototype	n	model	original	pattern	standard
protract	v	extend	lengthen	prolong	stretch
protracted	adj	drawn-out	extended	lengthy	long
protruding	adj	bulge	jutting	projecting	prominent
protuberance	n	bulge	bump	protrusion	swelling
provenance	n	derivation	origin	ownership	source
provender	n	feed	fodder	forage	victuals
proverb	n	adage	aphorism	saying	saw
proverbial	adj	familiar	famous	notorious	well-known
providence	n	economy	foresight	karma	prudence
provident	adj	economical	frugal	prudent	thrifty
providential	adj	fortunate	happy	lucky	opportune

provider	n	operator	purveyor	supplier	vendor
province	n	area	bailiwick	district	territory
provincial	adj	country	local	regional	rustic
provincialism	n	dialect	localism	parochialism	patois
provision	n	delivery	offer	providing	supply
provisional	adj	interim	temporary	tentative	transitional
proviso	n	condition	prerequisite	stipulation	qualification
provisory	adj	conditional	provisional	temporary	tentative
provocation	n	incentive	incitement	motivation	stimulus
provocative	adj	exciting	seductive	sexy	stimulating
provoke	v	annoy	arouse	incite	irritate
prowess	n	bravery	courage	heroism	valor
proximate	adj	adjacent	close	immediate	nearby
proximity	n	closeness	juxtaposition	nearness	vicinity
proxy	n	agent	deputy	representative	substitute
prude	n	goody-goody	moralist	prig	puritan
prudence	n	care	caution	discretion	wisdom
prudent	adj	careful	cautious	discreet	wise
prudential	adj	careful	circumspect	discreet	provident
prudery	n	modesty	moralism	primness	puritanism
prudish	adj	priggish	prim	puritanical	straitlaced
prurient	adj	carnal	lewd	lustful	sexy
pseudo	adj	counterfeit	fake	false	sham
pseudonym	n	alias	disguise	incognito	nickname
psyche	n	being	mind	soul	spirit
psychiatrist	n	analyst	psychologist	shrink	therapist
psychic	n	clairvoyant	diviner	fortuneteller	soothsayer
psychopath	n	lunatic	madman	maniac	sociopath
psychopathia	n	antisocial	apathy	brazenness	egocentric
psychopathic	adj	crazy	demented	insane	unbalanced
psychosis	n	insanity	lunacy	madness	mental illness
psychotic	adj	crazy	demented	insane	lunatic
puberty	n	adolescence	greenness	juvenility	youth
pubescent	adj	adolescent	downy	juvenile	teenage
puce	adj	carmine	crimson	red	russet
puckish	adj	impish	mischievous	naughty	playful

pudgy	adj	chubby	fat	stout	tubby
puerile	adj	childish	foolish	immature	silly
pugilism	n	boxing	fisticuffs	fistfight	spar
pugilist	n	battler	boxer	combatant	fighter
pugnacious	adj	aggressive	combative	hostile	quarrelsome
puissant	adj	dynamic	mighty	strong	vigorous
pulchritude	n	attractiveness	beauty	grace	loveliness
pullulate	v	abound	overflow	swarm	teem
pulp	n	mash	mush	paste	puree
pulp	n	cheap	sensational	trashy	rubbishy
pulpit	n	lectern	platform	podium	rostrum
pulsate	v	beat	palpitate	pulse	throb
pulverize	v	crush	crumble	grind	pound
pun	n	double enten-dre	joke	quip	wordplay
punch	v	hit	jab	smack	strike
punctilio	n	decorum	etiquette	formality	propriety
punctilious	adj	fussy	meticulous	particular	scrupulous
punctual	adj	exact	prompt	quick	timely
pundit	n	analyst	commentator	critic	reviewer
pungency	n	acridity	bite	bitterness	sharpness
pungent	adj	acrid	biting	penetrating	sharp
punitive	adj	disciplinary	harsh	penal	punishing
puny	adj	feeble	small	tiny	weak
pupa	n	chrysalis	larva	naiad	nymph
purblind	adj	dimwitted	myopic	obtuse	stupid
purgation	n	cleaning	clearing	evacuation	purification
purgative	adj	aperient	cathartic	cleansing	laxative
purgatory	n	hell	inferno	limbo	netherworld
purge	v	cleanse	clear	purify	remove
purify	v	clarify	cleanse	purge	refine
purist	n	pedant	perfectionist	prude	puritan
puritanical	adj	prim	proper	prudish	straitlaced
Puritanism	n	austerity	moralism	prudishness	strictness
purlieus	n	environs	neighborhood	surroundings	vicinity
purloin	v	lift	rob	steal	swipe

purple patch	n	brilliance	effectiveness	success	triumph
purport	v	allege	claim	profess	signify
purported	adj	alleged	claimed	hypothetical	supposed
purposeful	adj	deliberate	determined	intentional	resolute
purposive	adj	deliberate	intentional	purposeful	willful
purser	n	bursar	cashier	paymaster	steward
pursuant	n	following	prosecutor	pursuer	using
pursue	v	chase	continue	follow	track
purulent	adj	festering	infected	pussy	putrid
purvey	v	deliver	provide	provision	supply
purveyance	n	condition	stock	procurement	provision
purview	n	jurisdiction	range	responsibility	scope
pusillanimous	adj	cowardly	fainthearted	fearful	timid
putative	adj	deemed	reckoned	reputed	supposed
putatively	adv	allegedly	presumably	reportedly	supposedly
putrefy	v	decay	decompose	rot	spoil
putrescent	adj	corrupt	putrid	rotten	unclean
putsch	n	coup	rebellion	revolt	takeover
pygmy	adj	dwarf	midget	tiny	shrimp
quack	n	charlatan	fake	mountebank	pretender
quadrangle	n	four sided	square	courtyard	enclosure
quaff	v	drink	gulp	imbibe	swig
quagmire	n	dilemma	predicament	marsh	swamp
quail	v	cower	flinch	shrink	wince
quaint	adj	curious	eccentric	strange	old-fashioned
qualification	n	condition	degree	proviso	skill
qualified	adj	able	competent	eligible	skilled
qualify	v	fit	limit	modify	restrict
quality	n	attribute	feature	grade	trait
qualm	n	doubt	hesitation	misgiving	scruple
quandary	n	dilemma	perplexity	predicament	uncertainty
quantitative	adj	amount	numerical	quantified	volume
quantity	n	amount	mass	number	volume
quantum	n	amount	measure	quantity	volume
quarantine	n	insulation	isolation	segregation	sequestration
quarry	n	game	prey	target	victim

quarter	n	area	district	region	section
quarters	n	abode	home	house	room
quash	v	annul	cancel	reverse	suppress
quasi	adj	apparently	near	semi	supposedly
quatrain	n	four lines	four stanzas	four verses	poem
quaver	v	quiver	shake	shiver	tremble
quay	n	dock	jetty	pier	wharf
queasy	adj	nauseous	sick	squeamish	uneasy
queer	adj	curious	odd	peculiar	strange
quell	v	crush	squelch	subdue	suppress
quench	v	extinguish	quell	satiate	satisfy
queries	n	calls	inquiries	questions	requests
querulous	adj	complaining	cross	irritable	testy
questionnaire	n	form	inquiry	poll	survey
queue	n	file	line	rank	row
quibble	v	bicker	dispute	dodge	evade
quicken	v	accelerate	expedite	hasten	speed
quiddity	n	eccentricity	essence	quintessence	substance
quidnunc	n	busybody	gossip	talebearer	yenta
quiescence	n	dormancy	ease	quiet	rest
quiescent	adj	motionless	quiet	still	tranquil
quietus	n	death	decease	dissolution	rest
quill	v	encourage	excite	provoke	stimulate
quintessence	n	core	epitome	essence	heart
quintessential	adj	classic	exemplary	prototypical	typical
quintuplet	n	five	pentad	quint	quintet
quip	n	jest	joke	wisecrack	witticism
quirk	n	caprice	oddity	peculiarity	quality
quisling	n	betrayer	collaborator	double-crosser	traitor
quitclaim	n	disclaimer	renunciation	surrender	waiver
quittance	n	indemnity	payment	receipt	reparation
quiver	v	shake	shiver	shudder	tremble
quixotic	adj	idealistic	impractical	romantic	whimsical
quizzical	adj	bantering	jesting	joking	kidding
quizzically	adv	curiously	inquisitively	oddly	questioningly

quondam	adj	erstwhile	former	old	past
quorum	n	assembly	congregation	convention	meeting
quota	n	allowance	portion	ration	share
quotidian	adj	commonplace	daily	ordinary	trivial
rabble	n	crowd	masses	mob	riffraff
rabid	adj	frenzied	furious	mad	wild
racism	n	apartheid	bias	fascism	segregation
racketeer	n	blackmailer	gangster	mafioso	mobster
raconteur	n	narrator	novelist	spinner of yarns	storyteller
radical	adj	extreme	fanatical	rabid	revolutionary
radical	n	crazy	extremist	fanatic	revolutionist
raffish	adj	cheap	garish	rowdy	vulgar
ragamuffin	n	beggar	tramp	urchin	waif
rail	v	blast	denounce	rant	scold
raillery	n	badinage	banter	mockery	ridicule
raiment	n	apparel	attire	clothing	garb
rake	n	debauchee	libertine	playboy	profligate
rakish	adj	dashing	dissolute	jaunty	licentious
rale	n	level	rate	ratio	percentage
rally	n	assembly	gathering	meeting	muster
rambunctious	adj	boisterous	disorderly	rowdy	unruly
ramification	n	aftermath	consequence	result	outcome
ramify	v	branch	divide	separate	split
rampage	n	frenzy	fury	rage	uproar
rampant	adj	runaway	unbridled	uncontrolled	wild
rampart	n	barrier	bastion	bulwark	wall
ramrod	n	drumstick	foreman	overseer	rammer
ramshackle	adj	decrepit	dilapidated	rickety	shaky
rancid	adj	fetid	foul	putrid	rotten
rancor	n	bitterness	hatred	hostility	resentment
rancorous	adj	acrimonious	bitter	hostile	resentful
random	adj	casual	chance	haphazard	irregular
randy	adj	horny	lecherous	lustful	vulgar
rankle	v	annoy	irritate	nettle	vex
rant	v	bombast	rage	scold	spout

rapacious	adj	avaricious	grasping	greedy	predatory
rapidity	n	celerity	quickness	speed	swiftness
rapier	n	blade	dagger	saber	sword
rapine	n	looting	pillage	plundering	spoliation
rapport	n	accord	agreement	empathy	harmony
rapproche-ment	n	approach again	approximation	reconciliation	reestablish-ment
rapscallion	n	knave	rascal	rogue	scamp
rapt	adj	absorbed	engrossed	enraptured	immersed
rapture	n	bliss	ecstasy	happiness	joy
rarefaction	n	attenuation	depletion	dwindling	scarcity
rarefied	adj	esoteric	exclusive	private	select
rarefy	v	attenuate	distill	refine	purify
rash	adj	brash	hasty	foolhardy	reckless
rasp	v	abrade	grate	rub	scrape
rate	v	estimate	evaluate	price	value
ratify	v	approve	confirm	endorse	sanction
ratiocinate	v	calculate	deduce	reason	think
ratiocination	n	conclusion	deduction	logic	reason
ration	n	allowance	measure	portion	share
rational	adj	intelligent	logical	reasonable	sound
rationale	n	explanation	grounds	justification	reason
rationalism	n	freethinking	intelligence	logic	philosophy
rationalist	n	functionalism	positivist	realist	reasonable-ness
rationaliza-tion	n	justification	pretext	reason	resolve
rationalize	v	excuse	explain	justify	streamline
raucous	adj	harsh	hoarse	rough	strident
ravage	n	demolish	destroy	ruin	plunder
ravenous	adj	famished	hungry	insatiable	starved
ravine	n	canyon	gorge	notch	valley
ravish	v	captivate	charm	defile	rape
raze	v	demolish	destroy	level	wreck
reactionary	adj	die-hard	conservative	conventional	orthodox
realism	n	authenticity	literalism	naturalism	verisimilitude
realistic	adj	lifelike	practical	reasonable	sensible

realize	v	achieve	comprehend	know	understand
really	adv	actually	honestly	indeed	truly
realm	n	area	domain	kingdom	world
reap	v	collect	gather	harvest	obtain
reasonable	adj	intelligent	logical	rational	sensible
reata	n	lariat	lasso	noose	riata
rebarbative	adj	foul	loathsome	repellent	repugnant
rebuff	v	refuse	reject	snub	spurn
rebuke	v	censure	reprimand	reproach	scold
rebus	n	charade	enigma	puzzle	riddle
rebut	v	answer	deny	disprove	refute
rebuttal	n	answer	reply	response	retort
recalcitrant	adj	defiant	disobedient	stubborn	unruly
recant	v	recall	retract	revoke	withdraw
recapitulate	v	recap	repeat	restate	summarize
recede	v	ebb	retreat	subside	withdraw
receipt	n	bill	check	ticket	voucher
receive	v	accept	get	obtain	take
recension	n	amendment	editing	review	revision
receptacle	n	canister	container	holder	vessel
receptive	adj	flexible	open	responsive	yielding
recess	v	adjourn	prorogate	prorogue	suspend
recidivism	n	backsliding	lapse	relapse	reversion
recidivist	n	backslider	jailbird	relapser	repeater
recipient	n	beneficiary	donee	giftee	payee
reciprocal	adj	complementary	correlative	equivalent	mutual
reciprocate	v	exchange	interchange	retaliate	return
reciprocity	n	correlation	exchange	kinship	mutuality
recision	n	cancellation	recall	repeal	revocation
recital	n	account	narration	performance	story
recitation	n	enumeration	litany	narration	reading
reckon	v	calculate	estimate	figure	think
reckoning	n	account	calculation	computation	tally
reclame	n	accolade	applause	cheer	ovation
recluse	n	hermit	loner	outcast	solitary

reclusive	adj	antisocial	secluded	solitary	withdrawn
recognition	n	acknowledge-ment	appreciation	gratitude	recognizing
recognize	v	discern	distinguish	identify	perceive
recoil	v	flinch	rebound	retreat	wince
recollect	v	recall	remember	reminisce	think
recommend	v	advise	advocate	commend	suggest
recompense	n	compensation	redress	remuneration	requital
reconcile	v	adjust	balance	resolve	settle
recondite	adj	abstruse	arcane	deep	esoteric
reconnais-sance	n	espionage	exploration	observation	surveillance
reconnoiter	v	explore	scout	spy	survey
record	v	chronicle	file	note	register
recount	v	narrate	recite	relate	tell
recoup	v	recover	regain	restore	retrieve
recourse	n	appeal	expedient	resort	resource
recreancy	n	apostasy	cowardice	defection	perfidy
recreant	adj	coward	faithless	treacherous	unfaithful
recriminate	v	accuse	blame	censure	criminate
recrimination	n	accusation	censure	countercharge	incrimination
recrudesce	v	break	recur	resume	revert
recrudes-cence	n	flare-up	outbreak	recurrence	renewal
recruit	v	conscript	enlist	hire	raise
rectify	v	correct	improve	remedy	repair
rectilinear	adj	direct	perpendicular	square	straight
rectitude	n	honesty	integrity	uprightness	virtue
recumbent	adj	flat	prone	reclining	supine
recuperate	v	convalesce	heal	improve	recover
recuperation	n	convalescence	recovery	rehabilitation	restoration
recur	v	duplicate	redo	repeat	replicate
recusant	n	dissident	insurgent	rebel	revolutionary
red herring	n	decoy	distraction	diversion	misdirect
redact	v	censor	edit	obscure	remove
redeem	v	recover	rescue	retrieve	save
redeemer	n	Deliverer	demigod	rescuer	Savior

redemption	n	expiation	recovery	rescue	salvation
redemptive	adj	liberating	delivering	redeeming	saving
redintegrate	v	correct	recoup	rectify	restore
redolent	adj	aromatic	balmy	fragrant	sweet
redoubling	n	duplicating	increasing	intensifying	magnifying
redoubt	n	bastion	citadel	fortress	stronghold
redoubtable	adj	dread-some	fearsome	formidable	steadfast
redress	v	correct	equalize	rectify	remedy
redress	n	amends	compensation	reparation	restitution
reducible	adj	collapsible	convertible	diminishable	exchangeable
reduction	n	abatement	decrease	reducing	lowering
redundancy	n	discharge	dismissal	termination	unemploy-ment
redundant	adj	excess	extra	repetitive	unnecessary
reek	v	scent	smell	stench	stink
reel	v	lurch	roll	spin	stagger
reeling	adj	dizzy	giddy	light-headed	woozy
refectory	n	cafeteria	dining hall	lunchroom	mess hall
refer	v	apply	assign	cite	mention
reference	v	mention	note	refer	source
referendum	n	ballot	election	poll	vote
referent	n	meaning	prototype	referrer	significance
referred	v	cited	mentioned	pertained	related
referring	adj	alluding	allusive	denotative	indicative
refined	v	civilized	cultivated	polished	purified
refinement	n	cultivation	culture	elegance	sophistication
reflect	v	commentate	consider	image	mirror
reflection	n	consideration	observation	thinking	thought
reflective	adj	meditative	pondering	thinking	thoughtful
reflux	n	backflow	decrease	ebb	reflow
reform	v	amend	better	improve	repair
refracted	v	deflected	dispersed	scattered	separated
refraction	n	bending	deflection	deviation	dispersion
refractory	adj	disobedient	headstrong	obstinate	stubborn
refrain	v	abstain	avoid	cease	desist
refulgent	adj	brilliant	gleaming	radiant	sparkling

refund	v	rebate	reimburse	repay	return
refurbish	v	recondition	remodel	repair	restore
refuse	v	decline	deny	disallow	reject
refute	v	deny	disprove	contradict	rebut
regal	adj	grand	imperial	majestic	royal
regale	v	amuse	entertain	feast	treat
regalia	n	array	finery	formal dress	insignia
regardless	adv	anyway	however	irrespective	nevertheless
regenerative	adj	recovering	recuperative	replenisher	restorer
regime	n	administration	government	management	rule
register	n	chronicle	file	list	record
registered	adj	cataloged	entered	listed	recorded
regnant	adj	dominant	prevailing	reigning	ruling
regress	v	relapse	return	reversion	throwback
regressive	adj	backward	digressive	reactionary	retrograde
regretful	adj	contrite	remorseful	repentant	sorry
regrettable	adj	deplorable	lamentable	sad	unfortunate
regularly	adv	consistently	frequently	periodically	routinely
regulate	v	adjust	control	direct	manage
regulation	n	control	legislation	order	rule
regurgitate	v	disgorge	puke	upchuck	vomit
rehabilitation	n	convalescence	recovery	recuperation	rehab
rehash	v	recapitulate	reiterate	repeat	restate
rehearse	v	practice	recite	reiterate	repeat
reification	n	commodification	embodiment	incarnation	objectification
reify	v	commodity	embody	materialize	realize
reign	v	command	dominate	govern	rule
reimbursement	n	compensation	refund	payment	return
rein	v	check	control	curb	limit
reincarnation	n	approximation	impression	imprint	version
reinforce	v	enhance	improve	increase	strengthen
reinstitutionalize	v	commit	formalize	mainstream	regulate
reiterate	v	reaffirm	renew	repeat	restate
reiteration	n	echo	frequency	recurrence	repetition

reject	v	deny	dismiss	refuse	repel
rejoice	v	celebrate	enjoy	exult	revel
rejoinder	n	answer	comeback	response	retort
rejuvenate	v	refresh	renew	restore	revive
rejuvenated	v	enlivened	mended	refreshed	restored
rejuvenating	adj	enlivening	exhilarating	invigorating	refreshing
relapse	n	backsliding	recidivism	recurrence	regression
relative	adj	applicable	pertinent	proportionate	related
relatively	adv	fairly	pretty	quite	rather
relaxation	n	break	leisure	recreation	rest
relegate	v	banish	demote	dismiss	transfer
relent	v	give in	let up	slacken	yield
relenting	adj	agreeable	flexible	responsive	yielding
relentless	adj	determined	inflexible	rigid	unstoppable
relevance	n	applicability	importance	interest	significance
relevant	adj	applicable	appropriate	fitting	proper
relic	n	antique	keepsake	memento	souvenir
religiose	adj	godly	pietistic	pious	religious
religious	adj	devout	holy	pious	spiritual
relinquish	v	abandon	give up	renounce	surrender
reliquary	n	casket	container	sanctuary	shrine
relish	v	appreciate	enjoy	like	savor
reluctance	n	doubt	hesitation	misgiving	unwillingness
remanent	adj	permanent	persistent	remaining	residual
reminiscence	n	memory	recall	recollection	retrospection
reminiscent	adj	nostalgic	recalling	remindful	suggestive
remiss	adj	careless	lax	negligent	slack
remonstrate	v	disapprove	except	object	protest
remorse	n	guilt	regret	sadness	sorrow
remuneration	n	compensation	payment	reimbursement	reward
renascent	adj	budding	dynamic	resurgent	reviving
rendezvous	n	appointment	date	engagement	meeting
renegade	adj	deserter	rebel	traitor	turncoat
renege	v	back out	disavow	reverse	withdraw
renitent	adj	resistant	resistive	strong	tough

renounce	v	abandon	disown	forsake	relinquish
renovate	v	refurbish	recondition	repair	restore
renown	n	celebrity	distinction	fame	reputation
renowned	adj	celebrated	eminent	famous	illustrious
reparation	n	amend	atonement	compensation	renovation
repast	n	banquet	dinner	feast	meal
repeal	v	abolish	cancel	recall	revoke
repertoire	n	capabilities	masteries	proficiencies	talents
repertory	n	cache	collection	repository	stock
repetition	n	duplication	iteration	repeat	replication
repine	v	grieve	lament	languish	regret
replace	v	change	shift	substitute	switch
replenish	v	provide	refill	refresh	restore
replete	adj	abounding	complete	full	laden
repletion	n	glut	satiation	satiety	surfeit
replica	n	copy	duplicate	facsimile	reproduction
replicate	v	copy	duplicate	repeat	reproduce
repose	n	rest	tranquility	poise	composure
reprehend	v	censure	condemn	decry	denounce
reprehensible	adj	abominable	blameworthy	disgraceful	shameful
repress	v	restrain	stifle	subdue	suppress
repression	n	control	restraint	oppression	suppression
repressive	adj	arrogant	domineering	overbearing	restrictive
reprieve	n	clemency	pardon	stay	suspension
reprimand	n	denunciation	lecture	rebuke	scold
reprisal	n	counterblow	retaliation	revenge	payback
reprise	n	duplication	repeat	repetition	replication
reproach	v	blame	rebuke	reprimand	scold
reproachful	adj	accusatory	critical	disapproving	disparaging
reprobate	n	corrupt	degenerate	unprincipled	wicked
reprobation	n	blame	condemnation	denunciation	disapproval
reproof	n	rebuke	reprimand	reproach	scolding
reprove	v	castigate	censure	criticize	reproach
repudiate	v	deny	disown	refuse	reject
repudiated	v	checked	rejected	removed	withdrawn
repudiating	v	denying	disavowing	refusing	rejecting

repudiation	n	cancellation	denial	rejection	renunciation
repugnance	n	disgust	dislike	hatred	horror
repugnant	adj	disgusting	offensive	repulsive	revolting
repulse	v	dismiss	refuse	reject	repel
repulsion	n	aversion	disgust	repugnance	revulsion
repulsive	adj	disgusting	offensive	repellent	repugnant
reputation	adj	distinction	fame	repute	standing
repute	adj	fame	name	report	reputation
reputed	adj	alleged	presumed	putative	supposed
requiem	n	dirge	elegy	lament	threnody
require	v	demand	necessitate	need	want
requisite	adj	essential	necessary	required	vital
requisition	v	appropriate	claim	commandeer	occupy
requital	n	compensation	reprisal	retaliation	vengeance
requite	v	compensate	recompense	repay	satisfy
rescind	v	cancel	repeal	revoke	void
research	n	examination	inquiry	investigation	study
resentment	n	anger	bitterness	hostility	spite
reserve	n	constraint	discipline	restraint	self-control
reserved	adj	aloof	diffident	reticent	shy
reside	v	abide	dwell	live	stay
residual	adj	balance	leftover	remaining	surplus
residue	n	excess	remainder	remnants	surplus
resignation	n	abandonment	relinquish-ment	submission	surrender
resigned	adj	acquiescent	compliant	patient	yielding
resilience	n	elasticity	flexibility	springiness	strength
resilient	adj	hard	persistent	stiff	strong
resolute	adj	determined	resolved	settled	steadfast
resolutely	adv	decisively	determinedly	firmly	strongly
resolution	n	decision	determination	resolve	settlement
resolve	v	decide	determine	settle	unravel
resonant	adj	booming	resounding	reverberating	vibrant
resound	v	echo	resonate	reverberate	ring
resource	n	assets	funding	supply	wealth
resourceful	adj	clever	inventive	sharp	skillful

respectively	adv	accordingly	adequately	appropriately	properly
respire	v	blow	breathe	exhale	inhale
respite	n	break	pause	relief	rest
resplendent	adj	brilliant	dazzling	gorgeous	shining
respond	v	answer	acknowledge	react	reply
response	n	answer	feedback	reaction	reply
responsibility	n	accountability	duty	liability	obligation
responsive	adj	flexible	open	reactive	receptive
restitution	n	compensation	redress	reparation	satisfaction
restive	adj	agitated	anxious	nervous	restless
restoration	n	reconstruc-tion	recovery	rehabilitation	renewal
restore	v	rehabilitate	repair	return	revive
restrain	v	control	hinder	restrict	suppress
restrained	adj	controlled	inhibited	moderate	restricted
restraint	n	confinement	constraint	hindrance	restriction
restriction	n	constraint	control	limitation	restraint
restrictive	adj	contrary	exclusive	limiting	restraining
resume	v	continue	proceed	reopen	restart
resurgence	n	rebirth	renewal	resurrection	revival
resurrection	n	rebirth	renewal	revitalization	revival
resuscitate	v	reanimate	resurrect	revitalize	revive
resuscitation	n	renewal	restoration	revitalization	revival
retaliation	n	reprisal	retribution	revenge	vengeance
retch	v	cast	heave	gag	spew
reticence	n	hesitation	inhibition	reserve	restraint
reticent	adj	reserved	restrained	shy	uncommuni-cative
reticulation	n	grid	mesh	netting	network
retinue	n	cortege	entourage	suite	train
retire	v	leave	quit	retreat	withdraw
retiring	adj	modest	unassuming	shy	reserved
retort	n	answer	comeback	reply	response
retract	v	cancel	recall	revoke	withdraw
retreat	v	fall back	recede	retire	withdraw
retrench	v	diminish	keep	reduce	save
retribution	n	reprisal	retaliation	revenge	vengeance

retrieve	v	reclaim	recover	regain	restore
retrograde	v	decline	degenerate	deteriorate	worsen
retrogress	v	regress	relapse	retrograde	worsen
retrogression	v	decay	decline	degenerate	deteriorate
retrogressive	adj	backward	declining	reactionary	regressive
retrospect	n	flashback	recollection	remembering	review
retrospective	adj	pensive	reflective	retroactive	thoughtful
revamp	v	overhaul	repair	restore	revise
reveille	n	awakening	bugle call	morning	signal
revel	v	celebrate	delight	frolic	rejoice
revelation	n	disclosure	discovery	foreshadow-ing	prophecy
revelry	n	celebration	festivity	gaiety	merrymaking
revenant	n	apparition	phantom	specter	spirit
revenue	n	earnings	income	profit	yield
reverberate	v	echo	resonate	resound	ring
revere	v	adore	respect	reverence	worship
reverence	n	admiration	esteem	respect	worship
reverent	adj	devout	godly	respectful	worshipful
reverie	n	daydream	fantasy	musing	trance
revert	v	regress	retrogress	return	reverse
review	v	examine	inspect	recap	scan
revile	v	attack	abuse	defame	scold
reviled	v	derided	hated	injured	trained
revilement	n	abuse	insult	invective	vituperation
revise	v	amend	change	reconsider	review
revision	n	amendment	change	reconsider-ation	review
revitalize	v	refresh	rejuvenate	renew	revive
revive	v	reinvigorate	resurrect	resuscitate	revitalize
revivification	n	rebirth	resuscitation	revitalization	revival
revocable	adj	removable	rescindable	reversible	voidable
revoke	v	cancel	repeal	rescind	withdraw
revolution	n	insurrection	rebellion	revolt	mutiny
revulsion	n	abhorrence	aversion	mindset	repugnance
reward	n	bounty	compensation	prize	recompense
rhabdomancy	n	astrology	augury	crystal gazing	divination

rhapsodic	adj	ecstatic	happy	joyful	rapturous
rhapsodize	v	enthuse	gush	idealize	rave
rhapsody	n	ecstasy	heaven	rapture	transport
rhetoric	n	elocution	oratory	speech	address
rhetorical	adj	bombastic	declamatory	grandiloquent	oratorical
rheumatism	n	arthritis	gout	inflammation	lumbago
rhythm	n	beat	cadence	measure	tempo
ribald	adj	coarse	gross	indecent	vulgar
ribaldry	n	indecency	obscenity	raciness	smut
rickety	adj	decrepit	feeble	ramshackle	weak
ricochet	v	bounce	carom	rebound	skip
riddle	v	bore	perforate	puncture	screen
ridicule	n	contempt	mockery	sarcasm	scorn
ridiculous	adj	absurd	ludicrous	silly	stupid
rife	adj	abundant	prevalent	replete	widespread
riffraff	n	dregs	rabble	scum	trash
rifle	v	loot	pillage	plunder	ransack
rift	n	breach	break	crack	split
righteous	adj	fair	just	moral	upright
rigor	n	harshness	severity	sternness	stringency
rigorism	n	inflexibility	relentlessness	rigidity	stiffness
rigorous	adj	exact	harsh	severe	strict
rime	n	crust	frost	hoarfrost	incrustation
riparian	adj	coastal	near shore	riverside	waterside
riposte	n	answer	rejoinder	response	retort
risible	adj	amusing	laughable	ludicrous	ridiculous
risk	n	danger	exposure	hazard	threat
rite	n	ceremony	ritual	service	observance
ritual	n	ceremony	custom	formality	rite
rivalry	n	competition	conflict	contention	contest
rivet	v	fasten	fix	join	secure
robust	adj	persistent	sound	strong	vigorous
robustly	adv	actively	firmly	strongly	vigorously
rodomontade	n	arrogant	boasting	bragging	vainglory
roentgenog-raphy	n	fluoroscopy	radiography	radioscopy	X-ray photog-raphy

rogue	n	crook	rascal	scoundrel	villain
roister	v	binge	carouse	revel	wassail
roistering	adj	boisterous	noisy	raucous	rowdy
romantic	adj	dreamy	impractical	loving	visionary
romanticist	n	dreamer	escapist	idealist	visionary
romp	v	caper	frisk	frolic	gambol
rookie	n	apprentice	beginner	greenhorn	novice
roommate	n	buddy	chum	companion	comrade
roots	n	family	heritage	pedigree	stock
roseate	adj	auspicious	hopeful	optimistic	rosy
roster	n	list	record	roll	schedule
rostrum	n	dais	platform	podium	pulpit
rotate	n	revolve	spin	turn	twist
rotation	n	gyration	revolution	spin	turn
rotund	adj	fat	obese	plump	round
rouse	v	awaken	excite	stir	stimulate
roustabout	n	dockhand	laborer	longshoreman	stevedore
rout	n	defeat	disorder	overthrow	retreat
rout	v	beat	crush	overcome	vanquish
routinize	v	familiarize	profile	standardize	stereotype
royalist	n	cavalier	monarchist	tory	traditionalist
rubicund	adj	florid	flushed	red	ruddy
rubric	n	category	course	formula	title
ruck	n	company	crowd	gather	pack
rudiment	n	base	basic	element	fundamental
rudimentary	adj	basic	elementary	fundamental	undeveloped
rue	n	contrition	regret	remorse	repentance
rueful	adj	mournful	regretful	sad	sorry
ruffian	n	hooligan	roughneck	tough	thug
ruminant	adj	pensive	reflective	thoughtful	wistful
ruminate	v	contemplate	meditate	ponder	reflect
rumination	n	cogitation	contempla-tion	meditation	reflection
rumpus	n	commotion	disturbance	tumult	uproar
runic	adj	eerie	magical	mysterious	weird
runnel	n	brook	burn	rill	rivulet

ruse	n	artifice	ploy	stratagem	trick
rustic	adj	country	crude	pastoral	rural
rusticate	v	banish	leave	plebeianize	retire
ruthless	adj	brutal	cruel	merciless	savage
sabbatical	n	break	holiday	leave	vacation
saber	n	blade	broadsword	scimitar	sword
sabotage	v	destroy	subvert	undermine	wreck
saboteur	n	destroyer	traitor	vandal	wrecker
saccharine	adj	sentimental	sugary	sweet	syrupy
sacerdotal	adj	clerical	ministerial	pastoral	priestly
sack	v	loot	maraud	pillage	plunder
sacrament	adj	communion	ceremony	liturgy	observance
sacred cow	n	icon	idol	immune	taboo
sacrilege	n	blasphemy	desecration	impiety	profanation
sacrilegious	adj	blasphemous	disrespectful	irreverent	profane
sacrosanct	adj	hallowed	holy	inviolable	sacred
saddle	v	burden	load	lumber	weight
safari	n	expedition	journey	trip	trek
saga	n	epic	legend	story	tale
sagacious	adj	discerning	insightful	perceptive	shrewd
sagacity	n	discernment	insight	intelligence	wisdom
sage	n	adviser	thinker	savant	scholar
sage	adj	intelligent	judicious	sensible	wise
salable	adj	commercial	merchantable	marketable	sellable
salacious	adj	lascivious	lecherous	lewd	libidinous
salary	n	paycheck	payment	stipend	wage
salient	adj	notable	noticeable	prominent	remarkable
saline	adj	brackish	briny	salted	salty
sallow	adj	ashen	pale	pasty	sickly
sally	n	attack	charge	raid	sortie
salubrious	adj	beneficial	favorable	healthful	wholesome
salutary	adj	beneficial	good	healthful	wholesome
salutation	n	greeting	hello	salute	welcome
salvation	n	deliverance	redemption	rescue	saving
salve	n	balm	cream	lotion	ointment
salvific	adj	deliverance	delivery	rescue	saving

salvo	n	barrage	bombardment	fusillade	volley
sanctification	n	blessing	consecration	dedication	purification
sanctify	v	bless	consecrate	hallow	purify
sanctimonious	adj	feigned virtue	hypocritical	insincere	smug
sanction	v	approve	authorize	endorse	support
sanctioning	v	authorization	permission	license	endorse
sanctuary	n	haven	refuge	retreat	shelter
sanguinary	adj	cruel	bloodthirsty	bloody	murderous
sanguine	adj	cheerful	confident	hopeful	optimistic
sanity	n	balance	rationality	reason	soundness
sap	v	debilitate	enervate	enfeeble	weaken
sapid	adj	delectable	delicious	palatable	tasty
sapient	adj	discerning	prudent	sage	wise
sarcasm	n	irony	mockery	satire	ridicule
sarcophagus	n	bier	casket	stone coffin	tomb
sardonic	adj	biting	caustic	cynical	sarcastic
sartorial	adj	clothing	garment	tailored	style
sass	n	cheek	impudence	insolence	mouth
satanic	adj	fiendish	hellish	evil	wicked
satchel	n	pack	pouch	purse	sack
sate	v	fill	satiate	satisfy	stuff
satiate	v	gratify	satisfy	gorge	quench
satiety	n	glut	repletion	satiation	surfeit
satire	n	caricature	lampoon	pasquinade	sarcasm
satiric	adj	caustic	sarcastic	sardonic	scoffing
satirical	adj	biting	cutting	cynical	mocking
satirize	v	caricature	lampoon	mock	parody
satisfy	v	fulfill	meet	please	serve
satrap	n	emperor	governor	ruler	sovereign
saturate	v	drench	immerse	permeate	soak
saturnalia	n	bacchanal	merrymaking	orgy	revelry
saturnine	adj	gloomy	melancholy	somber	sullen
satyr	n	Casanova	lecher	lothario	philanderer
satyriasis	n	erotomania	nymphomania	licentiousness	wantonness
saucy	adj	brash	brazen	fresh	impertinent

saunter	v	ramble	stroll	hike	tromp
savant	n	authority	expert	intellectual	scholar
savor	v	appreciate	enjoy	like	taste
savory	v	appetizing	delicious	spicy	tasty
savvy	n	experience	expertise	know-how	skills
scabbard	n	case	cover	protectant	sheath
scabrous	adj	coarse	harsh	rough	rugged
scalar	n	amount	magnitude	measure	quantity
scale	v	ascend	climb	mount	rise
scan	v	examine	inspect	scrutinize	survey
scandal	n	disgrace	dishonor	opprobrium	reproach
scandent	adj	ascending	buoyant	climbing	rising
scanty	adj	inadequate	meager	scarce	sparse
scapegoat	n	fall guy	patsy	victim	whipping boy
scapegrace	n	knave	rapscallion	rogue	scamp
scarify	v	cut	incise	lacerate	scratch
scarify	v	alarm	frighten	scare	worry
scarp	n	bluff	cliff	crag	ridge
scathe	v	attack	castigate	excoriate	slam
scathing	adj	cutting	caustic	mordant	scornful
scatter-brained	adj	flighty	frivolous	giddy	silly
scavenger	n	collector	garbage man	junkman	rummager
scene	n	location	place	spot	stage
scepter	n	mace	rod	staff	wand
scheme	n	contrive	intrigue	machinate	plot
schism	n	division	rift	separation	split
schismatic	adj	apostate	dissident	sectarian	unorthodox
scholarship	n	education	erudition	knowledge	learning
scholastic	adj	academic	educational	intellectual	scholarly
scholiast	n	annotator	commentator	critic	referee
scimitar	n	broadsword	knife	saber	sword
scintilla	n	particle	shred	speck	trace
scintillate	v	gleam	glitter	shine	sparkle
scintillating	adj	brilliant	gleaming	glittering	sparkling
scion	n	descendant	heir	offspring	successor

sclerotic	adj	crusty	hard	inflexible	rigid
scoff	v	jeer	mock	ridicule	sneer
scolding	n	rebuke	reprimand	dress-ing-down	tongue-lash-ing
scone	n	biscuit	muffin	pastry	roll
scope	n	area	extent	range	reach
score	v	cut	gash	notch	scratch
score	n	incision	mark	account	total
scorn	n	contempt	disdain	mockery	ridicule
scoundrel	n	rascal	rogue	cheat	swindler
scour	v	clean	comb	rake	search
scourge	n	affliction	curse	pandemic	plague
scout	v	explore	look	spot	watch
screed	n	discourse	harangue	lecture	sermon
screwdriver	n	auger	blade	lathe	tool
scrivener	n	author	penman	scribe	writer
scruple	n	doubt	hesitation	misgiving	uncertainty
scrupulous	adj	careful	conscientious	principled	strict
scrutinize	v	examine	inspect	investigate	study
scurf	n	dandruff	mange	scabies	scale
scurrility	n	billingsgate	lewdness	obloquy	obscenity
scurrilous	adj	abusive	coarse	insulting	vulgar
scurry	v	barrel	bustle	rip	run
scurvy	adj	cheap	contemptible	despicable	dirty
sear	v	burn	char	scorch	singe
search	n	hunt	investigation	pursuit	quest
sebaceous	adj	fat	greasy	oily	oleaginous
secede	v	leave	part	separate	withdraw
seclude	v	confine	isolate	segregate	separate
secluded	adj	isolated	remote	lonely	solitary
seclusion	n	isolation	privacy	segregation	solitude
sect	n	denomination	faction	faith	group
sectarian	n	denomina-tional	fanatic	narrow-mind-ed	nonconform-ist
secular	n	nonreligious	profane	temporal	worldly
secularized	v	deconsecrat-ed	dissuaded	transferred	vulgarized

secure	v	achieve	ensure	fasten	obtain
sedate	v	quell	relax	soothe	tranquilize
sedation	n	calm	drowsiness	restfulness	torpor
sedentary	adj	fixed	immobile	inactive	stationary
sedge	n	bracken	grass	reed	rush
sediment	n	deposit	dregs	grounds	precipitate
sedimentary	adj	dense	deposited	heavy	impure
sedition	n	insurrection	rebellion	revolt	revolution
seduce	v	allure	beguile	entice	tempt
seduction	n	allurement	charm	enticement	temptation
sedulous	adj	assiduous	busy	diligent	industrious
seedy	adj	dilapidated	scruffy	shabby	sleazy
seemliness	n	appropriate-ness	fitness	propriety	suitability
seemly	adj	becoming	decent	fitting	proper
seethe	v	boil	fume	simmer	stew
seething	adj	boiling	bustling	fuming	furious
segregate	v	detach	dissociate	isolate	separate
segue	n	continuation	shift	passage	transition
seizure	n	attack	confiscation	fit	stroke
select	adj	best	choice	excellent	superior
self-abnega-tion	n	abstinence	continence	sobriety	temperance
self-aggran-dizement	n	arrogance	boastfulness	conceit	egotism
self-effacing	adj	bashful	diffident	modest	shy
semantic	adj	word meaning	phonetics	derivation	language
semblance	n	appearance	form	likeness	resemblance
semicolon	n	colon	pause	period	punctuation mark
seminal	adj	fundamental	important	original	primary
sempiternal	adj	endless	eternal	everlasting	perpetual
senescence	n	decrepitude	dotage	feebleness	senility
senescent	adj	aging	decrepit	elder	old
senile	adj	aged	old	decrepit	infirm
senility	adj	caducity	confusion	dotage	forgetfulness
seniority	n	precedence	priority	rank	superiority

sensational	adj	excellent	fantastic	outstanding	terrific
sense	n	feeling	reason	sensation	understanding
senseless	adj	absurd	foolish	idiotic	stupid
sensible	adj	rational	reasonable	sane	wise
sensory	adj	receptive	sensitive	sensorial	sensuous
sensual	adj	carnal	bodily	physical	sensory
sensualist	n	debauchee	hedonist	sybarite	voluptuary
sensuous	adj	luxurious	opulent	sumptuous	voluptuous
sentence	n	decree	judgment	ruling	verdict
sententious	adj	didactic	homiletic	moralizing	sermonic
sentient	adj	awake	aware	cognizant	conscious
sentiment	n	attitude	feeling	opinion	view
sentimental	adj	emotional	mushy	romantic	tender
sentinel	n	guard	lookout	sentry	watchman
sentry	n	guard	lookout	sentinel	watch
separate	adj	distinct	divided	individual	isolated
separation	n	disunion	division	partition	segregation
sepulcher	n	burial	grave	tomb	vault
sepulture	n	burial	entombment	funeral	grave
sequacious	adj	dependent	servile	subservient	unoriginal
sequel	n	conclusion	continuation	epilogue	follow-on
sequential	adj	consecutive	sequent	succeeding	successive
sequester	v	isolate	seclude	segregate	separate
sequestrate	v	confiscate	isolate	seize	withdraw
seraglio	n	bordello	brothel	harem	whorehouse
seraph	n	guardian	messenger	spirit	sprite
seraphic	adj	angelic	cherubic	divine	saintly
serendipitous	adj	fortunate	lucky	providential	unplanned
serendipity	n	accident	fluke	fortunate	good luck
serene	adj	calm	composed	cool	peaceful
serenity	n	calmness	composure	peacefulness	quietness
seriatim	adv	chronologically	consecutively	sequentially	successively
serious	adj	grave	heavy	severe	significant
serpentine	adj	crooked	curved	snaky	winding
serrate	adj	denticulated	jagged	notched	toothed

serried	adj	close	compact	crowded	packed
serum	n	antibiotic	antiseptic	cure	vaccine
serviceable	adj	effective	functional	helpful	useful
servile	adj	humble	slavish	submissive	subservient
servitude	n	bondage	enslavement	servility	thralldom
sessile	adj	attached	jammed	rigid	stuck
session	n	assembly	gathering	meeting	rally
settee	n	couch	davenport	love seat	sofa
settle	v	fix	reconcile	resolve	solve
sever	v	break	cut	separate	split
severance	n	disunion	division	partition	separation
shallot	n	bulb	chive	onion	scallion
sham	n	deception	fake	fraud	travesty
shambles	n	chaos	disorder	mess	muddle
Shanghai	v	abduct	hijack	lift	seize
shard	n	fragment	piece	scrap	sliver
share	n	part	portion	ration	quota
sheen	n	gloss	luster	polish	shine
sheepish	adj	diffident	modest	retiring	shy
sheik	adj	chief	head	leader	ruler
shibboleth	n	authentica-tion	catchword	custom	password
shipyard	n	boatyard	dockyard	dry dock	wharf
shirk	v	avoid	circumvent	escape	evade
shoddy	adj	cheap	inferior	poor	shabby
shoring	n	brace	shore	stay	support
shortcoming	n	failing	fault	inadequacy	weakness
shortsighted	adj	careless	myopic	nearsighted	thoughtless
shrapnel	n	chip	shard	sliver	splinter
shrew	n	bitch	hag	nag	vixen
shrewd	adj	clever	crafty	cunning	sharp
shriek	v	howl	scream	screech	yell
shrill	v	high-pitched	penetrating	piercing	strident
shroud	n	blanket	cloak	covering	veil
shrouded	adj	concealed	hidden	obscure	secret
shun	v	avoid	dodge	eschew	reject

shunt	n	alternative	branch	bypass	diversion
shyster	n	cheat	pettifogger	swindler	trickster
sibilant	n	fricative	hiss	spirant	whistle
sibyl	n	augur	prophet	seer	soothsayer
sickle	n	crescent	knife	machete	scythe
sidereal	adj	astral	diffuse	starry	stellar
sidle	v	creep	edge	slither	snake
siege	n	barrier	barricade	blockade	cordon
sieve	v	filter	screen	sift	strain
signatory	n	endorser	signature	signer	viewer
signet	n	emblem	hallmark	seal	token
significance	n	importance	matter	relevance	value
significant	adj	considerable	important	major	substantial
signification	n	denotation	import	meaning	sense
silhouette	n	contour	figure	outline	profile
simian	n	ape	chimpanzee	monkey	primate
simile	n	analogy	comparison	like	metaphor
similitude	n	affinity	likeness	representation	similarity
simper	n	grin	smile	smirk	sneer
simplistic	adj	facile	naive	superficial	unsophisticated
simulacrum	n	image	likeness	representation	trace
simulate	v	fake	imitate	model	replicate
simulation	n	duplication	imitation	replication	reproduction
simultaneous	adj	coincident	concurrent	contemporary	synchronous
sincerely	adv	genuinely	honestly	naturally	truly
sinecure	n	easy ride	good income	little work	cushy job
sinew	n	brawn	muscularity	strength	vigor
sinewy	adj	lean	muscular	strong	wiry
singe	v	burn	char	scorch	sear
single-minded	adj	determined	focused	resolute	resolved
singly	adv	alone	independently	individually	separately
singular	adj	extraordinary	peculiar	unique	unusual
sinister	adj	foreboding	menacing	ominous	threatening

sinuate	adj	serpentine	tortuous	unstable	wavy
sinuous	adj	crooked	lithe	tortuous	twisting
sinuous	adj	complex	complicated	intricate	winding
siphon	v	channel	drain	draw	tap
sire	v	beget	create	father	procreate
siren	n	enchantress	femme fatale	seductress	temptress
site	n	location	place	position	spot
situation	n	job	place	position	status
sizzling	adj	boiling	burning	hot	torrid
skeptical	adj	disbelieving	distrustful	doubting	suspicious
skepticism	n	doubt	reservation	suspicion	uncertainty
skim	v	browse	glide	fly	scan
skinflint	n	cheapskate	miser	niggard	tightwad
skirmish	n	battle	dispute	encounter	fight
skittish	adj	edgy	nervous	uptight	wary
skulk	v	creep	lurk	sneak	steal
skullduggery	n	chicanery	dishonesty	swindling	trickery
skyrocketing	adj	ascending	mounting	rising	soaring
slag	n	dross	refuse	sludge	waste
slake	v	assuage	quench	satiate	satisfy
slander	v	defame	malign	slur	smear
slate	v	list	program	record	schedule
slaver	v	dribble	drivel	drool	slobber
slavish	adj	obsequious	servile	submissive	subservient
slay	v	assassinate	kill	murder	slaughter
sleight	n	artifice	deception	deftness	dexterity
slew	n	abundance	heap	load	quantity
slip	n	blunder	error	mistake	oversight
slippage	n	glide	lapse	skid	slide
slither	v	creep	glide	slide	slip
sliver	n	bit	chip	fragment	scrap
slogan	n	catchword	motto	saying	watchword
sloth	n	idleness	inactivity	laziness	sluggishness
slothful	adj	idle	inactive	lazy	sluggish
slough	v	cast	discard	molt	shed
slovenliness	n	messiness	neglect	sloppiness	untidiness

slovenly	adj	dirty	messy	sloppy	unkempt
slue	v	pivot	rotate	swerve	veer
sluggard	n	idler	lazybones	loafer	slouch
sluggish	adj	inactive	lazy	slow	plodding
sluice	n	channel	conduit	drain	gutter
slur	v	charged	confused	placed	pointed
smattering	n	bit	dash	modicum	smidgen
smelt	v	found	melt	refine	reduce
smirk	v	simper	sneer	snicker	leer
smite	v	afflict	beat	hit	strike
smock	n	apron	housecoat	pinafore	robe
smug	adj	conceited	proud	self-satisfied	vain
snare	v	capture	catch	entrap	trap
snide	adj	malicious	mean	spiteful	unkind
snippet	n	bit	extract	morsel	scrap
snivel	v	blubber	sniff	whimper	whine
snub	v	disregard	ignore	neglect	slight
snuff	v	destroy	eliminate	extinguish	kill
soaring	adj	ascending	rising	lofty	towering
sobriety	n	abstinence	composed	gravity	moderation
sobriquet	n	alias	handle	moniker	nickname
socialite	n	aristocrat	blueblood	social climber	trendsetter
sockdolager	n	finisher	exceptional	outstanding	settler
sodality	n	association	fellowship	league	society
sodden	adj	saturated	soaked	soggy	wet
sodomy	n	bestiality	buggery	perversion	reaming
software	n	application	data processing	informatics	program
soigne	adj	elegant	fashionable	sleek	sophisticated
sojourn	v	abide	crash	dwell	lodge
sojourn	n	stay	stopover	visit	vacation
solace	n	comfort	consolation	relief	support
solder	v	fuse	join	unite	weld
solecism	n	blunder	faux pas	gaffe	indiscretion
solemn	adj	dignified	grave	serious	somber
solemnity	n	ceremony	earnestness	gravity	seriousness

solicit	v	beg	implore	petition	request
solicitous	adj	attentive	careful	concerned	considerate
solicitude	n	anxiety	care	concern	worry
solidarity	n	accord	harmony	oneness	unity
solidify	v	congeal	harden	set	thicken
soliloquy	n	lecture	monologue	talk to oneself	tirade
solitary	adj	alone	lonely	single	private
solitude	n	isolation	loneliness	privacy	seclusion
soluble	adj	answerable	explainable	resolvable	solvable
solve	v	answer	crack	resolve	unravel
solvent	adj	creditworthy	flush	in the black	reliable
somber	adj	anxious	attentive	concerned	thoughtful
sometimes	adv	intermittently	occasionally	periodically	sporadically
sommelier	n	barman	bartender	waiter	wine steward
somnolent	adj	dozy	drowsy	sleepy	sluggish
sonic	adj	acoustic	audible	auditory	sound
sonorous	adj	full	majestic	resonant	rich sounding
soothsayer	n	fortune-teller	oracle	prophet	seer
sop	n	boodle	bribe	concession	offering
sophism	n	deception	delusion	error	misconception
sophisticated	adj	complex	complicated	cultured	refined
sophistry	n	deception	delusion	fallacy	misleading
sophomoric	adj	childish	foolish	immature	young
soporific	adj	drowsy	narcotic	opiate	sleepy
sordid	adj	dirty	foul	dishonorable	sleazy
soritical	adj	analytical	conditional	deductive	inductive
sorority	n	fellowship	fraternity	brotherhood	sisterhood
sortie	n	attack	excursion	sally	outing
soubrette	n	actress	coquette	flirt	ingénue
soupcon	n	hint	speck	touch	trace
source	v	find	obtain	originate	reference
souse	n	alcoholic	boozer	drunkard	lush
sovereign	n	autocrat	monarch	potentate	ruler
spacecraft	n	capsule	rocket	satellite	spaceship
spar	v	box	clash	contend	fight

sparse	adj	poor	scanty	scarce	thin
Spartan	adj	disciplined	harsh	severe	stern
spasmodic	adj	changeable	erratic	intermittent	irregular
spate	n	flood	flow	stream	surge
spatial	adj	cosmic	dimensional	space	three-dimensional
spatula	n	blade	scoop	trowel	utensil
spawn	v	breed	generate	perform	produce
specie	n	change	coinage	form	money
species	n	class	kind	race	type
specificity	n	accuracy	explicitness	particularity	peculiarity
specify	v	define	determine	indicate	name
specimen	n	model	pattern	sample	representative
specious	adj	deceptive	fallacious	false	misleading
spectacle	n	circus	extravaganza	pageant	spectacular
spectral	adj	eerie	ghostly	supernatural	unearthly
spectrum	n	diapason	gamut	range	scale
speculate	v	hypothesize	ponder	suppose	theorize
speculation	n	guess	hypothesis	supposition	venture
speculative	adj	conjectural	hypothetical	suppositional	theoretical
speculator	n	gambler	gamester	investor	operator
spendthrift	n	extravagancy	spender	squanderer	waster
spew	v	discharge	disgorge	emit	eject
spindle	n	axle	shaft	pivot	spool
spindly	adj	gangly	lanky	spindling	thin
spire	n	apex	steeple	summit	tower
spirited	adj	animated	energetic	lively	vivacious
spiritual	adj	divine	holy	mental	religious
spirituous	adj	alcoholic	inebriant	intoxicative	vinous
spite	n	malice	hatefulness	malevolence	maliciousness
splay	v	divide	separate	spread	widen
spleen	n	anger	hatred	resentment	wrath
splenetic	adj	grumpy	irritable	peevish	touchy
splice	v	connect	join	marry	unite
splurge	v	indulge	spend	squander	waste
sponsor	v	finance	fund	patronize	support

sponsor	n	backer	guarantor	patron	surety
spontaneous	adj	extempora-neous	impulsive	involuntary	natural
spoor	v	follow	pursue	stalk	track
sporadic	adj	constant	infrequent	irregular	occasional
sportive	adj	frolicsome	merry	playful	sprightly
spouse	n	consort	mate	partner	significant other
spry	adj	agile	lightsome	lively	nimble
spume	n	foam	froth	lather	suds
spurious	adj	artificial	bogus	counterfeit	false
spurn	v	rebuff	refuse	reject	scorn
squabble	n	dispute	fight	quarrel	spat
squalid	adj	dilapidated	dirty	filthy	seedy
squall	n	gale	flurry	storm	tempest
squalor	n	dirtiness	filthiness	foulness	sordidness
squander	v	blow	spend	throw away	waste
squandering	adj	extravagant	lavish	unthrifty	wasteful
squash	v	beat	crush	press	squeeze
squeak	v	creak	peep	screech	squeal
squeamish	adj	nauseous	queasy	sick	woozy
squelch	v	check	crush	quell	stifle
stability	n	constancy	firmness	soundness	strength
stabilize	v	fix	secure	settle	steady
stable	adj	balanced	firm	secure	steady
staccato	adj	abrupt	disjointed	disconnected	separate
stage	v	perform	play	present	show
stagnant	adj	motionless	stationary	stale	foul
stagnation	n	inactivity	motionless	doldrums	slump
staid	adj	sedate	serious	sober	solemn
stalk	v	hunt	follow	pursue	track
stalwart	adj	robust	strong	stout	sturdy
stamina	n	endurance	energy	strength	vigor
stanch	v	halt	restrict	stem	stop
stanchion	n	column	pier	pillar	post
stanza	n	division	section	text	verse
stark	adj	bare	bleak	desolate	severe

startle	v	frighten	scare	shock	surprise
stasis	n	balance	counterpoise	equilibrium	stability
stately	adj	grand	imposing	majestic	noble
statement	n	announce-ment	declaration	evidence	report
static	adj	inactive	immobile	stationary	unchanging
stationary	adj	immobile	stable	standing	static
stature	n	importance	quality	rank	standing
status	n	condition	position	rank	standing
staunch	v	faithful	loyal	reliable	steadfast
steadfast	adj	firm	persistent	stable	steady
stealthy	adj	secrecy	sly	sneaky	underhand
stentorian	adj	booming	loud	roaring	sonorous
stereotype	v	catalogue	categorize	define	stamp
sterile	adj	barren	fruitless	impotent	infertile
sterile	adj	aseptic	germ-free	hygienic	sanitary
stigma	n	blot	brand	spot	stain
stigmatize	v	brand	defame	denounce	pillory
stimulate	v	animate	arouse	excite	stir
stimulus	n	incentive	incitement	inducement	provocation
stint	n	period	shift	spell	time
stipulate	v	establish	provide	require	specify
stir	v	excite	move	rouse	stimulate
stodgy	adj	dull	stuffy	turgid	unimaginative
stoic	adj	apathetic	unaffected	unemotional	unresponsive
stoical	adj	detached	indifferent	long-suffering	reserved
stolid	adj	apathetic	insensitive	unemotional	unresponsive
stoma	n	hole	opening	orifice	pore
straightfor-wardness	n	candor	frankness	honesty	openness
stratagem	n	ploy	ruse	scheme	trick
stratum	n	layer	level	plane	rank
strenuous	adj	difficult	hard	laborious	tough
striated	adj	fluted	ribbed	streaked	striped
strict	adj	exact	rigid	rigorous	severe
strictly	adv	exactly	rigidly	rigorously	precisely
stricture	n	censure	criticism	bind	draw tight

strident	adj	discordant	harsh	loud	shrill
strife	n	conflict	discord	dissension	warfare
striking	adj	attractive	impressive	magnificent	remarkable
stringent	adj	harsh	rigorous	severe	strict
strip	v	loot	pillage	plunder	ransack
strive	v	attempt	contend	endeavor	toil
strong	adj	firm	hard	persistent	powerful
strop	v	grind	hone	sharpen	whet
strophe	n	section	stanza	passage	provision
structures	v	constructs	makes	orders	plans
strut	v	prance	sashay	stalk	swagger
studious	adj	bookish	diligent	industrious	scholarly
studying	v	consider	examine	investigate	learn
stultification	n	abuse	damage	decline	harm
stultify	v	muzzle	repress	ridicule	stifle
stultifying	v	impairing	inhibiting	invalidating	offsetting
stunted	adj	diminutive	underdeveloped	undersized	wee
stupefaction	n	amazement	bewilderment	surprise	wonder
stupefy	v	amaze	astonish	dumfound	stun
stupendous	adj	astonishing	astounding	fantastic	prodigious
stupor	n	languor	lassitude	lethargy	torpor
stygian	adj	dark	gloomy	murky	pitchy
stylized	adj	abstract	amplified	beautiful	elegant
stymie	v	hinder	thwart	block	impede
suasion	n	incitement	inducement	persuasion	urge
suave	adj	debonair	refined	smooth	sophisticated
suavity	n	amenity	courtesy	diplomacy	tact
subdue	v	conquer	crush	overcome	suppress
subdued	adj	muted	quiet	restrained	soft
subject	v	dominate	subdue	subjugate	subordinate
subject	adj	dependent	likely	prone	subservient
subjective	adj	emotional	individualize	instinctive	personalized
subjugate	v	dominate	enslave	submissive	suppress
sublet	v	hire	lease	rent	sublease
sublimate	v	clean	elevate	purify	refine

sublimation	n	division	redirection	rerouting	transferal
sublime	adj	excellent	inspiring	magnificent	superb
subliminal	adj	hidden	involuntary	subconscious	unconscious
sublunary	adj	earthly	mundane	terrestrial	worldly
submarine	adj	deep	submerged	undersea	underwater
submissive	adj	compliant	flexible	meek	yielding
submit	v	introduce	present	provide	send
subordinate	adj	inferior	junior	minor	secondary
subordination	n	compliance	conformity	obedience	submission
suborn	v	bribe	buy	corrupt	instigate
subornation	n	application	bribery	cause	force
subpoena	n	process	summons	writ	warrant
subscribe	v	agree	endorse	sign	support
subsequent	adj	ensuing	following	posterior	succeeding
subservient	adj	docile	obedient	servile	submissive
subside	v	decline	diminish	lessen	sink
subsidiary	n	business	company	firm	holding
subsidiary	adj	accessory	ancillary	secondary	subordinate
subsidization	n	aid	allowance	award	funding
subsidize	v	back	finance	fund	support
subsidy	n	appropriation	financial	funding	subvention
subsistence	n	existence	maintenance	support	sustenance
substantial	adj	considerable	large	significant	strong
substantiate	v	authenticate	confirm	validate	verify
substantiated	adj	justified	proven	reasonable	supported
substantive	adj	essential	practical	significant	substantial
substitute	v	change	relieve	replace	switch
substrate	n	base	foundation	substratum	support
subsume	v	contain	embrace	include	involve
subterfuge	n	artifice	ploy	trickery	wile
subterranean	adj	below	beneath	buried	underground
subtle	adj	crafty	sly	fine	slight
subtlety	n	delicacy	nicety	nuance	refinement
subversion	n	mutiny	rebellion	sedition	treason
subversive	n	insurgent	radical	revolutionary	traitor
subvert	v	overthrow	pervert	sabotage	undermine

subway	n	metro	train	tube	underground
succedaneum	n	makeshift	replacement	substitute	surrogate
succeed	v	achieve	manage	prevail	win
success	n	accomplishment	achievement	triumph	victory
successive	adj	consecutive	sequent	sequential	successional
succinct	adj	brief	clear	compact	concise
succor	v	aid	comfort	help	relief
succubus	n	devil	fiend	incubus	nightmare
succulent	adj	delicious	juicy	luscious	tasty
succumb	v	die	surrender	submit	yield
suffice	v	adequate	do	satisfy	serve
sufficient	adj	acceptable	adequate	enough	satisfactory
suffrage	n	ballot	franchise	voice	vote
suffuse	v	fill	pervade	permeate	saturate
suffused	adj	filled	flush	pervasive	saturated
suggestible	adj	credulous	gullible	impressionable	susceptible
suggestive	adj	evocative	improper	lewd	risqué
suitable	adj	appropriate	fitting	proper	right
sullen	adj	gloomy	glum	moody	sulky
sully	v	dirty	foul	soil	stain
sultry	adj	hot	humid	stuffy	sweltering
summarily	adv	immediately	promptly	quickly	shortly
summary	adj	brief	compact	concise	curt
summon	v	call	convene	gather	muster
sumptuary	adj	conditional	exclusive	lavish	qualified
sumptuous	adj	grand	lavish	luxurious	rich
sunder	v	divide	part	sever	split
sundry	adj	assorted	diverse	several	various
superannuated	adj	antiquated	decrepit	obsolete	outdated
superannuation	n	allowance	benefit	pension	retirement
superb	adj	excellent	gorgeous	outstanding	splendid
supercilious	adj	arrogant	contemptuous	haughty	scornful
superego	n	conscience	difficulty	duty	scruples

supererogation	n	excess	overflow	overkill	spare
supererogatory	adj	excess	extra	spare	surplus
superficial	adj	frivolous	shallow	surface	trivial
superfluity	n	excess	pointless	unnecessary	waste
superfluous	adj	excessive	overabundant	surplus	unnecessary
superimpose	v	cover	overlap	overlay	superpose
superintend	v	head	handle	oversee	supervise
superlative	adj	excellent	matchless	superb	superior
supernal	adj	celestial	delightful	divine	heavenly
supernumerary	adj	excess	extra	spare	surplus
supersede	v	commute	displace	replace	succeed
superstition	n	fear	folklore	ignorance	irrational
supervene	v	ensue	follow	interrupt	succeed
supervisor	n	boss	chief	manager	superintendent
supplant	v	displace	replace	substitute	succeed
supplement	v	amplify	complement	enlarge	expand
suppleness	n	elasticity	flexibility	limberness	pliability
suppliant	adj	beseeching	entreating	pleading	prayerful
supplicant	n	applicant	beggar	candidate	petitioner
supplicate	v	beg	beseech	petition	plead
supplication	n	appeal	petition	plea	prayer
supply	v	deliver	furnish	give	provide
supply	n	amount	inventory	reservoir	stock
suppose	v	assume	believe	imagine	think
supposition	n	assumption	guess	hypothesis	theory
supposititious	adj	bastard	illegitimate	misbegotten	substitute
suppress	v	repress	restrain	stifle	subdue
suppurate	v	fester	infected	pus	putrefy
suppurating	adj	dirty	foul	infected	rotten
supremacy	n	authority	excellence	mastery	superiority
surcease	n	cessation	discontinuation	stoppage	suspension
surdity	n	deafness	hearing loss	obsolete	uncountable

215

surety	n	bond	deposit	guarantee	security
surfeit	v	cram	fill	gorge	stuff
surfeited	adj	full	glutted	gorged	satiated
surge	n	growth	rise	rush	upsurge
surgent	adj	critical	essential	pressing	serious
surly	adj	brusque	gruff	rude	sullen
surmise	v	assume	guess	presume	suppose
surmount	v	beat	conquer	master	overcome
surmounting	adj	better	excellent	extraordinary	unusual
surpass	v	beat	exceed	excel	outdo
surpassing	adj	exceeding	excellent	exceptional	superior
surreal	adj	dreamlike	fantastic	unreal	weird
surreptitious	adj	crafty	secretive	sneaky	underhand
surrogate	n	alternate	deputy	replacement	substitute
surveillance	n	observation	oversight	supervision	watch
survive	v	endure	exist	last	live
susceptible	adj	liable	receptive	sensitive	vulnerable
suspend	v	adjourn	prorogate	prorogue	recess
sustain	v	bear	maintain	support	uphold
sustenance	n	food	nourishment	subsistence	support
susurrant	adj	mumbling	murmuring	muttering	whispering
susurration	n	mumble	murmur	rustle	whisper
susurrus	n	murmur	soft	subdued	whisper
suture	v	darn	sew	stay	stitch
svelte	adj	lesson	lithe	slender	willowy
swank	v	boast	brag	swagger	swash
swanky	adj	elegant	glamorous	high-class	upmarket
swarthy	adj	dark	dusky	pitch-black	sable
swatch	n	patch	piece	strip	sample
sweltering	adj	boiling	fiery	hot	sultry
swimmingly	adv	favorably	splendidly	successfully	well
swindle	v	cheat	con	defraud	trick
swivel	v	rotate	spin	swing	turn
sybarite	n	deviant	immoralist	misbehaver	sensualist
sybaritic	adj	hedonistic	indulgent	luxurious	pleasure-seeking

sycophant	n	flatterer	fawner	parasite	yes-man
sycophantic	adj	fawning	obsequious	servile	subservient
syllabus	n	curriculum	outline	program	schedule
sylvan	adj	floral	pastoral	rural	rustic
symbiosis	n	cooperation	interaction	relationship	synergy
symbiotic	adj	associational	cooperative	interdependent	synergetic
symbol	n	emblem	figure	mark	sign
symmetrical	adj	balanced	harmonious	regular	uniform
symmetry	n	balance	harmony	proportion	unity
sympathy	n	compassion	liking	mercy	pity
symposium	n	conference	discussion	meeting	seminar
symptomatic	adj	characteristic	indicative	peculiar	suggestive
synchronize	v	coincide	coordinate	harmonize	match
synchronous	adj	coincidental	concurrent	contemporary	simultaneous
syncope	n	blackout	coma	faint	insensibility
syndicate	n	cabal	cartel	Mafia	ring
syndrome	n	complaint	disease	disorder	symptom
synecdoche	n	allegory	alliteration	allusion	analogy
synergism	n	collaboration	cooperation	coordination	teamwork
synergistic	adj	combined	collaborative	interdependent	reciprocal
synergy	n	collaboration	cooperation	symbiosis	teamwork
synesthetic	adj	aesthesis	sensation	physiology	psychology
synod	n	assembly	convocation	council	conclave
synonymous	adj	alike	equivalent	equal	similar
synopsis	n	digest	recap	outline	summary
synoptic	adj	brief	concise	short	summary
syntactical	adj	grammar	highlighting	structural	verbal
syntax	n	conjugation	grammar	language	sentence structure
synthesis	n	combination	fusion	integration	union
synthesize	v	arrange	combine	incorporate	make
system	n	arrangement	device	method	scheme
systematic	adj	methodical	orderly	organized	regular
systemic	adj	comprehensive	consistent	methodical	regular

tabernacle	n	church	sanctuary	temple	tent
table	v	defer	hold off	postpone	shelve
tableau	n	display	montage	portrayal	scene
tabloid	n	bowdleriza-tion	rag	scandal sheet	sensationalist
taboo	adj	forbidden	prohibited	proscribed	verboten
tabulate	v	arrange	classify	index	enumerate
tacit	adj	implied	silent	unsaid	unspoken
taciturn	adj	reserved	silent	speechless	withdrawn
taciturnity	n	quietness	reserve	reticence	silence
tactful	adj	considerate	diplomatic	discreet	sensitive
tactic	n	plan	ploy	scheme	strategy
tactile	adj	material	physical	sensory	touchable
tactless	adj	discourteous	rude	uncivil	undiplomatic
tailings	n	colliery spoil	debris	residue	waste rock
taint	v	contaminate	defile	pollute	tarnish
take	n	bounty	catch	haul	yield
talisman	n	amulet	charm	mascot	phylactery
talismanic	adj	magical	necromantic	sorcerous	witching
tally	n	census	count	record	score
talon	n	claw	heel	hook	nail
tamper	v	disturb	fiddle	interfere	meddle
tandem	n	double	pair	series	team
tang	n	bite	kick	taste	zest
tangent	n	aside	digression	divagation	excursion
tangential	adj	digressive	divergent	extraneous	peripheral
tangible	adj	concrete	material	real	touchable
tantalize	v	charm	entice	provoke	tease
tantalizing	adj	alluring	appealing	inviting	tempting
tantamount	adj	alike	equal	equivalent	same
taper	n	candle	light	long	slender
tardiness	n	idleness	lateness	slothfulness	slowness
tarn	n	lagoon	loch	pond	pool
tarnish	v	blemish	dull	stain	sully
tarnished	adj	damaged	darkened	marred	stained
tarry	n	linger	sojourn	stay	visit

taskmaster	n	boss	chief	manager	overseer
tassel	n	border	edge	margin	fringe
tattered	adj	ragged	seedy	shabby	threadbare
taunt	v	jeer	mock	ridicule	tease
taut	adj	rigid	stiff	tense	tight
tautological	adj	circular	redundant	repetitious	verbose
tautology	n	redundancy	repetition	pleonasm	wordiness
tawdry	adj	cheap	flashy	gaudy	showy
technical	adj	engineering	industrial	professional	specialized
technique	n	approach	manner	method	way
technological	adj	engineering	mechanical	scientific	substantive
technology	n	engineering	machinery	method	scheme
tedious	adj	boring	dull	tiresome	uninteresting
tedium	n	boredom	doldrums	ennui	weariness
teem	v	abound	crawl	overflow	swarm
teetotaler	n	abstainer	nondrinker	prohibitionist	straightedge
telecast	n	broadcast	cablecast	television	transmission
telepathy	n	clairvoyance	ESP	foreknowledge	foresight
telltale	adj	denotative	indicative	reflective	significant
temerarious	adj	audacious	brash	foolhardy	reckless
temerity	n	audacity	boldness	gall	recklessness
temper	v	moderate	soften	harden	toughen
temperament	n	character	disposition	nature	tendency
temperance	n	abstinence	moderation	restraint	sobriety
temperate	adj	calm	composed	moderate	sober
tempest	n	squall	storm	tumult	uproar
tempestuous	adj	agitated	furious	stormy	turbulent
tempo	n	beat	cadence	pace	rate
temporal	adj	earthly	mundane	secular	worldly
temporary	adj	brief	fleeting	momentary	short-lived
temporize	v	delay	filibuster	procrastinate	stall
tempt	v	attract	entice	invite	lure
tenable	adj	defensible	reasonable	upheld	valid
tenacious	adj	determined	firm	persistent	tough
tenaciously	adv	persistently	steadfastly	strongly	stubbornly

tenacity	n	determination	perseverance	persistence	stubbornness
tenant	n	inhabitant	occupant	renter	resident
tendentious	adj	biased	opinionated	partial	partisan
tendentiously	adv	exclusively	halfway	partially	unfairly
tendril	n	coil	runner	shoot	thread
tenebrific	adj	desolate	dismal	dreary	gloomy
tenebrous	adj	dark	dim	gloomy	obscure
tenement	n	apartment	flat	overcrowded	run-down
tenet	n	belief	doctrine	opinion	principle
tensile	adj	flexible	pliant	stretchable	yielding
tentative	adj	provisional	temporary	hesitant	undecided
tenuous	adj	flimsy	slender	thin	weak
tenure	n	hitch	stint	term	tour
tepid	adj	apathetic	halfhearted	indifferent	lukewarm
tergiversate	v	defect	equivocate	evade	pussyfoot
tergiversation	n	abandonment	defection	desertion	equivocation
termagant	n	dragon	shrew	virago	vixen
terminate	v	cease	conclude	end	stop
terminology	n	jargon	language	nomenclature	vocabulary
terrain	n	ground	landscape	territory	topography
terrestrial	adj	earthly	secular	temporal	worldly
territory	n	county	field	land	patch
terse	adj	abrupt	blunt	brief	curt
tessellated	adj	checked	mosaic	plaid	variegated
testament	n	covenant	evidence	proof	witness
testimony	n	affirmation	confirmation	evidence	proof
testy	adj	cranky	grouchy	irritable	petulant
tether	v	bind	lash	strap	tie
thaumaturge	n	enchanter	magician	sorcerer	wizard
theatrics	n	drama	showmanship	stage	theatre
theism	n	belief	faith	piety	religion
theme	n	idea	matter	subject	topic
theologian	n	ecclesiastic	priest	scholastic	studier of religion
theology	n	divinity	doctrine	dogma	religion
theoretical	adj	academic	conceptual	hypothetical	speculative

theory	n	hypothesis	proposition	supposition	thesis
therapeutic	adj	corrective	curative	healing	restorative
therapy	n	cure	rehabilitation	remedy	treatment
therefore	adv	accordingly	consequently	hence	thus
thesis	n	assumption	dissertation	proposition	theme
thespian	adj	dramatic	histrionic	staged	theatrical
thespian	n	actor	mummer	player	trouper
thew	n	beef	brawn	force	muscle
thither	adv	now	then	there	where
thorny	adj	difficult	hard	tough	trick
thorough	adj	careful	complete	comprehensive	full
thought	n	concept	idea	notion	opinion
thrall	n	bondage	servant	servitude	slavery
thralldom	n	bondage	enslavement	servility	yoke
threadbare	adj	ragged	seedy	shabby	tattered
threnody	n	dirge	elegy	lament	requiem
thrifty	adj	careful	economical	frugal	sparing
throes	n	agony	anguish	pain	pangs
throng	n	crowd	flock	mob	swarm
throttle	v	choke	garrote	strangle	suffocate
throwback	n	atavism	regression	reversion	setback
thwart	n	check	foil	frustrate	hinder
tiara	n	anadem	crown	coronet	diadem
tidings	n	news	information	intelligence	word
tier	n	class	grade	rank	row
tiff	n	argument	disagreement	dispute	quarrel
timbre	n	pitch	resonance	sound	tone
timid	adj	bashful	cowardly	fearful	shy
timorous	adj	apprehensive	cowardly	fearful	shy
tintinnabulation	n	chime	jingle	peal	ringing
tirade	n	harsh	lecture	sermon	speech
titan	n	colossus	giant	hulk	monster
tithe	n	alms	charity	duty	tenth
titillate	v	electrify	excite	thrill	tickle
titillation	n	excitement	bang	kick	thrill

221

titivate	v	adorn	beautify	decorate	dress up
tittle	n	bit	grain	speck	trace
toady	n	bootlicker	flatterer	flunky	yes-man
tocsin	n	alarm	signal	siren	warning
tolerance	n	allowance	indulgence	kindness	patience
tolerate	v	allow	bear	endure	suffer
tome	n	book	publication	volume	work
toothsome	adj	delectable	delicious	palatable	tasty
torpid	adj	dull	inactive	lazy	sluggish
torpor	n	dull	laziness	sloth	sluggishness
torque	n	rotating force	spin	turning	twisting
torrid	adj	burning	fiery	hot	scorching
tortuous	adj	serpentine	sinuous	twisting	winding
torturous	adj	agonizing	excruciating	harrowing	painful
totem	n	emblem	ritual object	symbol	talisman
tout	v	praise	brag	promote	advertise
toxic	adj	deadly	harmful	poisonous	venomous
track	v	follow	shadow	trail	dog
tract	n	area	region	essay	pamphlet
tractable	adj	compliant	flexible	submissive	yielding
traditional	adj	common	conventional	customary	usual
traduce	v	defame	disgrace	humiliate	slander
tragedy	n	affliction	calamity	disaster	misery
training	n	teaching	instructing	educating	disciplining
traitor	n	betrayer	deserter	renegade	turncoat
tranquil	adj	calm	peaceful	quiet	serene
tranquility	n	calm	peacefulness	quiet	serenity
tranquilize	v	calm	anesthetize	settle	soothe
transaction	n	contract	compact	bargain	operation
transcend	v	exceed	excel	outdo	surpass
transcen-dence	n	excellence	perfection	superiority	supremacy
transcendent	adj	abstract	idea	divine	supreme
transcenden-tal	adj	abstract	idea	sublime	surpassing
transcending	v	passing	topping	exceeding	bettering
transcribe	v	copy	duplicate	record	reproduce

transferred	v	moved	shifted	maneuvered	transmitted
transfigure	v	transform	exalt	transfer	convert
transfix	v	impale	hold	grip	arrest
transfuse	v	insert	infuse	permeate	saturate
transgress	v	disobey	offend	trespass	violate
transgression	n	crime	offense	sin	trespass
transient	adj	fleeting	momentary	temporary	itinerant
transitory	adj	brief	fleeting	momentary	temporary
translation	n	change	conversion	interpretation	transformation
transliterate	v	interpret	render	transcribe	translate
translucent	adj	clear	crystalline	see-through	transparent
transmute	v	change	transform	translate	convert
transom	n	crossbeam	lintel	skylight	window
transparent	adj	apparent	evident	obvious	plain
transparent	adj	clear	crystal	see-through	translucent
transpire	v	happen	develop	emerge	occur
transplant	v	graft	relocate	transfer	uproot
transport	v	carry	haul	transmit	transfer
transpose	v	convert	interchange	invert	translate
transubstantiate	v	convert	metamorphose	transform	transmute
transverse	adj	crosswise	horizontal	oblique	slanted
trappings	n	equipment	gear	outfit	paraphernalia
trauma	n	injury	shock	stress	upset
traumatic	adj	alarming	distressing	harrowing	painful
travail	n	drudgery	effort	toil	work
traverse	v	cross	negotiate	travel	walk
travesty	n	caricature	farce	parody	mockery
treacherous	adj	deceitful	dishonest	perfidious	traitorous
treacle	n	molasses	sugar	sweetness	syrup
treason	n	betrayal	perfidy	traitor	treachery
treat	v	consider	handle	regale	regard
treat	n	dainty	delicacy	morsel	tidbit
treatise	n	book	discourse	disquisition	dissertation
trek	n	expedition	journey	travels	trip
trellis	n	grid	lattice	mesh	netting

tremble	v	quiver	shake	shiver	shudder
tremendous	adj	enormous	gigantic	great	huge
tremor	n	quake	quiver	shake	temblor
tremulous	adj	nervous	quavering	shaky	trembling
trenchant	adj	acute	incisive	keen	penetrating
trencherman	n	glutton	gourmand	gourmet	sponge
trend	n	incline	lean	slant	tend
trepidation	n	apprehension	dread	fear	fright
triage	n	group	relief	safety	sorting
tribulation	n	trial	visitation	ordeal	crucible
tribunal	n	bar	bench	court	forum
tributary	n	affluent	branch	feeder	stream
tried	adj	experienced	proven	reliable	tested
trifling	adj	insignificant	paltry	trivial	unimportant
tripartite	adj	three-way	triangular	trilateral	triple
tripe	n	drivel	nonsense	rubbish	trash
triplet	n	three	triad	trinity	trio
triptych	n	threesome	triad	trilogy	trio
trite	adj	clichéd	commonplace	stale	stereotyped
triturate	v	beat	crush	grind	pulverize
triumvirate	n	trio	threesome	triple	trinity
trivial	adj	little	insignificant	trifling	unimportant
triviality	n	frivolity	faith	trivia	frippery
troglodyte	n	cave dweller	crude	primitive	seclusion
troglodytic	adj	alone	desolate	lone	solitary
trolley	n	carriage	cart	tram	truck
trollop	n	floozy	harlot	hussy	tramp
trope	n	bromide	cliché	platitude	shibboleth
troth	n	betrothal	engagement	espousal	pledge
troubadour	n	bard	minstrel	musician	poet
troublous	adj	disquieting	distressing	troublesome	upsetting
trounce	v	thrash	beat	defeat	overcome
troupe	n	company	gang	group	team
truant	n	absent	fugitive	no-show	runaway
truckle	v	yield	fawn	kowtow	bootlick
truculence	n	brutality	ferocity	cruelty	viciousness

truculent	adj	belligerent	ferocious	fierce	savage
truculently	adv	aggressively	belligerently	sharply	strong
trudge	v	march	slog	plod	toil
truism	n	self-evident	truth	stereotype	commonplace
truly	adv	actually	genuinely	really	sincerely
truncate	v	abbreviate	abridge	condense	shorten
truncheon	n	baton	bludgeon	club	nightstick
truss	v	band	bind	tether	tie
tryst	n	meeting	rendezvous	appointment	engagement
tsunami	n	breaker	ground swell	surge	tidal wave
tumbler	n	beaker	glass	goblet	mug
tumbril	n	barrow	buggy	cart	dray
tumefy	v	grow	increase	rise	swell
tumid	adj	swollen	tumescent	turgid	varicose
tumult	n	commotion	disturbance	fuss	turmoil
tumultuous	adj	disorderly	stormy	tempestuous	turbulent
tundra	n	moor	plain	prairie	steppe
turbid	adj	clouded	muddy	murky	obscure
turbulence	n	agitation	commotion	disorder	disturbance
turbulent	adj	confused	stormy	tempestuous	tumultuous
tureen	n	bowl	casserole	dish	platter
turgid	adj	bloated	inflated	puffy	swollen
turkey	n	failure	fiasco	flop	washout
turncoat	n	apostate	betrayer	renegade	traitor
turnover	v	deliver	give	supply	provide
turpitude	n	depravity	vice	immorality	corruption
turret	n	belfry	spire	steeple	tower
tussle	n	fight	grapple	scuffle	wrestle
tutelage	n	guardianship	education	instruction	training
twain	n	brace	couplet	pair	twosome
twinge	n	pain	ache	stitch	pang
tycoon	n	baron	industrialist	king	mogul
typical	adj	general	normal	common	usual
tyrannical	adj	dictatorial	absolute	totalitarian	autocratic
tyrannize	v	bully	dominate	intimidate	oppress
tyranny	n	oppression	dictatorship	autocracy	despotism

tyro	n	amateur	apprentice	beginner	novice
ubiquitous	adj	common	omnipresent	prevalent	universal
ukase	n	command	decree	edict	order
ulterior	adj	concealed	covered	covert	hidden
ultimate	adj	extreme	final	last	terminal
ultimately	adj	conclusively	eventually	finally	lastly
ultimatum	n	claim	demand	stipulation	warning
ululate	v	bay	howl	wail	yowl
ululation	n	howl	lament	moan	wail
umbra	n	shadow	adumbration	shade	penumbra
umbrage	n	displeasure	irritation	offense	resentment
unabashed	adj	brazen	blatant	forward	shameless
unabated	adj	constant	incessant	perpetual	relentless
unabridged	adj	complete	entire	unabbreviated	uncut
unaccus-tomed	adj	different	irregular	rare	strange
unaffected	adj	natural	simple	sincere	unemotional
unalloyed	adj	complete	perfect	pure	total
unanimity	n	accord	agreement	consensus	unity
unanimous	adj	agreeable	compatible	harmonious	united
unappealing	adj	disagreeable	unappetizing	unattractive	unpleasant
unassailable	adj	incontestable	indomitable	invincible	secure
unassuming	adj	humble	lowly	meek	modest
unavailing	adj	futile	unsuccessful	useless	worthless
unaware	adj	suddenly	unexpectedly	ignorant	unfamiliar
unbecoming	adj	unfitting	inappropriate	unsuitable	improper
unbiased	adj	fair	impartial	just	objective
unblemished	adj	immaculate	perfect	pure	spotless
unbosom	v	disclose	expose	reveal	unveil
unbridled	adj	unrestrained	wild	uninhibited	uncontrolled
unbury	v	disinter	excavate	exhume	unearth
uncanny	adj	eerie	mysterious	strange	weird
uncompro-mising	adj	inflexible	rigid	stubborn	unyielding
unconscio-nable	adj	monstrous	ridiculous	unreasonable	unscrupulous

unconven-tional	adj	bizarre	eccentric	strange	unusual
uncouth	adj	uncultured	crude	raw	rough
unction	n	balm	cream	oil	salve
unction	n	earnestness	fervor	passion	zeal
unctuous	adj	ingratiating	insincere	obsequious	phony
undaunted	adj	brave	bold	courageous	fearless
underground	adj	buried	covered	secret	undercover
undermine	v	impair	sabotage	sap	weaken
underpin	v	bolster	prop	support	sustain
underscore	v	accentuate	emphasize	stress	underline
understate-ment	n	minimization	subtlety	trivialization	underempha-sis
understudy	n	backup	replacement	reserve	stand-in
undertaker	v	embalmer	funeral direc-tor	gravedigger	mortician
underworld	n	criminal world	demimonde	gangland	netherworld
underwrite	v	countersign	finance	guarantee	subsidize
undoubtedly	adv	certainly	clearly	definitely	surely
undue	adj	excessive	extravagant	immoderate	inordinate
undulate	v	fluctuate	roll	surge	wave
unduly	adv	disproportion-ately	excessively	overly	unreasonably
unenlight-ened	adj	ignorant	naive	uneducated	uniformed
unequivocal	adj	certain	clear	definite	direct
unerring	adj	accurate	exact	infallible	precise
unethical	adj	crooked	dishonest	immoral	unprincipled
unexception-able	adj	faultless	flawless	pure	spotless
unfailing	adj	certain	steadfast	sure	reliable
unfair	adj	inequitable	partial	unethical	unjust
unfathom-able	adj	deep	infinite	mysterious	puzzling
unfeigned	adj	genuine	heartfelt	honest	sincere
unflagging	adj	indefatigable	persistent	tireless	untiring
unflappable	adj	calm	composed	laid-back	nerveless
unfledged	adj	callow	immature	inexperienced	unripe

unfortunately	adj	regrettably	sadly	unhappily	unluckily
unfrock	v	depose	dismiss	drop	release
unfurl	v	expand	open	spread	unfold
ungainly	adj	awkward	clumsy	gawky	ungraceful
unguent	n	balm	cream	ointment	salve
unheralded	adj	unannounced	unanticipated	unexpected	unpredicted
uniform	adj	consistent	even	regular	unchanging
uniformity	n	consistency	harmony	regularity	standardiza-tion
unilateral	adj	one-sided	partial	single	unidirectional
unimpeach-able	adj	blameless	exemplary	faultless	irrefutable
uninterested	adj	apathetic	casual	indifferent	unconcerned
unique	adj	exceptional	sole	special	unusual
unison	n	accord	agreement	harmony	unity
universal	adj	comprehen-sive	general	widespread	worldwide
universalism	n	amplitude	breadth	gamut	spectrum
univocal	adj	absolute	definitive	specific	straightfor-ward
unjaundiced	adj	detached	fair	just	objective
unkempt	adj	messy	sloppy	slovenly	untidy
unlettered	adj	ignorant	illiterate	uncultivated	uneducated
unlikely	adj	doubtful	incredible	remote	unbelievable
unmitigated	adj	complete	perfect	sheer	total
unmoved	adj	apathetic	impassive	indifferent	unconcerned
unnerving	adj	alarming	creepy	disturbing	frightening
unobtrusive	adj	humble	modest	quiet	unassuming
unorthodox	adj	peculiar	uncommon	unconven-tional	unusual
unprecedent-ed	adj	new	novel	unique	unparalleled
unremitting	adj	constant	continuous	persistent	unceasing
unremittingly	adv	continuously	endlessly	incessantly	steadily
unrequited	adj	silent	unanswered	unresponsive	unreturned
unrestrained	adj	free	uncontrolled	uninhibited	wild
unsavory	adj	disagreeable	distasteful	offensive	unpleasant
unscathed	adj	unharmed	unhurt	uninjured	whole

unscrupulous	adj	corrupt	deceitful	dishonorable	untrustworthy
unseat	v	depose	dethrone	displace	oust
unseemly	adj	improper	inappropriate	indecent	unbecoming
unselfishness	n	care	consideration	generosity	kindness
unsettling	adj	disturbing	troubling	upsetting	worrisome
unsound	adj	defective	faulty	invalid	weak
unstinting	adj	bountiful	charitable	generous	liberal
unstudied	adj	impromptu	offhand	unaffected	unplanned
unsullied	adj	immaculate	pristine	pure	spotless
unsung	adj	nameless	unacknowl-edged	unknown	unrecognized
untenable	adj	indefensible	illogical	invalid	unfounded
untoward	adj	annoying	inappropriate	unfortunate	unseemly
unusually	adv	abnormally	extremely	surprisingly	uncommonly
unwarranted	adj	baseless	groundless	needless	unjustified
unwieldy	adj	awkward	clumsy	cumbersome	ungainly
unwitting	adj	ignorant	oblivious	unconscious	unintentional
unwonted	adj	odd	rare	uncommon	unusual
upbraid	v	criticize	rebuke	reprimand	reprove
upright	adj	ethical	honest	moral	righteous
upshot	n	consequence	effect	result	outcome
upstart	n	arriviste	nobody	nouveau riche	parvenu
urban	adj	city	metropolitan	municipal	town
urbane	adj	refined	polished	sophisticated	worldly
urbanity	n	civility	cosmopolitan-ism	polish	sophistication
urge	n	craving	desire	longing	yearning
usable	adj	functional	operable	practicable	serviceable
use	v	apply	employ	exercise	utilization
useful	adj	appropriate	beneficial	helpful	valuable
useless	adj	futile	pointless	unnecessary	worthless
usual	adj	common	normal	ordinary	regular
usurer	n	bookie	loan shark	moneylender	shylock
usurious	adj	illegal	exorbitant	extortionate	outrageous
usurp	v	confiscate	grab	seize	take over
usurpation	n	appropriation	assumption	commandeer-ing	seizure

229

usury	n	extortion	loansharking	moneylending	overcharging
utilitarian	adj	functional	practical	serviceable	useful
utility	n	advantage	benefit	service	usefulness
utopia	n	bliss	Eden	heaven	paradise
utopian	adj	fanciful	idealistic	romantic	visionary
utter	adj	absolute	complete	full	total
utterance	n	articulation	statement	voice	word
uttered	adj	oral	spoken	vocal	voiced
vacillate	v	fluctuate	hesitate	stagger	waver
vacillation	n	fluctuation	hesitation	uncertainty	wavering
vacuity	n	emptiness	vacancy	vacuum	void
vacuous	adj	devoid	empty	unintelligent	vacant
vagabond	n	beggar	drifter	tramp	vagrant
vagabondage	adj	doubtful	dubious	unsettled	unstable
vagary	n	fancy	notion	quirk	whim
vagrancy	n	homeless	loitering	ramble	straying
vague	adj	hazy	indefinite	indistinct	unclear
vain	adj	conceited	empty	otiose	proud
vainglorious	adj	conceited	egotistic	proud	self-important
vainglory	n	conceit	egotism	pride	vanity
valedictory	adj	departing	farewell	last	parting
valetudinar-ian	n	convalescent	hypochon-driac	invalid	malingerer
valetudinar-ian	adj	feeble	frail	sickly	weak
valiant	adj	courageous	fearless	bold	brave
valid	adj	authentic	legitimate	sound	true
validate	v	authenticate	certify	confirm	verify
valor	n	boldness	bravery	courage	heroism
value	n	amount	figure	price	worth
vandal	n	criminal	defacer	hooligan	thug
vandalism	n	desolation	destruction	devastation	hooliganism
vane	n	blade	weathercock	weather vane	wind vane
vanguard	n	avant-garde	forefront	lead	point
vanity	n	conceit	egotism	narcissism	pride
vanquish	v	beat	conquer	defeat	overcome
vantage point	n	angle	perspective	position	viewpoint

vapid	adj	bland	dull	flat	uninteresting
vapor	v	blow	boast	brag	flourish
variance	n	altercation	conflict	discrepancy	divergence
variant	adj	different	distinct	divergent	irregular
varicose	adj	enlarged	swollen	tumescent	turgid
variegated	adj	dappled	diverse	spotted	streaked
various	adj	assorted	different	miscellaneous	varied
vary	v	alter	change	differ	modify
vassal	n	follower	servant	subject	subordinate
vast	adj	enormous	gigantic	huge	immense
vaticination	n	presage	prediction	prognostication	prophecy
vaticinator	n	diviner	oracle	prophet	seer
vaunt	v	blow	boast	brag	crow
vaunted	v	acclaimed	celebrated	flaunted	hyped
vector	n	bearing	course	direction	trajectory
veer	v	bend	deviate	swerve	turn
vegetation	n	botany	flora	growth	plants
vehemence	n	fervor	forcefulness	intensity	violence
vehement	adj	fierce	intense	urgent	violent
vehemently	adv	fervently	fiercely	strongly	vigorously
veiled	adj	concealed	covered	hidden	obscure
vellicate	v	jerk	pinch	titillate	twitch
venal	adj	bribable	corruptible	degenerate	mercenary
venality	n	corruption	degradation	disgrace	immorality
vendetta	n	argument	disagreement	dispute	quarrel
veneer	n	facade	facing	finish	surface
venerable	adj	aged	old	respected	revered
venerate	v	adoration	regard	respect	revere
veneration	n	adoration	homage	reverence	worship
vengeance	n	retaliation	retribution	requital	revenge
vengeful	adj	hostile	retaliatory	revengeful	spiteful
venial	adj	excusable	forgivable	pardonable	understandable
venom	n	malice	poison	spite	toxin
vent	v	air	discharge	outlet	release
ventral	adj	abdominal	forward	front	underside

231

venture	n	adventure	enterprise	risk	speculation
venturesome	adj	audacious	bold	brave	daring
venue	n	forum	place	site	spot
veracious	adj	accurate	genuine	honest	right
veracity	n	authenticity	honesty	reality	truthfulness
veranda	n	gallery	lanai	piazza	porch
verbal	adj	oral	spoken	vocal	wordy
verbatim	adv	exactly	literally	precisely	word for word
verbiage	n	circumlocu-tion	gobbledygook	redundancy	wordiness
verbose	adj	talkative	long-winded	windy	wordy
verbosity	n	talkativeness	long-winded-ness	windiness	wordiness
verdant	adj	fresh	grassy	green	lush
verdict	n	decision	judgment	sentence	ruling
verge	n	brink	border	edge	margin
veridical	adj	exact	precise	right	strict
verifiable	adj	certain	confirmable	demonstrable	true
verify	v	authenticate	confirm	prove	validate
verisimilitude	n	authenticity	likelihood	plausibility	realism
veritable	adj	authentic	genuine	real	true
verity	n	conviction	fact	reality	truth
vernacular	n	common	dialect	informal	slang
vernal	adj	fresh	spring	young	youthful
versatile	adj	adaptable	dexterous	flexible	variable
versatility	n	adaptability	adjustability	compliance	flexibility
verse	n	lyric	poem	rhyme	stanza
vertex	n	apex	crest	peak	top
vertiginous	adj	dizzy	giddy	light-headed	woozy
vertigo	n	dizziness	giddiness	lightheaded-ness	wooziness
vesicle	n	blister	bubble	cyst	sac
vespers	n	evensong	orison	prayer	service
vespertine	adj	crepuscular	dim	faint	gloomy
vest	v	authorize	belong	devolve	empower
vested	v	authorized	committed	ordered	provide
vestibule	n	entry	foyer	hall	lobby

vestige	n	hint	remnant	relic	trace
vestigial	adj	latent	nonfunction-ing	residual	rudimentary
veto	v	decline	deny	disallow	reject
vex	v	agitate	annoy	bother	confound
vexatious	adj	annoying	irksome	irritating	troublesome
viable	adj	hard	persistent	sound	strong
viaduct	n	bridge	crossing	overpass	underpass
viand	n	foodstuff	nourishment	sustenance	provision
vibrant	adj	active	energetic	lively	resounding
vicarious	adj	delegated	indirect	secondary	substitute
vicinity	n	area	neighborhood	proximity	region
vicious	adj	evil	ferocious	spiteful	wicked
vicissitude	n	alternation	change	fluctuation	variation
victuals	n	edibles	food	provender	provisions
vie	n	compete	contend	rival	strive
vigil	n	guard	lookout	surveillance	watch
vigilance	n	alertness	attentiveness	qui vive	watchfulness
vigilant	adj	alert	attentive	cautious	watchful
vigilante	n	avenger	castigator	chastiser	punisher
vignette	n	description	design	picture	sketch
vigor	n	energy	force	power	strength
vigorous	adj	active	energetic	lively	strong
vilification	n	defamation	maliciousness	slander	smearing
vilify	v	attack	defame	disparage	slander
villa	n	castle	country house	manor	mansion
villain	n	knave	rascal	rogue	scoundrel
vim	n	energy	vigor	vitality	zip
vincible	adj	exposed	liable	vulnerable	weak
vindicate	v	acquit	excuse	exonerate	justify
vindicated	adj	absolved	acquitted	cleared	exonerated
vindictive	adj	mean	retributive	sinister	spiteful
violate	v	defile	disobey	infringe	transgress
virago	n	harpy	shrew	termagant	vixen
virile	adj	male	manly	masculine	potent
virtually	adj	almost	nearly	practically	substantially

virtue	n	excellence	goodness	merit	quality
virtuosity	n	genius	skill	talent	technique
virtuoso	n	ace	expert	genius	master
virtuous	adj	honest	moral	pure	righteous
virulent	adj	deadly	malignant	poisonous	venomous
visage	n	countenance	expression	face	look
visceral	adj	instinctive	internal	intuitive	unreasoning
viscid	adj	gummy	sticky	syrupy	thick
viscosity	n	consistence	density	fluidity	thickness
viscous	adj	glutinous	sticky	syrupy	thick
visible	adj	apparent	evident	manifest	obvious
vital	adj	critical	essential	important	necessary
vitality	n	animation	energy	life	spirit
vitiate	v	corrupt	contaminate	ruin	spoil
vitreous	adj	glassy	translucent	transparent	pellucid
vitriol	n	cunning	dislike	evil	hatred
vitriolic	adj	acid	caustic	nasty	scathing
vituperate	v	abuse	blame	castigate	insult
vituperation	n	abuse	obloquy	outburst	vitriol
vituperative	adj	abusive	contumelious	invective	scurrilous
vivacious	adj	active	animated	lively	spirited
vivid	adj	brilliant	bright	clear	graphic
vivisection	n	biopsy	dissection	division	operation
vocalist	n	crooner	chorister	singer	songster
vocation	n	aptitude	business	career	occupation
vociferate	v	bawl	cry	roar	shout
vociferous	adj	boisterous	clamorous	loud	noisy
vogue	n	fashion	rage	style	trend
void	adj	barren	clear	empty	vacant
void	v	annul	cancel	quash	vacate
volatile	adj	changeable	fickle	flighty	unstable
volatility	n	fickleness	instability	unpredict-ability	variability
volition	n	choice	decision	determination	will
volubility	n	articulacy	eloquence	fluency	loquacity
voluble	adj	chatty	fluent	long-winded	talkative

volubly	adv	copiously	enthusiastically	garrulously	mildly
voluminous	adj	extensive	great	large	massive
voluntary	adj	free	intentional	spontaneous	willful
voluptuary	n	debauchee	hedonist	sensualist	sybarite
voluptuous	adj	lewd	lustful	sensual	sexy
voluptuously	adv	carnally	fleshly	lushly	sensually
voracious	adj	greedy	hungry	insatiable	piggish
votary	n	adherent	disciple	follower	partisan
voucher	n	chit	coupon	receipt	ticket
vouchsafe	v	allow	give	permit	promise
voyeur	n	peeper	spy	viewer	watcher
vulgar	adj	coarse	crude	indecent	rude
vulgarity	n	coarseness	crudeness	grossness	rudeness
vulgarize	v	degrade	generalize	popularize	simplify
vulnerable	adj	exposed	susceptible	unprotected	weak
waffle	v	dither	equivocate	vacillate	waver
wag	n	comedian	comic	humorist	wit
wager	n	bet	gamble	risk	stake
waggish	adj	droll	humorous	jocular	witty
waif	n	foundling	ragamuffin	stray	urchin
wainscot	n	lining	paneling	partition	sheathing
waive	v	defer	forgo	postpone	relinquish
wallow	v	delight	indulge	flounder	roll
wan	adj	ashen	cadaverous	pale	sallow
wane	v	decline	decrease	dissipate	wither
wangle	v	contrive	engineer	finagle	manipulate
waning	adj	declining	dying	fading	weakened
want	n	deficiency	lack	need	scarcity
wanton	adj	abandoned	immoral	loose	promiscuous
warble	n	melody	song	strain	tune
wariness	n	alertness	caution	prudence	vigilance
warlock	n	magician	sorcerer	witch	wizard
warn	v	advise	alert	caution	inform
warrant	v	authorize	guarantee	justify	sanction
wary	adj	alert	careful	cautious	watchful

waspish	adj	irritable	peevish	petulant	touchy
wastrel	n	idler	prodigal	profligate	spendthrift
watershed	n	defining moment	landmark	milestone	turning point
waver	v	dither	hesitate	tremble	vacillate
wax	v	become	expand	increase	turn
waxen	adj	livid	pale	pallid	sickly
waylay	v	accost	ambush	intercept	surprise
wayward	adj	contrary	disobedient	perverse	unruly
wean	adj	detach	disaffect	divide	estrange
weathered	adj	battered	beaten	seasoned	worn
weekend	n	holiday	tour	travel	vacation
weir	n	barrage	barrier	dam	dike
welcome	adj	agreeable	pleasant	pleasing	nice
welkin	n	blue	firmament	heaven	sky
welter	n	commotion	confusion	flurry	hodgepodge
Weltschmerz	n	boredom	doldrums	melancholy	weariness
wharf	n	berth	dock	landing	pier
wheedle	v	cajole	coax	persuade	flatter
whence	adv	certainly	then	thus	very
whet	v	grind	quicken	sharpen	stimulate
whiffle	v	break	falter	stagger	vacillate
whim	n	fancy	impulse	notion	quirk
whimsical	adj	erratic	fanciful	fantastic	fickle
whimsy	n	caprice	fancy	freak	quaintness
whit	n	iota	jot	modicum	tittle
whited sepulcher	n	corruption	hypocrite	impostor	Pharisee
wholesome	adj	beneficial	fit	good	healthy
widespread	adj	general	popular	prevailing	universal
wield	v	exert	handle	manipulate	utilize
wildlife	v	animal	creature	fauna	nature
willful	adj	deliberate	insistent	headstrong	obstinate
wily	adj	crafty	cunning	shrewd	sly
wince	v	cringe	flinch	recoil	shrink
winch	n	crane	derrick	hoist	windlass
windfall	n	bonanza	bonus	boon	godsend

winnow	v	examine	select	separate	sift
winsome	adj	attractive	charming	engaging	winning
wise	adj	astute	intelligent	sensible	smart
wistful	adj	contemplative	melancholy	pensive	yearning
wither	v	decay	fade	shrivel	wilt
witty	adj	amusing	clever	funny	humorous
wizened	adj	dried	shriveled	shrunken	withered
woe	n	distress	grief	misery	sorrow
wonders	n	marvels	miracles	prodigies	questions
wont	n	custom	habit	practice	way
woo	v	court	encourage	invite	pursue
worker	n	employee	hand	laborer	operative
worry	n	anxiety	concern	fear	trouble
worthwhile	adj	advantageous	profitable	rewarding	valuable
wrack	v	demolish	destroy	ruin	wreck
wraith	n	apparition	ghost	specter	spirit
wrangle	n	argue	bicker	fight	squabble
wrath	n	anger	fury	indignation	rage
wreak	v	cause	exact	impose	inflict
wrest	v	extort	seize	snatch	wrench
wretched	adj	desolate	despicable	miserable	worthless
wright	n	consultant	craftsman	mechanic	operator
writ	n	injunction	subpoena	summons	warrant
writhe	v	agonize	squirm	twist	wriggle
wroth	adj	furious	irate	livid	mad
wrought	adj	done	made	molded	shaped
wry	adj	askew	crooked	lopsided	twisted
wunderkind	n	talent	phenomenon	prodigy	whiz
xeric	adj	arid	desert	dry	thirsty
xyloid	adj	arboraceous	forested	ligneous	woody
xylophone	n	marimba	glockenspiel	vibraharp	vibraphone
yahoo	n	barbarian	philistine	savage	vulgarian
yammer	v	blab	chatter	complain	gossip
yarn	n	anecdote	fable	story	tale
yaw	v	deviate	swerve	veer	weave
yawl	n	dandy	jolly boat	sailboat	yacht

yclept	v	baptized	christened	named	titled
yearn	v	crave	desire	long	want
yearnings	n	cravings	desires	hungers	longings
yeasty	adj	barmy	frothy	spirited	zesty
yelp	n	bark	cry	squeal	yap
yen	n	craving	desire	longing	yearning
yeoman	n	attendant	bodyguard	clerk	escort
yield	v	concede	submit	succumb	surrender
yogi	n	guru	mahatma	pandit	swami
yoke	v	connect	couple	join	link
yokel	n	bumpkin	hayseed	hick	rustic
yore	n	auld lang syne	history	past	yesteryear
Young Turks	n	radicals	rebels	reformers	revolutionists
yowl	n	cry	holler	howl	yell
zany	adj	goofy	foolish	funny	madcap
zeal	n	eagerness	earnestness	enthusiasm	passion
zealot	n	enthusiast	fanatic	maniac	nut
zealous	adj	devoted	eager	enthusiastic	passionate
zenith	n	culmination	maximum	peak	summit
zenithal	adj	apical	extreme	highest	preeminent
zephyr	n	breeze	draft	gust	waft
zest	n	enthusiasm	gusto	keenness	passion
zing	n	verve	vigor	vitality	zip
zoophagous	adj	carnivorous	flesh-eating	meat-eating	predacious

BIBLIOGRAPHY

Wordlist Sources

Bader, W., Burt, D. S., & Killoran, D. M. (2006). *Master the Miller analogies test*. Lawrenceville, NJ: Thomson/Petersons.

Barrons Educational Series. (1994). *Barrons: How to Prepare for the Mat: Miller Analogies Test*. Hauppauge, NY.

Bramson, M. (1981). *How to prepare for the Miller analogies test*. San Diego: Harcourt Brace Jovanovich.

Bromberg, M., & Gordon, M. (1987). *1100 Words you need to know*. New York: Barrons Educational Series.

Buckley, W. F. (1998). *The lexicon:*San Diego, CA: Harvest Books.

Cambridge Educational Services. (1998). *Gre testprep plus*. New York.

Elster, C. H., & Elliot, J. (1994). *Tooth and nail a novel approach to the new Sat*. San Diego: Harcourt Brace & Co.

Kolby, J. (2000). *Vocabulary 4000: the 4000 Essential for an Educated Vocabulary*. Nova Press.

Martz, G. (1995). *Sat verbal workout*. New York: Random House.

River City Publ. (1998). *Easy prep flash cards GRE*. St. Louis, MO.

Robinson, A. (2012). *Word Smart: How to Build an Educated Vocabulary.* Princeton Review.

staff, K. (2016). *Mat Strategies, Practice & Review with 7 Practice Tests.* Kaplan Publishing.

Waldhorn, A., & Zeiger, A. (1957). *Word mastery made simple.* Garden City, NY: Doubleday.

Zahler, K. A. (2006). *McGraw-Hills Mat: Miller Analogies Test.* New York: McGraw-Hill.

Synonym Sources

Jellis, S. (2002). *Microsoft Encarta college thesaurus.* New York: St. Martins Press.

Dictionary by Merriam-Webster: America's most-trusted online dictionary. (n.d.). Retrieved from https://www.merriam-webster.com/

Power Thesaurus. (n.d.). Retrieved from https://www.powerthesaurus.org/